BLACK ICE

BLACK ICE

THE LIFE AND DEATH OF
JOHN CURRY

Elva Oglanby

VICTOR GOLLANCZ

LONDON

First published in Great Britain 1995
by Victor Gollancz
A Division of the Cassell group
Wellington House, 125 Strand, London WC2R OBB

A catalogue record for this book is
available from the British Library

ISBN 0 575 05907 9

Photoset in Great Britain by
Rowland Phototypesetting Ltd
Bury St Edmunds, Suffolk
Printed and bound in Great Britain by
Mackays of Chatham plc, Chatham, Kent

To David Spungen,
who contributed so greatly
to the writing of this book.
As with the John Curry Skating Company, it
was for both of us a labour of love.
Nil desperandum.

Contents

Acknowledgements

Under this heading, I would like to take the opportunity to acknowledge not only the people who made it possible for me to complete this book, but also those who made such important contributions to the work of the John Curry Skating Company. Both endeavours were, in every sense, a team effort.

Top of both lists must go my friend and partner, David Spungen, who at all times put the welfare of the company before his own, and whose commitment to this book has been unconditional. I must also mention here my family, who have likewise offered unfailing support throughout both projects.

On behalf of the John Curry Skating Company, I would like to thank those people who offered vital support and advice and those who contributed financing at critical moments in our history. In alphabetical order, they are: April Allen, Rita Anichini, Shelley Cammacker, Michael Cohl, Pat Dobson, Mark and Sara Grayson, Bill Hallock, Bob Harley, Roger Gettys Hill, Kevin Kossi, David Krebs, Jerome Landau, Steve Leber, Billy Rappaport, Michael Rosenberg, Jack Sakazaki, Bob Strauss, Vernon Taylor, George and Lisa Webster, Bob Williams and Kit Wright. In addition, I must mention the beneficence of five extraordinary allies, whose generosity was ongoing and crucial to the survival of the company: Sander Jacobs, Bill Kenwright, Lewis Rappaport, Bill Weylock and Jack Wilson.

I could not have written the book without the constant help and advice of my editor, Vicki Harris, who has been patient and supportive beyond the call of duty. I would also like to thank my agent, Octavia Wiseman, and the team at Victor Gollancz. Especial mention must go to Elizabeth Dobson, the Production Director, and Sarah Abel, who have fought so valiantly against impossible time constraints; to Alex Huggins, the publicist; and to Nick May of the art department and Brian Robins, who created such a brilliant cover design. Finally I would like to thank Nerina Shute for her valuable advice and support, and my friend Jocelyn Williams for her constant words of encouragement.

This list cannot be concluded without paying my respects to my dear friend and mentor, Bill Judd, who died in January 1987. He was a visionary and a dreamer who recognized artistic talent in its infancy; he was a gifted impresario and a fine human being and he is sadly missed. There is no doubt that, but for him, the John Curry Skating Company would never have existed.

Preface

John Curry and I often discussed the possibility of writing his auto-biography together, and over the years he spent hundreds of hours telling me about his life. I learnt of his pain and frustration, his loneliness and his longing for a permanent partner; of his constant search for professional fulfilment and his overwhelming desire to be at peace. I came to know the human being behind the public façade: a shy, self-effacing man who was also a driven and dedicated perfectionist, an idealist in a world ruled by the necessity for compromise.

When John died in April 1994, little was known about him beyond the fact that he was an Olympic gold-medallist who had perfected skating as an art form. I looked through the dozens of folders filled with notes from our sessions, and realized that he had already told his story, and that I had sufficient material to complete the project we had started almost twenty years earlier.

The book seemed to divide itself naturally into three sections: John's life before I met him, our years of working together and the period following the collapse of the John Curry Skating Company. The first part is told entirely from John's own point of view. I have tried, wherever possible, to preserve his distinct way of speaking; but occasionally, for the sake of continuity, I have taken poetic licence. What was important to me was that the content of this book would have satisfied John's own sensibilities.

In the final analysis I believe that, had he still been alive, he would have been pleased with the result.

Part One

The dream is always the same. I am standing on the platform of an underground station, holding my father's hand. Strange people are milling around us, pushing us closer and closer to the edge. I am tugging at my father's hand, trying to get his attention. He turns to look at me and I see tears streaming down his face. He is trying to say something to me but I can't hear the words. I want to comfort him, to stop him from crying, but he turns away from me again. Suddenly a train comes roaring out of the tunnel towards us and he falls silently forward on to the tracks and disappears under the wheels. I open my mouth to scream but no sound comes out. I look round desperately for help, but the people have all gone and the carriages are empty. I run up and down the train and then I see my father's hand, stretched out towards me. I reach down to grasp it but, just as I am about to touch his fingers, I wake up, sweating and terrified, and convinced I should have done something to save him.

1

John Curry was born on 9 September 1949, in a leafy suburb of Birmingham called Acock's Green. According to the astrological calendar, he was a triple Virgo.

'I don't really believe in astrology, but I suppose there's no denying that I have all the Virgo characteristics: difficult, moody, idealistic, stubborn. People tell me I'm a perfectionist, but I'm never really certain if I should take it as a compliment or a criticism. Certainly I can't bear it when things aren't done properly. Perhaps that's why I love teaching so much. There's nothing in the world more satisfying than to be able to nurture talent. To watch artists unfold, like flowers, and persuade them to trust their own instincts.'

John was the youngest of three boys. When his mother, Rita, brought him home from the hospital his two brothers inspected the new arrival solemnly. After a few minutes Michael, the eldest, went off to play, but Andrew, who was still a toddler himself, stayed to watch. He was delighted with his baby brother.

'Andrew and I were always close. He would try to look after me when we were tiny and he loved to push me round the park in my pram. Michael was another story. I suppose if I'm honest I would have to admit I was scared of him. He would tease me unmercifully and devised all manner of tortures for me. His favourite thing was to dangle me by one arm from an upstairs window and threaten to drop me. The more I screamed, the more he liked it. I made the mistake of telling him I was terrified of the dark, and after that he would take fiendish delight in locking me into small cupboards for hours on end. He would shout through the door, telling me that I should be careful of poisonous spiders. Michael was the apple of my father's eye. He was always saying, "Why can't you be more like Michael?" Mother didn't have a favourite. She loved us all equally, no matter what we did. She was always very kind and supportive, but she could never be persuaded to contradict my father.'

Rita was always very busy and John spent a great deal of time on his own. Because of this he developed a vivid imagination and would hold long conversations with invisible friends.

'I wasn't the least bit interested in toys as such, but I had shelves full of books. I read anything I could get my hands on. I wrote stories, too. And plays. I made a little model theatre out of balsa-wood, with a stage and lights and a curtain that went up and down. I spent so many happy hours with that theatre. I made miniature characters and they would perform in the plays I wrote. I was so engrossed in them that I believed they were real, and I would often lie awake at night trying to catch one of them moving.'

Ironically, it was John's father, Joseph, who taught him to love the theatre. Later, when John was a performer himself, Joseph was terribly unhappy about it; but at that point John was the only one in the family who would go to the theatre with him.

'He had a passion for musicals. We saw everything in the West End of London and we never missed a performance of the Birmingham Light Opera. I must have seen the *Desert Song* fifteen times. I loved it all just as much as he did – all the colour and excitement and energy. It was an enchanted world to me. The odd thing, though, was that my father refused completely to go to the ballet. He wouldn't even contemplate it. Something about it offended him.'

Dancing came naturally to John, and from the time he was able to walk he would move instinctively every time he heard music. His feet would tap, his body would sway and he would skip up and down the stairs.

'It was like breathing to me. No one taught me, it just came from somewhere inside of me. I would turn on the radio and start dancing around without thinking. It made me happy. Whenever my father saw me dancing, though, he would get very angry. His face would turn red, the colour of raw liver, and a pulse in the base of his neck would start to twitch. I couldn't understand why he felt that way, but I thought I must be doing something very wrong. I felt ashamed of myself because I knew I couldn't help dancing.'

When he was five, John saved his pocket money each week until he had enough to buy a recording of *Swan Lake*. It was his favourite music and he wanted to be able to play it on the gramophone. He carried the precious disc home and showed it to his mother.

'She loved it as much as I did. We would listen to it together and I would show her how I thought the swans would dance, even though I had never seen a ballet at this point in my life. She told me all about Tchaikovsky and about the first performance of *Swan Lake* in the Maryinsky Theatre in St Petersburg. One day my father arrived home when we were in the middle of one of these sessions and he flew into a terrible rage. I had never seen him so angry. He snatched the record from the turntable and broke it in half. I was so shocked I didn't even cry. "I don't want you listening to this any more. It's not good for you," he shouted. "You should be outside playing football." I didn't know it then, of course, but my father was homophobic.'

Joseph owned an engineering firm in Birmingham that made precision parts for cash registers. Although the business was successful, it was not a fulfilling career and he felt empty and frustrated.

'My father was a brilliant inventor, a hugely accomplished man, who was forced by convention to channel his talents into a traditional field. The fact that he earned a great deal of money almost made things worse for him. We lived a very comfortable existence, with a large house, servants and cars. I think it would have been easier for him if we had been poor and he had been forced to fight for the basic necessities of life. He would have somehow felt more useful.'

In some ways John led the life of an only child, spending hours in his room in a world of his own invention. Everyone around him seemed too busy to pay him much attention.

'I thought our family was close-knit, but looking back now I am shocked by the degree to which we were isolated from each other. Michael was always off somewhere; Andrew was quiet and shy and seemed preoccupied with his own problems; Mother was rushing madly from one end of the day to the other; and I would invariably have my head stuck into a book. And my father was desperately lonely, unable to communicate with any of us. He was a misfit, an extraordinary man in an ordinary world, and his strong creative urges clashed against his ingrained traditional values. For some reason, I seemed to be the major cause of his unhappiness and no matter how hard I tried I could never seem to please him. Everything I did

5

seemed to upset him. We appeared to have a chasm between us, yet in reality we were uncannily alike.'

In 1956, Joseph and Andrew caught TB. They were put into isolation at one end of the house and Rita added the role of nurse to her other duties.

'It was a highly contagious disease, of course, and I was not allowed to go into the annexe. I would watch Mother scurrying back and forth with a mask over her face, carrying supper trays and bedpans. She always looked tired.'

Because everyone in the household was at risk, they were given regular tests to make sure they were all right. At one point John became convinced that Andrew had died and that the news was being kept from him. He was caught trying to unlock the annexe door and his mother solemnly assured him that if he so much as touched it again he would be sent away until they were better.

'It wasn't long before I grew used to being alone in the rest of the house with Mother. Michael was seldom in, and I realized to my delight that I could play all the music I wanted. I could dance all over the place without anyone even noticing me. I revelled in the freedom and I think it was one of the few times in my life that I have been truly happy.'

While Joseph was ill, his business suffered. Some of the luxuries the family was used to had to be cut out, and economies were introduced. Andrew could not go to school so the money had to be found for a tutor to teach him at home. Although Joseph seemed to recover physically, the illness had a devastating effect on his emotional health. It left him severely debilitated and he became prone to violent mood swings. He was either euphoric or morbidly depressed. It seemed that the inner demons he had always been able to subdue now rose up and overpowered him, and the slightest incident would blow up out of all proportion.

'It was around this time that I went with Mother to see a performance of the *Nutcracker*. I remember the ballet so clearly. It mesmerized me and I could think of nothing else for weeks. I decided then that I wanted to spend the rest of my life as a professional dancer. I wanted to join the Royal Ballet School and eventually become part of the company. It was so important to me that I kept it to myself for weeks until one day I got up the courage to broach the subject to my parents. To my absolute dismay, my father said no without

6

even considering it. There could be no discussion on the matter. It was out of the question. I looked at Mother hoping she could somehow change his mind, but all she said was, "Your father has said no, John. You must accept that." I was devastated. I had expected my father's reaction but I had been relying on Mother to win him over. It hadn't occurred to me that she would agree with him. I opened my mouth to protest but my father stopped me angrily. "I forbid you to ever mention the subject again," he said, and that was the end of that. I felt as though I had been punched in the stomach. I cried for days.'

The disappointment over the dancing lessons was to persist through the winter. Concerned over John's unhappiness, Rita arranged to take him to see Margot Fonteyn dance. They went down to London to a matinée performance and she cautioned John not to say anything to anyone: 'There's no sense in creating a problem where one doesn't need to exist. This can be our secret.' Fortunately, Joseph was away at the time so it was not difficult to arrange.

'I don't even remember the ballet she was in now – I think it was *Romeo and Juliet* – because she was so charismatic that I could see only her. She was the most beautiful creature I could imagine, and to this day I view her as the consummate example of true artistry. She was so light and graceful, expressing emotion without apparent effort, floating across the stage in a perfect fusion of style and form. It was as though she was dancing inside a cloud of music where nothing else existed.'

Not long after the visit to see Margot Fonteyn, John saw an ice pantomime on television. He had seen them before and thought of them as a disjointed assembly of mediocre ice dancers and speciality acts. This time, however, he was drawn to the performance of the star.

'I think the pantomime was *Aladdin*. It had been the usual mixture of silly comedians, exploding cars and precision dancers and I wasn't really paying much attention to it. Suddenly this amazing woman came on to the ice and skated so beautifully that I got goosebumps. She had this extraordinary way of moving in strong, flowing lines and of being able to stay motionless while at the same time being in flight. I thought it was the most thrilling thing I had ever seen and I decided I wanted to learn to skate myself. I had a new passion.'

John waited patiently for the right moment to ask for lessons. He was terrified his parents would say no. He offered to do extra chores and was especially quiet and well-behaved. Finally, one afternoon, he broached the subject to his mother.

'I think I stopped breathing altogether while I waited for her answer. Her face gave nothing away and she took what seemed like a long time before she said anything. Then, to my astonishment, she said she thought it was a very good idea and that she thought my father would like it too. She went off to talk to him about it and when she came back she was smiling. "He agrees," she said. "He thinks it will be very good for you." I was dumbfounded, at a loss to understand his apparent change of heart, but later I realized that he found skating acceptable because it fell under the umbrella of sport. My poor father had no way to know that I intended to pursue ice as an art form.'

2

Now that John had permission to have skating lessons he was frantic to start, but it was to be several months before Rita could find the time to take him. He thought of nothing else, imagining himself gliding effortlessly across a sheet of ice. He was possessed. Finally, just before his seventh birthday, she told him the time had come to go for his first lesson.

'When we walked through the door of the old Summerhill Ice Rink I was literally shivering with excitement. I still remember every detail of that day – the swirl of colours as people made their way around the ice, some hanging on to the sides and others sailing along on their own. They jumped and span, stumbled and fell, and I passionately wanted to be part of it all. I felt as though I belonged. It's peculiar, but the thing I remember most vividly is the smell of the rink. It filled my nostrils and my psyche with its pungent mixture of damp air, wet coconut matting, sweaty bodies and stale coffee. I thought it the most wonderful smell in the world.'

Rita knew nothing of the relative merits of the Summerhill coaches. She looked down the list and selected one who fell within the middle price range. It turned out to be an inspired choice.

'By an extraordinary stroke of luck, Mother had signed me up with one of the best teachers in the area. Ken Vickers had a near-perfect technique, with the body always correctly positioned. He taught me the vital relationship between style and innovation that was later to form the basis of my work as a professional.'

Boots that fit well are fundamental to the success of a skater, and John was fortunate that his mother was willing to address this issue at such an early stage. Ken Vickers took John to the skate shop and fitted him on that first day, and although Rita was on a tight budget she paid for them without hesitation.

'As soon as I had those boots on I had the peculiar feeling that they were actually a part of me. I held on to Ken Vickers' hand for a few minutes until I had the feel of the ice. Then I let go of him and launched off on my own. I felt perfectly secure. It seemed to me to be the most natural thing in the world.'

Since John had no school on Wednesday afternoons, Rita chose that day for his weekly skating lesson. It was the most important event in his life, and he could never bear to miss it, no matter what the reason. One Wednesday morning he woke up with a sick headache and a temperature. He knew he had the flu, but he also knew that if he didn't go to school he wouldn't be allowed to go to Summerhill in the afternoon. He forced himself to eat breakfast and went off trying to look normal. He sat through arithmetic and reading, his head feeling as if it were on fire. By the time he got to the ice rink he could barely stand up, let alone skate. Ken Vickers looked at him sternly. 'You are far too sick to skate today, young man,' he said firmly. 'You should be at home in bed.' John looked as though he were about to burst into tears and Ken put his arm round his shoulders. 'I tell you what,' he said kindly, 'you can have a double lesson next week for the price of one, providing your mother thinks that would be all right.'

'I have always believed that the first teacher you have in any discipline is by far the most important. It's a sad fact that most people don't recognize this. What you learn at the beginning when you are at your most impressionable and most susceptible will colour everything you do afterwards. It is rather like a house of cards – if the foundation is weak, sooner or later the whole house will collapse. I was unbelievably lucky to have Ken Vickers at that point in my training, because what he taught me has formed the basis of my own teaching. Hopefully I have inspired some of my students to pass this knowledge on to others. Like all great teachers, Ken Vickers' instructions were actually very basic and straightforward. He taught from the heart because he loved and respected skating and he instilled this attitude in his pupils. His three cardinal rules were fundamental to his method: keep the back straight; bend the knees; use the upper body freely. Never just skate *on* the ice. Make it an extension of yourself. Become a part of it. It was this simple credo that took root in my heart at the age of seven and grew like a tree inside of me.'

John and his family spent Christmas in Suffolk that year. He took his skates with him because he could never bear to be parted from them, and he was delighted to find the mere frozen over. He raced around the great expanse of ice at high speed, the cold wind whistling past his ears and stinging his eyelids. Beneath his blades he could hear the crunch of powdered ice.

'It was so exhilarating, like flying. I imagined I was a bird, darting and swooping all over the place. When my father discovered what I was doing he told me such a terrifying story that I was never able to enjoy outdoor skating again. He said that ice doesn't just break and splinter, leaving a hole for the skater to fall through. It snaps open like a revolving door and hurls you into the freezing water underneath. Then it swings shut again and seals you in without any escape. I suppose he was trying to make me cautious. At any rate, he scared me so much that whenever I returned to the mere I would stay very close to the edge.'

'What are you doing, John?' Ken Vickers asked one afternoon. John had just been skating round the rink to show Ken some new steps he'd made up. He looked at Ken in surprise. 'A piece from *The Sleeping Beauty*. I heard it on the radio.' Ken seemed puzzled. 'But you had no music playing . . .'

John laughed. 'Oh, but I did! I can hear it in my head, every note of it. I don't need a tape.'

'I've always had this odd ability to retain music that I like, and ever since my first lesson I had been skating to my internal "recordings". I'd seen other children skating their competitive programmes

to the tape deck at the rink so I decided to make up my own programme. Ken Vickers was fascinated and told me it was probably
time I started competing. He suggested it would be better if I used
a proper cassette, though, so that the judges could hear what I was
skating to!'

John won the first competition he entered, at the age of seven and
a half. It was a simple programme, just a few steps and one or two
little spins. Even though some of the other competitors had far more
difficult programmes, it was John's unusual lyrical quality that gave
him the advantage.

'People came up to me and asked who had choreographed my
piece, but of course I had no choreography. I just had a natural
inclination to move to music. I would pretend the great dancers from
the Royal Ballet were watching me and I would perform for these
invisible judges. I seemed to know instinctively what they would
want me to do, and I won many competitions under their scrutiny.'

The next five years passed in a pleasant, unremarkable whirl. The
family had regained some of their financial stability, and it seemed
to John that a few of the pressures had disappeared from their lives.
Rita now had some help in the house again, and Andrew continued
to study under his private tutor. John's life now revolved around
skating and he had, without realizing it, risen up the competitive
ladder to the point where he was being discussed by those who
considered themselves the keepers of the realm. He was persuaded
to move on to new coaches, none of whom took to him. They found
him to be too innovative, and the very things that had so delighted
Ken Vickers proved to be offensive to them.

'My new mentors were horrified by the way I moved and told me
repeatedly that it was simply not the way a boy was expected to
skate. It was not suitable. I hadn't the faintest idea what they were
talking about – I skated the only way I could. Intuitively. It was the
music that dictated where and what I did.'

Each coach in turn tried desperately to modify John's style. When
all efforts failed, they suggested that he quit altogether. He was taken
on by yet another coach who would hit him sharply every time he
made an expressive movement with his arms.

'I began to dread my lessons for the first time since I had started
skating. This dreadful man would scream at me whenever I did
anything the least bit lyrical. What I considered beautiful he con-

demned as outrageous. He was determined to turn me into a jumping robot. There were days when I went home covered in bruises, but nobody seemed to think it was the least bit out of order. I have often worried since how many potentially good skaters have been ruined by such methods.'

When it became obvious that John's individual style was not responding to remedial training, Rita was sent for. John was now seen by the coaches as a difficult student. His belief in his own artistic sense was deemed to be a stubborn refusal to learn anything new. Rita was told that John had great potential as a competitor if he could only be moulded correctly. In order to make this happen, his coaches believed he needed to see a psychiatrist. After lengthy debate, Rita agreed.

'I don't have great faith in psychiatry, but on this occasion I was fortunate enough to encounter a fellow-traveller. I remember him vividly. He was small and wiry and we sat at the kitchen table drinking Earl Grey tea with lots of sugar. We chatted about television programmes for a while and then he said, "Why does it bother you that your coaches don't approve of you?" I was startled. I had never considered I had a right to an opinion of my own. After a moment's thought I said, "I suppose because it's important to me that they understand what I am doing."

'"And if they don't?" he asked.

'"Then I will just keep on doing it anyway."

'He laughed out loud. "That's exactly the answer I was hoping for," he said. "There's nothing wrong with you, John, and certainly nothing I would want to change. What you have is a creative talent, and you will have to accept that people are always going to be threatened by that. You've stepped outside the norm and that frightens them. It won't be easy for you, but if you stick to what you believe in I know you'll make it."'

3

By the time John was twelve, his father had become an alcoholic. The sadness that pervaded his life had become too much for him to bear, and he found a measure of escape in drinking. It was never openly discussed and all John would be told was that his father was ill and was not to be disturbed. Sometimes he disappeared for days, and at those times a weight seemed to lift from the house. Rita, who had become tense and rather nervous, began to hum to herself as she went about her chores.

'I know it seems a terrible thing to say now, but we actually dreaded the sound of my father's key in the front door. Although Mother spoke to me in riddles about his condition, I knew he was drinking. It terrified me, and I went to the library and found a book on alcoholism. I sat in the gloom at the back of the stacks and read it from cover to cover. What I learnt from it was that my father had a serious disease which had no known cure, and could be controlled only if the sufferer acknowledged its existence. Since this was unlikely to happen in my father's case, the prognosis was dire. As I understood it, he would become progressively more dependent until he died from it. I replaced the book, walked out of the building, went home and climbed into bed. I wanted to stay there for ever.'

When he was made to come downstairs for supper, John sat through the meal wondering how he could tell his mother what he had read. He was convinced she had no idea how serious the situation was, and finally decided the truth was too upsetting for her to cope with. He buried his knowledge deep inside himself, where it gnawed at him. He told no one, and carried it with him like a guilty secret, unable to voice it and powerless to do anything to help.

'I have since come to believe that one has a duty to tell the truth at all times, no matter how much it might hurt. I don't think there is any situation where it is better to keep a secret. People have a right to know everything that concerns them. I was only a child at the time, but if I had spoken to Mother about my fears, perhaps she would have felt compelled to seek professional advice. At least she would have felt less alone.'

As a result of the tensions at home, John began to frequent the cinema. He discovered one that showed classic films and offered a discount for multiple visits.

'I discovered the Ingmar Bergman films, which were rather dark and depressing, but which had a quality that perfectly suited my mood at the time. I wallowed in them. I saw everything – Garbo, Dietrich, Monroe, Swanson. I adored Astaire and admired Brando enormously. One day I saw *East of Eden* and identified so strongly with the James Dean character that I found myself crying. I went back to see it again and in a funny way I was comforted because he made me feel I wasn't alone in the world.'

John was finding it difficult to concentrate at school. He had never been a model student, but he had always managed to keep up. Now he found himself slipping behind and he seemed to have lost the ability to study. He would sit at his desk trying desperately to focus and forcing himself to listen. His mind wandered continuously, and he would find himself thinking about a new piece of choreography, going over the steps and rearranging the sequences.

'I was always happy on the ice. I would feel a huge surge of joy as I stepped out on to the rink and glided away. It was my own private world, one I could control and monitor. I belonged there. My coaches had stopped trying to change me, at least for the moment, and I was still doing well in competitions. Sometimes, however, the situation at home would get the better of me and I would perform abysmally. On very bad days I would lose concentration altogether and fall on the simplest of steps. On one particular occasion, during an event at Wembley, I fell so often that the routine resembled a scene from a *Marx Brothers* movie. For the majority of the time, though, I was secure with my skates on. I would be swallowed up by the rarefied atmosphere of the ice rink and all the pressures would be left behind.'

John was a lonely child. He knew other children, of course, but they were not in any sense what could be described as friends. At school he was considered rather strange.

'I was known as a snob or a weirdo, depending on the point of view. I wasn't part of the social life of the class and was rarely invited to parties. To be fair, this wasn't really surprising, as I refused to invite anyone back to my own house. I was terrified someone would see my father drunk. My position at school was difficult enough, but had that happened it would have become intolerable. "How come you never have a birthday party, Curry?" they would demand. I would shrug my shoulders with what I hoped was a very superior air. "Oh, I haven't got time for that sort of thing," I would say. "I'm much too busy skating." Fortunately, they left it at that.'

John's mother had a profound influence on him at this stage of his life. Her love of the arts and her sense of style impressed him deeply.

'I thought her very beautiful. She had great dress sense and favoured simple, elegant lines. I loved the way she combined colours, and she had a flair for making the plainest outfit look expensive. We would collaborate on my skating costumes, experimenting with different looks. Men's costumes tended to be boring and uniform in those days, and so we caused renewed alarm in my skating coaches. One particular costume had a white line swirled around a dark blue body-suit, and when I span it gave the effect of a Catherine wheel. I thought it very effective, but the judges were not at all happy about it. Costume is hugely important to the overall look of a skater. It must be exactly the right weight, it must "move" with the skater, taking into account the speed of the air displacement, and it must never, ever obscure the line of the body. It always makes me very sad when I see a really fine performance ruined because the skater is obliterated by an unsuitable costume.'

By the time he was thirteen, John was taking an active part in school athletics. He had always been good at sprinting and hurdling, but now he added both high and long jump to his roster. He seemed to have a natural aptitude for any activity that required him to move through space. He was selected for the track team and managed to fit the practices into his busy schedule. One day he chanced to over-hear the team coach discussing him with a colleague. 'John seems to be able to jump higher and run faster than anyone else in the school,' he said. 'It's because of his build,' was the reply. 'He carries no excess flesh at all, yet he has wonderful muscle tone. It gives him much greater momentum.'

'This casual remark made a lasting impact on me. For some reason I thought of it as a compliment and gave no thought to its accuracy. I began to eat less, weighing myself every morning in secret. I panicked if I gained an ounce, and was convinced in my heart that I had to be very, very thin if I was to skate well. That day I started an obsession with weight that took me years to conquer. And, like

15

so many other things in my life, it gained an added significance because I was unable to discuss it with anyone.'

To John's intense delight, his father began to take an interest in his progress on the track team. He was in a relatively good frame of mind at the time, and seemed to be pulling himself together. One evening at practice, John looked up to see Joseph sitting in the stands, watching.

'I couldn't believe he was there, and I kept checking to make sure he hadn't left. When he caught my eye he would lift his hand to acknowledge me, and I was ecstatic. At the end of the session he came down on to the tracks and clapped me on the back. For the first and only time in my life he told me he was proud of me. I could hardly breathe for fear something would spoil the moment. Afterwards he drove me home and we stopped on the way for an ice-cream. "John, you must concentrate on athletics from now on," he told me. "You could be a champion." Some instinct stopped me from protesting that it was skating I wanted to pursue. I wanted to leave the experience intact, so I said nothing. I had waited so long to do something that pleased him that I was afraid of upsetting the equilibrium again. I went to bed feeling happier than I had for many months, but by the next morning my father had disappeared again. What I had imagined to be a turning point in his life proved only to be a short intermission.'

4

In spite of Joseph's apparent improvement, his condition took a decided turn for the worse, and by the time John was fourteen the periods of relative normality had all but disappeared. There were no more outings to the theatre. Alcohol, which had always caused him to be unpredictable and illogical, now made him fly into violent rages.

'I dreaded these outbursts. I knew when they were coming because the expression in his eyes would change and his face would turn dark red. You could almost see the venom rising inside of him. Anything could set him off – it was usually something quite trivial which would take on a dimension of its own and escalate into a full-scale battle. He wouldn't allow us to ignore him, yet if we protested it would just provoke him further. He was deeply paranoid, and accused us of terrible things. He would hide things from us and forget where he had put them and refused to believe anything we said. We were often at our wits' end, with no idea at all how we should handle him. Mother never answered him back and she did her best to shield us from the situation and pretend that everything was all right. We lived in this sad little charade because to acknowledge what was going on would have been unthinkable. As long as we didn't talk about it we somehow convinced ourselves that it would go away.'

John spent a great deal of time at the ice rink, mostly in an effort to avoid the trauma. He dreaded having to go home and was frequently the last one to leave the rink. One night he arrived home particularly late to find his father lying full-length on the living-room carpet.

'He was paralytic. The smell of stale alcohol was nauseating and his speech was so thick and slurred that I couldn't understand a word he was saying. Mother was trying to get him up but every time she got him into a sitting position he would slump right back on the floor with a thud. It was like trying to handle a very heavy rag doll.'

Somehow, between them, they managed to get him upstairs and haul him on to his bed. He lay there cursing at them until he passed out. John pulled off his socks and shoes and opened his collar. Then he covered him with the quilt.

'He was breathing in deep, rasping gulps and I was afraid he would choke. I sat with him for a long time until his breathing was quieter. When I knew he wasn't going to die, I went downstairs to look for Mother. She was sitting at the kitchen table, crying silently. The look on her face almost broke my heart. She said, "You mustn't blame him, John. It isn't his fault. Whatever he does, he loves us all very much. He's just very unhappy." I didn't argue with her, but at that moment I found it impossible to feel any sympathy for my father's behaviour. It seemed to me that if he really cared for us he would stop drinking.'

John began to notice changes in his mother. The strain showed on her face and affected her usually cheerful disposition. She became impatient and found it difficult to pay attention to anything. She was constantly tired.

'My father was an insomniac. This hadn't bothered Mother before, because he would creep downstairs and read or catch up on some work. But now he was parading about noisily in a state of manic excitement. Sometimes he didn't go to bed at all. He was plagued by ideas all the time, one after the other. He could never stop them. He felt compelled to write them all down in case he forgot them, so he had notebooks all over the house. Sometimes it got so bad that he would pound his head against the wall and beg it to go away. "It" was the presence he always felt inside him. The thing that refused to leave him in peace.'

The manic highs were inevitably followed by severe depressions, often lasting for months. John tried desperately to bring him out of them but nothing seemed to work. The sadness was too deep-seated.

'On very rare occasions I managed to get him talking about something he enjoyed – his favourite musical, *Desert Song*, or the dogs he'd looked after as a child. He would forget the depression for a while and he could even get quite animated, but as soon as the conversation stopped it would be right back there again, just as though it had never left. I have to admit I had begun to feel it was hopeless.'

For the first time that he could remember, John's parents began to quarrel. His mother had unwittingly become a participant in his father's dramas and John found it deeply disturbing.

'I would hear the voices escalate and cover my ears to shut out the sound. I wanted to go downstairs and make my father apologize to Mother and have everything be all right again, but I knew it would only make things worse. I wanted so much to have a father like everybody else – someone boring and reliable and predictable, not a brilliant eccentric who invented things and drank too much. I was terribly angry with him for being so different.'

One evening John woke to hear raised voices and the sound of a crash. He crept downstairs and saw his parents standing in the living room with the remains of a porcelain vase between them.

'Mother was trying to persuade him to see a counsellor and he was furious. The very suggestion that he had a drinking problem always met with the same reaction, but I suppose she had to keep

18

trying. I heard him tell her to mind her own business. "I'm not an alcoholic," he yelled, "and I don't need some bloody quack poking his nose into my affairs." She put her hand on his arm to soothe him and he pushed her away so roughly that she fell against the sofa. I was appalled and ran to help her up. My father was far more powerful than me, but I stood in front of Mother and told him to leave her alone. He'd always thought of me as what he referred to as a wimp, so I think he was caught off guard. At any rate, it seemed to work because he slumped into his armchair and eventually fell asleep.'

After that John frequently intervened. His father was becoming increasingly abusive and it was impossible to contain his outbursts, let alone avoid them altogether. Everything John had so admired in him was obliterated by the ugly moods and he often became the focus of his wrath.

'I know it sounds terrible, but I actually began to hate my father. I couldn't help it. I hated him for making Mother so unhappy and for allowing himself to get into such a state. I think I hated him most of all for not being strong enough to fight against it. For virtually giving up. It made me feel as though he had abandoned us, and I suppose in a way he had.'

John was so worried about his mother that he took to sleeping with his door open. He tried locking the front door so his father couldn't get in, but this so angered him that he stood in the front garden shouting obscenities until it was opened again. Sometimes he would disappear completely for days on end and then the atmosphere in the house relaxed again.

'No one would have admitted it, but we all felt an immense sense of relief when my father went off on one of his trips. We knew he had gone to London, but had no idea where he went or what he did when he got there. All we knew or cared about in those days was the fact that he wasn't at home. It was a blessed relief.'

One night John had fallen asleep early, believing Joseph to be in London. About two in the morning he woke with a start to see his father standing over his bed.

'It frightened the life out of me. I could see his eyes glittering in the dark and could smell the whisky on his breath. He reached down suddenly and caught hold of my arm, yanking me out of bed on to the floor. I was so shocked I didn't even protest. He kicked at me with his boots and I tried to crawl under the bed to get away from him. He pulled me back and punched me so hard that I couldn't get my breath. He slapped me around the face and shook me violently, screaming at the top of his voice that he knew I had betrayed him. It was only because Mother intervened at this point that he stopped. She was appalled at what might have happened to me.'

John never found out exactly what had triggered the incident, but it was to be repeated many times over the next few months. Even as she struggled to protect him, his mother cautioned him to tell no one about the situation inside the house, just that his father was 'ill'.

'Mother believed that to discuss my father's behaviour with strangers was tantamount to treason. I understand the instinct, because to some extent I shared it. Looking back now, though, this attitude just served to conceal a problem that, had it been discussed openly, might have been treated.'

In the autumn, John was packed off to boarding school. His mother had agonized over the decision, but in the end had decided that it would be far better for him to be in a protected environment where he could lead a safe and productive life, and where she hoped he could put the situation at home out of his mind. The only disadvantage she could see was that he would not be able to skate.

'The truth is that I didn't even miss skating once I went to boarding school. I was so happy to be there, away from all the pressures, that I blossomed. I absolutely loved it and used to skip about humming to myself all day. I suppose some people regarded me as peculiar but nobody ever said anything. I found a friend there, someone who was also a bit of a loner, and for the first time I had the pleasure of having someone to share things with, someone who was on my own wavelength. We made up codes and passwords and lived in a secret world known only to the two of us. It was heaven, and I dreaded the end of the term when I would have to go back to Birmingham. I wasn't sure I could bear it.'

Academically, John thrived in boarding school. He discovered art for the first time, and spent hours sculpting and potting. He also read voraciously – Buchan, Stephenson, Byron, Hardy and Shakespeare.

'I began a love affair with Dickens at that school. To this day he is my very favourite writer. He created such vivid portraits of Victorian life and the characters were so sharply drawn that I felt

I belonged there. I still carry a volume of Dickens wherever I go and if I am lonely or depressed I open it up and read. It always makes me feel better.'

As Christmas approached John began to worry about going home. He was in the nativity play and found that he loved being on a stage and had a natural ability to retain and deliver lines. He was also in the school choir.

'I had a terrible singing voice, but no one seemed to notice. We went round the local hospital wards, singing carols to the sick. I don't think we were particularly good at it, but everyone seemed to enjoy it. We were all given three cheers and a bag of sweets.'

John's mother wrote to say she would be coming to pick him up for the holidays on the last day of term. She told him not to worry because they were all going to have a lovely Christmas.

'Just before I went home, I gave my friend his Christmas present. We were both fans of Byron, and I had found a very old, illustrated copy of *The Prisoner of Chillon* in a second-hand bookshop. I spent hours trying to think what to write in it and in the end I put "To my eternal spirit of the chainless mind, with love, John." I think it must have frightened him because when I went back after Christmas, he had left.'

The next term passed quickly and as Easter approached John again worried about going home. His father's condition had deteriorated even further and he was now experiencing full-blown paranoia.

'I don't know how Mother coped with it all, but somehow she managed. I think it was the stubborn belief that he would somehow recover that kept her moving forward. Without that to hold on to, I think she would have collapsed.'

In the middle of the holidays, a letter came from the school announcing that John would not be allowed to return. His mother explained to him that she had not been able to pay the fees and that her application for a scholarship for him had been turned down.

'I was heartsick. I couldn't believe I would have to go back to the local school and live at home all the time. I begged Mother to do something about it and finally she managed to get me into a new boarding school. I don't know how she wangled it, but I was duly packed off at the end of April. I was so relieved.'

John liked the new school even more than the first one. He joined the athletics team and made another close friend. He was, to his astonishment, quite popular. He decided to found a drama group and their first production was *The Importance of Being Earnest*.

'I played Lady Bracknell, and I rather enjoyed it. If I say so myself, I made quite a good job of it. I began to understand the timing necessary for comedy and I loved the energy that came back from an audience. It was more intimate than the response one got for skating. At ice rinks people will applaud anyone who can jump in the air. They could be wearing the most dreadful costume and have no idea of how to perform, but if they can turn round twice and land on one leg, the audience is always thrilled. I've always found that very depressing. When it comes to acting, though, you have to deliver a good performance or the audience won't clap. It's much more rewarding.'

As the summer wore on, John became part of the fabric of school society and enjoyed the easy ebb and flow of his days there. He had found, at last, a measure of security.

'I had fun at that school. I laughed easily and, even if I cried occasionally, it would soon be over. The important thing was that I had stopped feeling guilty about my father. I still worried about Mother, of course, but she wrote often and always gave the impression that everything was all right. For long stretches of time I actually forgot about it all. I suppose it sounds callous, but the truth is that I had managed to create another life for myself.'

5

John went home for the summer holidays. He had been invited to visit friends in Sussex, but he turned them down. He was concerned about the length of time he had been absent from skating, and also thought his mother might want him to spend some time at home.

'I suppose I felt rather guilty because I had spent so long in school. I had put everything out of my mind, including skating, and now I felt I must make up for it. The atmosphere at home was terrible. My father's condition had deteriorated even further, and Mother looked ill. I worried about the long-term effect it would have on her. My father seemed either to be preparing for a drinking bout or recovering from one. There wasn't very much in between.'

John quickly got back into the rhythm of the rink again and was soon spending several hours a day on the ice. He entered a competition in August and won with a very dashing programme. His coaches were impressed and urged him to enter the Novice Cup at Wembley.

'That competition turned out to be a significant event in my life. First, and most important, my father turned up to see me skate, and I won. Second, I was approached right after the competition by a scout for *Holiday on Ice*, offering me a professional contract. I have to admit it was tempting.'

John considered *Holiday on Ice* carefully. At the time, this was the only permanent professional ice show in Europe. The money was decent enough and the contract would have been for three years. Finally he responded with a conditional acceptance – he would take up the offer if he was allowed to design his own costumes and choose his own music and choreography. The reply was polite but definite: 'Either you come on our terms, or you don't come at all.' John opted for the latter.

'The offer from *Holiday on Ice* threw my aspirations into perspective. I now knew what I didn't want to do, and that was trail around Europe in a children's ice show that was more about circus than skating. I realized that if I was ever to be taken seriously in the ice world, ever to have a voice, then I would have to win the Olympic Games. It was that simple.'

John's father was going through a phase of total abstinence and during this period he went twice to see John skate. At the Novice Cup he sat close to the edge and was deeply moved by his son's performance.

'It meant so much to me that he came. I skated very close to where he was sitting and I could see how pleased he was. Not because he was putting on an act, but because he was deep down genuinely proud. I knew then that in spite of everything he really did love me.'

On the way home from Wembley, John told his parents of the

Holiday on Ice offer. He was startled by their negative reaction.

'It wasn't that I wanted to be in the show. Far from it. Quite honestly, it would have been unthinkable for me unless the money had been astronomical. Maybe even then. But I thought my parents were pleased with my skating and knew how committed I was. Instead they made it clear that they both felt I should give up any ideas of making a career on the ice. I'm afraid their attitude only served to make me more determined than ever to spend my life developing skating as an art form, no matter what the consequences.'

John loved boarding school, but he worried about the ice time he missed. It was with a certain reluctance that he returned for the autumn term, but once there he settled easily into the academic routine and found pleasure in rediscovering his friends.

'It was a happy time for me, on the whole. I was taken to hear my first symphony concert, which was a wonderful evening of Strauss waltzes. I vowed that someday I would skate to a live symphony orchestra. I was also introduced to the delights of Jane Austen and thought her just as wonderful as Dickens. I got such pleasure from those books, perhaps because I had never been exposed to them as a child. I think it's vitally important to read the classics to young children, even if they can't actually understand them. Something will rub off and the essence of the literature will be absorbed. Unfortunately, Mother was far too busy to read to me; I had to teach myself. I can't even remember when I started, but I must have been five or six.'

In November, Rita wrote to say John's father was in a very bad state. He was refusing to eat and spent almost all day in bed. He was clearly suffering from clinical depression.

'Mother's letter was particularly disturbing in light of my father's apparent improvement during the summer holidays. It was difficult to know what to make of his condition – whether it was the result of his drinking problem, or the cause of it. I tended to believe that some great sadness must be buried inside him. Something even he wouldn't acknowledge. I wished there was something I could do to help, but I knew it was impossible.'

Christmas approached and Rita tried to arrange a holiday in Suffolk. Joseph's condition precluded any long journeys, however, and even if he had been well enough to travel he almost certainly would not have agreed to go. He barely left the house any more. In the end, the family gathered in Acock's Green and celebrated Christmas the best way they could.

'It wasn't a deliriously happy holiday, but at least there was a kind of peace. On Boxing Day Mother asked me to take my father's supper to his room and see if I could get him to eat it. I knocked on his door, expecting him to be in bed, but I found him sitting in his armchair staring out of the window. He looked terribly sad. "Do you know how much I love the night sky?" he said. "There was a time when I could name all the stars, but now I seem to have forgotten them." I sat with him, coaxing him to taste his food. He hadn't been drinking, but his hands shook as he tried to hold his knife and fork. I realized with a shock that he seemed to have shrunk and I noticed deep shadows under his eyes. I thought I had never seen him so vulnerable.'

The next day Joseph began another drinking bout. He drained the remains of the Christmas liquor and when it had all gone he dressed and went out. When he returned it was nearly midnight and he could barely stand. John helped his mother get him into bed, as they had done so many times before. He made no protest, allowing them to undress him before he turned on his side and lay motionless, crying silently.

'I expect it sounds perverse, but I found myself wishing he was angry. This quiet grief was far more upsetting. Mother looked so worn out that I made her go to bed and I sat for a long time beside my father, watching him. I don't think he knew I was there because after a while he suddenly focused on me and seemed surprised to see me. "I was just thinking about the prison camp," he said. I was startled. I had no idea what he could possibly mean. He sighed deeply. "We spent three years there, you know. They used to do some very bad things to us. They always seemed to be angry, but I got away. I wanted to come home." He stared at me, puzzled. "Isn't it funny? Now that I'm here, I can't remember why I wanted to come." He closed his eyes and fell asleep. I sat, stunned, unable to grasp what I'd heard. Until that moment I had never heard that my father was a prisoner of war. If it was true, I thought it explained a great deal.'

John found his mother reluctant to discuss the subject with him. Eventually she said, 'You have to accept the fact that your father didn't want anyone to know about it. Not even you. He was a prisoner in Germany for three years. He escaped in 1944 and had the most terrifying journey before he made it home. He hasn't really been himself since then.' He must have looked shocked because she added, 'You can be proud of him, you know. He was only a corporal but he was awarded a medal. It seems he was very brave.'

'It felt strange to be hearing this from Mother. I was sad, because it would have made such a difference to me had I known about it before. It somehow seemed to make me closer to him, but I felt cheated that such a significant phase in his life had never been shared with me.'

Joseph continued to drink through the rest of Christmas week and his melancholy was replaced by an abusive paranoia. Several times John had to intervene between his parents and twice he was woken from his own sleep to find himself being dragged from his bed and beaten. He longed for school to start again.

'It was as if my father were two people, unconnected with one another. I loved and respected one and feared and resented the other. On the afternoon of 29 December, he flew into a particularly violent rage and frightened Mother so badly that she broke down in tears. It was too much for me. I turned on him and told him exactly what I thought of his behaviour and that I wished he would just go away and leave us all alone. Then I went to the ice rink and skated for two hours until I felt calmer. When I got home, he had gone to London.'

It was with a feeling of intense relief that the family sat down to dinner that evening. Music played on the radio and a cheerful fire burnt in the hearth. John went to bed early, exhausted from the trauma of the previous days and anxious to take advantage of a good night's sleep. At three o'clock in the morning he woke up with a start to see his father standing in the bedroom doorway.

'I flinched, because I was certain I was about to get another beating, especially in view of my outburst the day before. But he made no move and just leant against the door, smiling at me. He didn't look at all angry, in fact he actually looked quite relaxed. Eventually he left without saying anything. I felt a great peace settle over me and I lay down and slept deeply for seven hours.'

The next morning John went downstairs late and made himself

some coffee. Rita came in and offered to make him eggs and John asked where his father was. She looked at him in surprise. 'Still in London,' she said.

'Well he was here last night, because he came into my room.'

Rita shook her head. 'You must have had a dream, John. The front door was bolted. He wouldn't have been able to get in.' Just then, the phone rang and she went to answer it. When she came back her face was ashen and she was trembling. She sat at the kitchen table and tried to speak, but no words would come out.

'It took me a long time to calm Mother down. When she could finally speak she said, "I don't know how to tell you this, John, but something dreadful has happened. Your father is dead. He was found this morning in a hotel room in Paddington." I sat there, horrified, while the reality of her words sank in. All I could think was that now his pain would be over.'

6

Joseph's body was found by a chambermaid in the Great Western Royal Hotel in Paddington. He was sprawled, fully clothed, across a bed and appeared to have been alone when he died. He had ingested a massive amount of chloral hydrate, a powerful hypnotic drug, and had expired at approximately three o'clock on the morning of 30 December 1965. He was fifty years old.

'My father had left nothing to indicate what could have driven him to do such a thing. As far as we knew he had spoken to no one, and there was no sign of a suicide note. An inquest was ordered for 7 January, and somehow or other we all managed to live through the days in between. New Year's Eve, which was never my favourite time anyway, was the worst of all. I realized my father would never see another year and I felt so unbearably sad to think that he died on his own, with no one to help him.'

The coroner for Inner West London, George Thurston,

confirmed that the chloral poisoning had been self-administered. It was virtually impossible for it to have been an accident.

'My father's suicide had a devastating effect on us. It left us with a permanent sense of grief which will never go away, no matter what we do. I can never rid myself of the feeling that I somehow let him down.'

Once the inquest was over, Rita tried to pick up the pieces of her shattered life. There was very little money and Joseph's business had deteriorated over the last three years to the point where it was barely viable. She had to make some far-reaching decisions. Top of her list was to take John out of boarding school.

'I wasn't terribly upset about leaving the school at that point, because I felt I should be at home with Mother. I knew we were going to be on a very tight budget, but there was enough to pay for me to skate every morning until noon. Andrew had finished his formal education by this time, so I inherited his tutor and we would work together at the kitchen table every afternoon until four. We loathed each other and as a result nothing very much was ever accomplished. I can't imagine that I was cut out to be an academic, so it didn't really matter very much.'

Because Joseph had died in London, Rita managed to keep the story out of the local papers. She told everyone that he had died suddenly of TB and most people assumed the illness had recurred. Certainly no one asked any questions.

'Mother forbade us to talk about the suicide again. This was difficult for me because I abhorred lies of any kind and I was being forced to tell people my father had died of tuberculosis. However, I did honour her wishes as far as her own circle of friends was concerned. It struck me that it wasn't a good idea to pretend that something so traumatic had never happened. It fell into the same category as not talking about my father's war experiences. If things are not faced, they tend to fester in the subconscious and become gangrenous.'

John brooded continuously on what could have driven his father to take his own life. It was not by any means an easy deduction.

'No matter how hard I tried, I couldn't figure out what had happened. The most obvious thing would have been the depressions, which were almost continual towards the end of my father's life. If you add the amount of alcohol he consumed, then you must assume that it aggravated a potentially lethal situation. Yet somehow I didn't see that as the trigger. I thought about the war experiences, which had recently flared up in his memory, and about the financial difficulties he was in, which must have been worrying him for a very long time. And, quite apart from all these possibilities, there was the fact that my father was appalled by the severity of his own black rages and longed to be able to lead a normal life. But underneath all this was the terrible nagging fear that in some way my last heated exchange with him had robbed him of the will to go on.'

Because Joseph had committed suicide, the insurance company would not allow Rita to collect on his policy. With this last potential source of income gone, she had to make further economies, and all non-essentials were pared away.

'With virtually no money left, Mother had to let my tutor go and I was mercifully spared from any further exposure to his teachings. I don't know which of us was happier that the arrangement had come to an end. With his departure I felt the last trappings of my childhood fall away, and a new sense of freedom and purpose entered my life. I made up my mind to find a really good skating coach and concentrate my efforts on international competition. I believed that, with a great deal of hard work, I could make it all the way to the Olympics. If needs be, I would get a job and pay for the training myself.'

John asked everyone he could think of to recommend coaches to him, and one name kept coming up over and over again. Armand Perrin was a noted Swiss trainer, teaching in Streatham, south London, and John decided he would be an ideal choice. He packed his bags and caught a train to London.

'I was so keen to study with Mr Perrin that I didn't contact him ahead of time. I was afraid he would turn me down. Instead I arrived in Streatham unannounced and rented a furnished room the size of a broom cupboard. The next morning I presented myself at the ice rink at eight o'clock and asked Mr Perrin if he would take me on. He was very charming and kind and told me he would be delighted to have me as a student – the only problem was that he was moving to Solihull Ice Rink in six weeks' time. I had to laugh at the irony of it, because Solihull was only fifteen minutes' drive from our house in Acock's Green.'

John stayed the full six weeks in Streatham and found Armand

Perrin a first-rate teacher. At the end, he packed his bag and followed him back to Birmingham. He was not sorry to leave Streatham behind.

'I have to admit I was rather homesick by this time. Outside of boarding school, I had never lived away from home before and I missed having my things around me. I was more than happy to go back.'

For the next six months John worked hard, commuting twice a day to the Solihull rink. His skating improved dramatically, and his style evolved into a seamless fusion of technique and artistry. He moved across the ice in beautiful, unbroken lines and with a lyrical quality unique in the amateur world.

'I was satisfied with the direction I was taking, even though I was very much aware of the tut-tutting that went on behind my back. I'm sure the powers that be must have taken Mr Perrin aside and warned him that I was a lost cause. Nothing anyone could have said would have convinced me that I was wrong, however. I skated instinctively, and I skated to please myself. What I was doing was not right for everyone, but it was right for me.'

John spent his seventeenth birthday quietly at home. After tea, he told his mother that he would have to go back to London again, this time for a much longer period. His school figures – the tracing of specific loops and circles on the ice – which were vital to the success of a competitor, had been neglected recently and he wanted to go to Richmond and study under the world's foremost teacher, Arnold Gerschwiler.

'Mother was terribly unhappy about it, but of course she couldn't have stopped me. I knew exactly what I wanted to do. I wrote to Mr Gerschwiler to ask if he would take me as a pupil and to my delight he wrote back immediately to say he would be pleased to have me. I arranged to go straight away.'

Rita tried to talk to John about the dangers of setting his sights on such a singular ambition. She was deeply concerned about what would happen to him if he failed in his bid to win an Olympic title. She knew he had no desire to skate in a traditional ice show, and worried that the alternative, life as a coach, would not be something John could handle.

'I suppose to some extent I understood Mother's reservations. How could she really know the true depth of my commitment? I really had no choice because I was being driven internally to follow this particular path and I couldn't possibly contemplate failure. I had to be strong and determined and I had to be prepared to make sacrifices. I knew that at the outset.'

This time John set off for London with many of his favourite possessions packed in his bags. He went knowing he would have to get a job to support himself and that he would have to live frugally if he was to survive, because his mother had virtually nothing she could contribute.

'In spite of all the hardships I seemed to be facing, I left for London in high spirits and filled with hope. I didn't know it then but I had just, as they say, left home.'

7

John arrived in Richmond with two suitcases, a holdall and his skate bag. He was immediately enchanted by the old-world charm of the town and managed to find some inexpensive digs within easy reach of the ice rink.

'I loved everything about Richmond. Technically it was part of Greater London but in reality it was a self-contained world of its own, curled around a stretch of the River Thames that was a favourite subject for painters. I thought it was all very beautiful.'

In order to pay for his lessons and his digs, John had to find a source of income. He had no working experience at all, but he did have a combination of charm and resourcefulness which soon landed him a job in a small supermarket.

'I was amazed that they took me on. Perhaps I was just in the right place at the right time – at any rate, I soon became expert at stacking shelves and operating the till. My wages were very small – just enough to cover the barest of essentials – but I was lucky enough to be given the day-old bread and the things that were about to go out of date. In this way I managed to survive.'

The Richmond Ice Rink was situated in a picturesque spot on the Thames, right beside the Richmond Bridge, and was within walking distance of John's lodgings.

'It would have been difficult to imagine a more idyllic setting. Richmond Rink is a kind of mecca for skaters, having been the site of the earliest indoor competitions and the training ground for many international champions. It was steeped in history and every time I walked into the building I could feel the ghosts all around me.'

Under Mr Gerschwiler's patient tutelage, John's school figures improved steadily. He worked hard at them and developed a new sense of respect for their importance.

'Like many skaters I tended to look on school figures as a necessary evil, some archaic ritual designed to hamper the growth of a performer. Now I began to see them in a different light and to understand that without this vital grounding there could be no real artistry. Figures are to skaters as scales are to pianists. Without them to underpin the choreography, the artist will lack the quality of line so essential to beautiful movement.'

John was desperate to find a job with a higher salary and more flexible hours. His father's company had made components for the National Cash Register Company in Marylebone Road, and he approached them to see if they had a suitable vacancy. To his surprise they not only offered him employment, but also agreed to schedule his hours to fit in with his training programme.

'It was a very demanding arrangement, but it did allow enough time for everything I needed to accomplish. I got up at five in the morning and skated at Richmond until twelve. Then I snatched a quick lunch and took the train to the NCR offices where I worked from two until five. I usually fell asleep on the train home so it was lucky that mine was the last stop on the line. The job was not particularly distinguished – it consisted mainly of looking after clients who were waiting to see someone other than me – but I knew that if I stuck it out I would eventually be paid enough money to rent a bedsitter of my own. The thought of achieving that measure of independence, however illusory, kept me going forward.'

At first John enjoyed an unusually good relationship with Arnold Gerschwiler. He was an accomplished and graceful free-skater, in sharp contrast to the majority of students in the Gerschwiler stable, and brought a refreshing new dimension to the free-style sessions.

'In December, I was invited to join Arnold's annual winter school in Davos, Switzerland. I was very flattered to be asked, but of course there was no way that I could afford to go. I stayed behind and made myself skate every day. I can't say I enjoyed being alone, but I wanted to surprise Mr Gerschwiler when he came back. It was a long three months.'

During this period, John became obsessed with his weight again. He had chanced to overhear a conversation between two of his fellow-students in which they remarked that John was looking healthier than when he arrived. This seemingly innocent comment began a chain reaction that culminated in him starving himself for days at a time.

'I have no idea what was going on in my head. I just know that I suddenly felt terribly fat. My landlady was very kind and would cook huge evening meals for me, mostly consisting of starch. I had no way to refuse these offerings without hurting her feelings, so I would consume them as quickly as I could, excuse myself from the table, go into the bathroom and vomit it all up again as quietly as possible. I think I weighed eight stone at the time, but I felt like a blimp.'

John became the British Junior Champion of 1967 and was once again offered advice by the skating hierarchy. To date his climb up the competitive ladder had not been a smooth one, and his continued refusal to compromise led to clashes with leading British officials.

'It was all such a nonsense really. It had nothing to do with good skating, but everything to do with power trips and the superimposing of one will upon another. I was told that if I was ever to make an impact on the international circuit I must change everything about myself – my attitude, my costumes, my choreography. I actually laughed out loud at one point. I couldn't help it. If I was such a disaster, how was it that I had managed to get this far? "In spite of yourself," I was told.'

John was determined to stick to his own inimitable style on the ice, and in 1968 he won the coveted Jennings Trophy for free-skating at Nottingham Ice Stadium. He couldn't resist sending a postcard to one of his critics. It said, 'Pleased to let you know that I have just won the Jennings Trophy in spite of myself. John Curry.'

'Nothing could have convinced me at that point in my career that I was on the wrong track. I knew, without any doubt at all, that what

I was doing was working for me. It made me happy to skate the way I did, and I hoped it might give others pleasure too.'

John became concerned about the amount of time he was absent from his job at the NCR, but they made it plain to him that they understood the requirements of his competitive life and were more than happy to hold open his job while he was away. In 1969 they awarded him a pay rise and he was at last able to rent a bedsitter.

'It was late October, and extremely mild for the time of year. I found a very nice, private bedsitter, convenient for both ice rink and station, and soon had it looking like home. I set out my books, put a box of teabags by the stove, set up my little radio and made up the bed. I celebrated my first night there by cooking myself a large mushroom omelette, making a pot of tea, turning on the radio and relaxing in the old brown armchair. It was such bliss to have my own space and I felt that I was finally free.'

By November the weather had turned cold. The extra cost of the bedsitter had more than eaten up John's increase in salary and unless he could put coins in the gas meter he was without heat, hot water and cooking facilities.

'I devised ways of economizing. Someone had given me an old flask, so I was able to keep my tea hot all day. I ate salad and sandwiches to save on the gas, and when I did use it I would brew up a huge pot of vegetable stew, enough to last a week. I frequently went to bed early to avoid turning on the gas fire. I would lie, huddled under the blankets, reading by candlelight. I seemed to be eternally cold – I washed in cold water in a cold room, ate a cold breakfast and went to skate at a cold rink. I suppose it was all rather unbearable but I kept telling myself that I was happy.'

John made an excellent showing in the British Championships and was invited to represent Britain in the European Championships. Because of this, it became imperative that he accompany Arnold Gerschwiler to Davos for the winter training session, to gain the advantage of working with some of the world's leading competitors.

'The prospect was daunting. I had no money and I had a job. I would be gone for three months. I had no idea how I could possibly arrange it all. But the NCR was extremely supportive and gave me a leave of absence. They also gave me a bonus, which I was quite certain I wasn't entitled to. However, it made it possible for me to go. I set off in high spirits, filled with anticipation. I looked forward to a fantastic experience and had no inkling at that stage that it would all turn out to be a nightmare.'

8

Davos, high in the Swiss Alps, has always been a popular destination for winter-sports enthusiasts. Until the 1960s this included competitive skaters anxious to prepare themselves for the hazards of outdoor championships. The large rink in Davos was perfect for the purpose, being exposed to a succession of high winds, blowing snow, freezing temperatures and an irregular ice surface. By the time John arrived, however, the International Skating Union had already eliminated outdoor championships altogether.

'Working under those conditions for an extended period of time was not only superfluous, it was actually damaging. It seemed to me to be a cruel and inhuman folly to insist we go there when the training was so obviously inappropriate. The whole thing was appalling. The cold was so intense it made me gasp.'

John loathed being in Davos. He resented the strict schedule Arnold Gerschwiler had devised, making his students rise at six a.m. and walk through the frigid morning air to the rink.

'Mr Gerschwiler himself seemed immune to the harsh temperatures and expected his students to adapt. He believed that such a regimen would increase our strength and endurance and make us more successful in competition. It was like being in the Marine Corps or on a survival training course for the SAS. I was horrified to find myself in the middle of it.'

In the early morning, the rink was intensely cold and the air was arctic. Later in the day, when the sun had warmed the atmosphere, the situation was considerably more pleasant.

'We could have skated at any point in the day, but Mr Gerschwiler insisted that we must all be on the ice before seven a.m. I have no idea what possessed him, because the misery was indescribable. My eyes would water and then my eyelashes would freeze shut. My lungs felt as though they were on fire and when I breathed my nostrils would immediately seal themselves together. I wondered what on earth I was doing there.'

John's relationship with Arnold Gerschwiler began to deteriorate rapidly under the spartan conditions. The mutual admiration they had previously enjoyed seemed to disappear and they fought repeatedly.

'I was inconsolable. I would whinge until he lost his temper and then we would start shouting at one another. He was extremely unhappy with me and openly dismissive of my attitude which he considered to be very poor indeed. I can't say I blame him really – I was constantly complaining and I must have been a nightmare to deal with that season.'

John's skating began to show the strain alarmingly. He was completely unable to overcome his aversion to the conditions and even his free-skating suffered.

'It would not be an exaggeration to say that I simply collapsed. I couldn't seem to skate any more and I was falling all over the place. Even the most rudimentary moves were beyond me. I had lost the will to go on, and I suppose it is entirely possible that I had suffered some kind of nervous breakdown.'

Somehow John survived the ordeal, and in March he packed his bags thankfully and headed back to Richmond. He was delighted to be back in the sanctity of his own bedsitter, among his own possessions, and for a while he didn't notice the cold.

'Everything is relative. The first two weeks I was back, I actually thought my room was warm. It wasn't long, however, before I began to shiver again and I faced the usual problem of how to find enough coins for the gas meter. I managed to get through the last few days of winter by wearing my coat and scarf indoors. Whenever I became depressed by it, I reminded myself that it could have been much worse – I could have been in Davos.'

John worked furiously to regain his previous form on the ice. He was determined to counteract the damage done in Davos and to hold on to his position as the heir apparent to the British title.

'Mr Gerschwiler and I put our feud on hold. We didn't discuss it, but we both knew that if I was to have any chance at all of moving up the international ladder a ceasefire was essential. I was terrified that I had lost the ability to skate altogether, and dreaded the prospect of a life entirely dominated by cash registers. After two weeks of fruitless struggling, I began to panic. Then suddenly, without warning, it was as if a block had been removed and it all came flooding back to me. It's hard to describe the relief I felt.'

1970 was a significant year for John. He skated an outstanding free-style programme in the British Championships and took the Men's title for the first time. As a result he was picked to represent Great Britain in the European Championships, and was seeded in the top group of competitors. His free-skating programme, to the music of *Scheherazade*, dazzled the crowd and catapulted him into third place above some of the much more experienced Russian and German entries. He was now in line to make his first bid for the world title in Lyon in March 1971.

'I was both thrilled and appalled by the prospect. It was a double-edged sword – on the one hand I would be one step closer to my ultimate ambition; and on the other, I would now be forced to spend yet another winter season in Davos with Mr Gerschwiler. I wasn't at all sure that I could bear it, and I have no doubt he felt the same way. However, it seemed to be one of those dreadful twists of fate that assault one's life just when one is beginning to feel better about things. I didn't appear to have any choice in the matter, though, and I decided I would just have to get through it the best way I could.'

John now had a number of good friends in London, including his close companion Penny Malec. She suggested that he persuade them all to spend their vacations in Davos, and he waxed so lyrical about the beauty of the scenery that everyone agreed.

'The early-morning skating sessions were still anathema to me, but at least I knew that when they were over I could go off and have fun with my friends. It made the training almost tolerable, although my reservations about the wisdom of this particular site grew daily. If I was a serious contender for the World Championships it seemed to be perverse to subject me to a regime that a year earlier had virtually destroyed my ability to compete. I had no heart to continue arguing about it, however, and I decided that, if this was what Mr Gerschwiler wanted me to do, I would go through the motions and stop worrying about the consequences.'

John enjoyed what he referred to as his 'après-skate' activities. His friends came out to Davos in a steady stream, one after the other, so that he was rarely without congenial company. They rented skis and John immediately tried his hand at the more difficult slopes, finding he had a natural aptitude for the sport. He plunged, laughing aloud, down the runs and somehow managed to stay upright. He went on long cross-country treks and would drag a toboggan to the top of a precipitous, icy slope and hurtle at break-neck speed to the bottom. He would sometimes veer off the run on the way down and be thrown into a deep pile of soft snow up to his neck.

'I was having a fantastic time. I was doing what people are supposed to do when they go to ski resorts and I loved every minute of it. In the mean time, my skating grew worse and worse and Mr Gerschwiler and I began to have furious arguments again. I blamed the conditions and he blamed the fact that I was disobeying his strict instructions not to ski or toboggan. In fairness to him, I have to admit that these activities are unwise for any competitive skater – the risk of injury is far too great – but I was stubborn and refused to contemplate the potential of this. I insisted that what I did in my own time was my business. He was livid.'

The snow that fell relentlessly during February made the tracing of school figures on the ice practically impossible. Before a figure was even finished, it had been obliterated by the blowing drifts. It rendered the whole exercise futile.

'One morning I was battling to cut a path through the layer of snow which covered the ice, my vision seriously impaired by the fierce wind which drove yet more snow into my face. I was freezing to death and having great difficulty in holding my balance. Suddenly I realized how ridiculous it all was and I skated to the edge of the rink and took off my skates. "What do you think you are doing?" Mr Gerschwiler roared. I was too angry to reply, and simply walked quickly away in the direction of the hotel. He never forgave me for challenging his authority in that way, and by the time we left for Lyon in March we were barely able to exchange a civil word.'

Lyon was a disaster. None of the Davos graduates performed well and John was no exception. He turned in an uninspired programme and missed most of his jumps. As for his school figures, he had done better tracings five years earlier. It seemed like an appropriate moment for he and Arnold Gerschwiler to part company permanently.

9

During the traditional exhibition performances at the end of the Lyon championships, John was approached by Skee Goodheart, the owner of *Holiday on Ice*. He had heard rumours that John was thinking of quitting amateur competition.

'Mr Goodheart invited me to lunch, and I went because I was seriously considering the option of joining a show. I hadn't actually decided what to do, but my showing in the Worlds had left me with a huge dent in my confidence. I thought I should at least listen to what he had to say.'

Lunch was pleasant and the conversation was amicable and incidental. When the coffee arrived, John became impatient and decided to find out what this meeting was all about.

'I asked if he was interested in employing me and, if so, on what terms. He seemed taken aback, and proceeded to tell me that I needed *Holiday on Ice* because it was the only show that would offer me any kind of a forum. He then told me that I must accept the fact that I was an inferior competitor and could never hope to make any mark in the Olympics. I would be well advised to take his offer and his advice and join the cast of his show without making ridiculous and impossible artistic demands. I was so insulted that I immediately decided I was going to win the Olympics if it killed me. I thanked him politely for the lunch and excused myself from the table. One thing I knew for certain was that I would never, under any circumstances, join the cast of *Holiday on Ice*. I would rather wash dishes.'

During the practice sessions in Lyon, John had been impressed by a Canadian coach who taught in New York. His name was Peter Dunfield and he worked with many of the top international competitors. John decided to approach him to see if he would consider taking him as a student.

'Peter was very kind and friendly. I liked him right away. To my surprise he invited me to join him in New York for the summer season, with a further six weeks in Toronto. I accepted without hesitation, even though I had no idea where the money was to come from.'

John plucked up courage to ask his bank manager for a loan, and to his amazement he got it. He still needed an additional £300, which he managed to borrow from a friend and in addition the NCR gave him another small bonus.

'By my standards I was rich, so I set off for New York filled with hope and renewed determination. I felt it was an important turning point in my life.'

John's only misgiving as he flew across the Atlantic concerned accommodation. He had no idea how Americans lived, especially as students, and feared he might be billeted in a depressing room in a bad area.

'I had visions of myself ploughing through pimps and prostitutes on the Lower East Side. I had read horror stories about it and also about Harlem and the Bronx. However, I needn't have worried because I found myself staying with a wonderful family in one of the nicest homes I have ever been in. Frank and Nancy Streeter welcomed me in and made me part of the family, and I was given a room and bathroom of my own, very nicely furnished, and full run of the remainder of the house. I thought of it as a sanctuary, and although I didn't know it then it was to remain my New York head-quarters for as long as I continued to skate.'

The Streeter family lived in East 73rd Street, close to the junction with Third Avenue. It was a fashionable and safe area, near to the famous Bloomingdale's store. The whole area was filled with antique- and bookshops, boutiques and coffee houses. John loved to browse, especially in the bookstores, and would often stop for a cappuccino. He would sit at a table watching the people passing by.

'I was fascinated. New York is a twenty-four-hour city and has a throbbing pulse that never seems to stop beating. I loved nothing better than to sit and observe. It was like a show, a parade of endless variety. It was very hot that summer, in that steamy, oppressive way that is peculiar to the city, but I hardly noticed it. I was so happy to be there and to be part of all that.'

The Sky Rink is New York's only full-size indoor ice facility. It sits on top of a sixteen-storey building on the west side of the city and is frequented by every serious skater in the area. John loved it immediately and looked forward eagerly to spending six weeks work-ing there.

'The atmosphere was friendly and the place was relatively warm. Some very good skaters practised there and I enjoyed watching them and noting the different styles. Everything seemed to be perfect at first and I felt confident that my borrowing spree would be well worth the investment.'

Unfortunately, things began to go seriously wrong when Peter Dunfield appeared on the scene. He was a somewhat unorthodox coach, employing very modern methods. This system of teaching was exactly what had attracted John to him in the first place.

'We didn't get on at all. Not the least bit. We disagreed on every-thing and I felt he was insulting to the point of being rude. He was used to tearing people down in order to build them up again, but it had a totally demoralizing effect on me. He made no bones about the fact that he felt I was too old to learn anything new, and told me point-blank that I had already picked up far too many bad habits on the ice. There was little hope for me, as far as he could see. I have no idea what this approach was meant to achieve, but all it did was humiliate and depress me. He had, after all, agreed to take me and presumably must have considered there was something he could teach me. I was incensed that I appeared to have spent several hundred pounds to be subjected to a lot of psychobabble.'

The Streeter family made sure that John was comfortable and entertained when he was not at the Sky Rink, and this served to counteract the effects of his training sessions. He was taken to see a wide variety of ballet companies and was especially delighted with the more contemporary groups who visited the city during the sum-mer season. In July, he had to uproot once again and fly to Toronto with Peter Dunfield.

'There was nothing actually wrong with Toronto. It is a perfectly nice city – clean, safe and attractive to look at. But the trouble for me was that it wasn't New York. I had fallen in love with Manhattan and I found the sanitized atmosphere of Toronto stultifying in con-trast. I also missed living with the Streeters.'

The relationship between John and Peter grew worse. John's skating was deteriorating rapidly and he was often reduced to tears.

'I was embarrassed, but I couldn't help it. They were tears of frustration and panic. I couldn't believe that my skating was falling apart again. I couldn't seem to do anything about it, and the worse I got the more vicious were Mr Dunfield's comments. He seemed to despise me and I shrivelled up inside. Finally, there came a day when I couldn't bear it any longer. I think I would have become suicidal if I'd stayed there, so I decided to cut my losses and go home. Two hours later I was sitting in Toronto Airport waiting for a charter that was due to leave for London in twenty minutes. I had told no one I was going.'

John was too miserable to return to Richmond, and since he no longer had a coach there, there seemed little point. He realized he was homesick and caught a train to Birmingham.

'Mother wasn't there when I arrived, but I had my own key and let myself in. The house seemed deserted and the fridge was empty. I made no attempt to go out and buy anything. I was in a black depression and I didn't care about eating. I lay on my bed fully clothed, and cried until I fell asleep, and when I woke up the next day I started to cry all over again. I felt I was at the bottom of a deep pit and I had no interest in climbing out. I just wanted to crouch there until I died.'

John's mother returned three days later to find him in a terrible state. He was hungry and unkempt and his eyes were swollen from crying. She couldn't remember ever seeing him like that before and she was deeply concerned.

'Poor Mother. She had imagined me to be safely in Toronto, working with Mr Dunfield. I think I gave her quite a shock, and I must have looked terrible. The first thing she did was insist that I eat, even though I didn't want anything. I was so miserable I threw it all up again.'

Rita tried hard to bring John out of his depression but nothing seemed to work. He sat for hours, just staring into space. One evening he stirred himself and told her that he felt his life no longer had any true meaning. He added that he would be better off dead.

'Mother flew at me. I have rarely seen her angry but that night she was livid. I suppose that in my total self-absorption I had forgotten how any talk of death, especially suicide, would resurrect the most gruesome memories for her. It was stupid of me and when I realized what I had done I apologized. I promised her that I was just being silly and that she shouldn't take any notice of me. The exchange must have stirred something in me, because the next morning I washed and shaved and returned to Richmond. I thought I would have one more try.'

John had befriended a coach at the rink called Alison Smith. He admired her technique, and her warm, caring approach to her students appealed to him. He approached her now with the hope that she would agree to teach him.

'Alison's response to my request was immediate. She was honest enough to tell me that she couldn't guarantee she could achieve anything with me, but that if I was willing to try she would take me on. I told her I would do my very best and we shook hands. It was one of my happiest decisions.'

Richmond rink, like any major competitive rink, is controlled by an élite group of insiders. Head of this particular group was Arnold Gerschwiler, and when he discovered that John had now transferred to Alison Smith he was furious. He called Alison in and confronted her.

'Mr Gerschwiler had taught Alison, so he was irate at the idea she thought she could succeed with me where he had failed. "What makes you think you can control John Curry?" he demanded. "He's impossible to teach." Alison thanked him politely for his concern and told him that she had made up her mind to try. She added that she believed my style was absolutely right for me, and that she would encourage me to develop it. Mr Gerschwiler took her honesty to be a gauntlet hurled at his feet and he reacted disdainfully. He rarely spoke a civil word to Alison after that.'

John had always enjoyed skating at Richmond, but now it seemed to him that the atmosphere was decidedly unfriendly. People who had once greeted him with a smile now ignored him or gave him a curt nod.

'I noticed other coaches going out of their way to avoid me, and Alison was afforded the same treatment. We had become untouchables. On the ice we would be bumped into and pushed aside, and it seemed that people were always yelling at us. We began to dread going in, and there were days when we simply chose not to. I suppose we had been sent to Coventry for breaking the unwritten law of the ice-rink jungle – you don't transfer from one teacher to another within the same rink. Particularly if that teacher controls the skating school.'

In spite of their difficulties at the rink, John and Alison got along well together and under her careful guidance John made rapid progress. She was openly supportive of his style and encouraged his excursions into the realm of dance. She refused to allow him to listen to other opinions, warning him that it would just lead to confusion. It was important at this stage to be totally insular.

'I loved working with Alison, but the political hive at the rink was demoralizing. It smacked of everything that is wrong with British skating. Instead of encouraging Alison, who was one of their finest teachers, they chose instead to intimidate her and criticize her until she couldn't stand it any longer. A couple of years later she was forced to leave England, as many other good teachers have been obliged to do, and the country lost a rare talent. For some reason I cannot fathom, the British applaud mediocrity and punish achievement. No matter what anyone says, it is an indisputable fact.'

10

John's long climb up the competitive ladder was not an easy one. His refusal to compromise led to clashes with officials, and he made no secret of his disdain for the entire ice establishment. Alison, however, persuaded him to use a certain amount of discretion.

'I always seemed to be angry, but Alison taught me to contain it. The stupidity and ignorance we both encountered in Richmond made me seethe, but I did as she asked and kept it to myself. It seemed such a sad thing that the skating world was controlled by people who seemed not to understand the first thing about the needs and priorities of a skater. This was not only true of Richmond – it was unfortunately the norm wherever I went. Skating was in the hands of philistines, and I feared for its future.'

With the 1973 World Championships in Bratislava on the horizon, John asked the National Skating Association to find him a sponsor. His financial situation was a constant worry and he was desperate to find some kind of relief from the crippling expense of international competition. Coaches, travel, ice time, accommodation, boots and costumes would cost a leading competitor as much as £50,000 a year.

'I was always penniless. I pinched and scrimped on food, heat, clothing and transport. I walked everywhere and haunted the charity shops. There was nothing left to cut back on. As the day came for us to leave for Bratislava, I realized that I was not going to get sponsorship. It simply wasn't going to happen.'

John was tense going into the competition, but he managed to turn in a solid set of figures that were scored well. In the short compulsory programme, which lasted two minutes, he completed all but one of the required moves. He was well positioned for the final phase, the free-skating.

'Alison had a very calming influence on me. She gave me strength and focus. She forbade me to watch the other performances and made me wait backstage until it was my turn to go out on to the ice. I skated my best performance in years, and although I missed a medal I did finish in fourth place. I felt that I was at last beginning to make some real progress.'

The crowd at the Worlds responded enthusiastically to John's performance in the exhibition phase of the championship. The first four from each category are invited to skate in this special show, and since there is no judging, the atmosphere is always relaxed. In the audience that afternoon was a man called Ed Mosler, an American philanthropist who had supported many leading US skaters.

'After I had skated, I was approached by a man who congratulated me and said he would like to meet me at the hotel for a chat. I was sceptical, to say the least, because I couldn't think what a complete stranger would want to talk to me about. I told him I was very busy but I would try to give him a call later. The next morning he came up to me in the hotel lobby and apologized for not explaining who he was. He told me he had a charitable foundation which supported promising skaters and that, although they normally only awarded grants to American skaters, he had been so impressed with my performance that he was going to ask them to make an exception in my case. "I was thinking of five hundred pounds," he told me. "Do you think this would be of any help to you?" I was so shocked that for a moment I couldn't say anything. Suddenly all the years of struggling seemed to be coming to an end. Five hundred pounds was a small fortune to me in 1973.'

John hardly dared to think about Ed Mosler's offer for fear that something would go wrong. He had been poor for so long that the

45

prospect of having enough money to make his life comfortable was hard for him to grasp.

'Poverty had become a way of life to me. The gnawing worry that I wouldn't have enough money for the train, or the gas meter, or groceries, was always there. Luxuries of any kind had so long been denied me that I no longer had a taste for them. The financial cushion given to me by Mr Mosler's five hundred pounds would last me for at least two years, and I was determined not to waste any of it.'

As a matter of courtesy, John informed the National Skating Association that he had found a sponsor. He assumed the process was a formality, but to his consternation he was told that it might be better not to accept the offer.

'It was quite ludicrous. When pressed for a reason, the only one they could come up with was that Mr Mosler was an American. No matter that I had been existing on tea and toast for years, it seemed that I was to lose my sponsor simply because he came from the wrong side of the Atlantic. I argued vehemently with them and in the end they gave in. My sponsorship was officially endorsed.'

Alison and John worked at Richmond for another year and tried hard to ignore the negative atmosphere at the rink. John's skating had evolved dramatically since Bratislava, and they left for the European Championships with high hopes.

'I felt good in Zagreb. Strong and much more relaxed than usual, thanks to Alison's calming influence. I did well in figures, missed the combination jump in the compulsory segment, and pulled up again in the free-skating to take my first major international medal. Suddenly I realized that I was in the running for the Worlds, which were to be held in Munich in March. If nothing went wrong, I stood a good chance of improving on my fourth position in Bratislava.'

About a week before he left for Germany, John began to panic. So much hinged on his performance in Munich that he was beset by nerves and misgivings. Had he chosen the wrong music? Would his costume please the judges? Was his free-style programme too lyrical and over-simplified? He was no longer sure of himself or his direction, but it was too late to change anything. He would have to go with what he had.

'I was a nervous wreck. I couldn't sleep – I would wake up in a cold sweat, always having had the same dream. I was about to start my free-skating programme, poised in the centre of the ice. My music started and I tried to push off but nothing happened. I looked down at my feet and saw that I was wearing dance shoes instead of skates. I looked across to the judges for help, only to see that they were all my father. They started to laugh at me, and the laugh got louder and louder until I screamed at them to stop. At that point I woke up, trembling. I had that dream over and over again, and I became afraid to go to sleep at all. I was in a dreadful state. I couldn't keep any food down, and when I did I immediately felt fat and bloated although I know that I was actually very thin. Alison kept asking me what was going on, but I just couldn't bring myself to discuss it with her.'

John would avoid practices because he couldn't bear to face the other competitors. His Canadian friend, Toller Cranston, who was himself an artistic maverick, sought him out and asked him to come to one of the evening practices held at an arena outside the city. He was about to unveil his own free-style programme and he wanted John's opinion. John had no intention of skating himself, but he agreed to go with Toller. He was curious to see what the flamboyant Toronto skater had choreographed.

'It was one of those times that you remember all your life. I wasn't really expecting anything, although I knew Toller to be a highly unusual performer. When we arrived at the arena, almost two thousand people were inside. I was shocked, because very few people outside the competitive fraternity will normally come to a practice session. Eventually it was Toller's turn, and the other skaters cleared the ice. As he came out there was an audible gasp from around the building. He was dressed in black, and was in white face make-up with a tear painted on one cheek. For four minutes he skated to the music of *Pagliacci* like someone possessed, bringing to life in exquisite cameo the tragedy of Leoncavallo's clown. It was as much about his strength as an actor and a mime as it was about his ability as a skater, although this too was original and thrilling as he cut strange, asymmetrical shapes in the air. As he finished, the crowd stood and cheered and I found myself choking back sobs. I felt I had just witnessed the future of skating.'

When the first day of competition came, John was literally frozen with fear. His school figures were mediocre and he missed the combination jump in the compulsory segment. As he prepared to go out on to the ice for the free-skating programme, he was panic-stricken. His mind seemed to go blank.

'I begged Alison to let me withdraw. When the music started I couldn't remember my choreography and for once my instinctive feeling for the ice deserted me. I skated the worst performance of my life and ended up dropping four places to finish eighth. I was completely humiliated.'

The judges came to John after the performance and told him point-blank that he should quit. No one, they insisted, could possibly recover from such a disaster. It would be unprecedented.

'I really wasn't interested in what the judges had to say. I had already decided that I would have to give up, because I didn't feel I could go on taking money from Mr Mosler after such a poor showing. It was that aspect that bothered me: I felt I had let him down. Mr Mosler, however, surprised me. He came especially to find me and told me that he hoped I had not been deterred by the Munich competition, because he had found parts of my programme to be deeply moving and very beautiful. It was hard for me to accept the sincerity of this comment, and I repeated my intention of retiring. He looked very sad and said, "Just promise me that you will think it all over for a while before you decide. If you carry on, I will be delighted to continue to support you."'

John went to New York to stay with the Streeters. Here he felt that he was in a protected and caring environment and that he could think clearly. He stayed for several weeks, brooding about his future and deeply depressed about the state of his career.

'As I sat quietly in the sanctity of the Streeters' living room, I slowly came to the realization that, whatever had happened in Munich, I was not about to retire from the ice because of it. I was capable of much better things, and I was determined to change my skating in whatever way was necessary to achieve acceptance. After a great deal of thought, I decided to ask Slavka Kahout for advice.'

Slavka Kahout was an extraordinarily gifted teacher, who had taught the legendary American skater Janet Lynn. She had recently married the double Olympic gold-medallist, Dick Button, and was expecting her first child when John went to see her. From the beginning, she made it clear that she was not in the market for another pupil.

'Slavka was in the process of winding down her teaching obligations and was therefore unable to help me personally. She seemed to understand my needs, however, and she was not afraid to tell me what she considered to be my weaknesses. "Your jumping is far from strong," she said. "And your figures are still a problem. Since no one teacher can give you everything that you require, what you need to find is a combination of coaching talents. I suggest Gus Lussi for jumps and Carlo Fassi for figures." It turned out to be inspired advice.'

11

Lake Placid is a beautiful mountain village in the heart of New York State. It is the major centre for winter-sports training in the eastern USA, and the vast Olympic Ice Arena is home to several of the world's top figure-skating coaches. It was there, in the autumn of 1974, that John spent six weeks working with the legendary Gus Lussi.

'The first day I was there I was asked to run through my repertoire of jumps. I could see Mr Lussi was far from impressed and he told me bluntly that we would have to start from scratch: I must forget everything that I had been taught so far and begin again. I was panic-stricken. How could I possibly afford the time for such a course of action? He looked at me sternly and said, "If you don't do as I suggest, you may as well give up any hope of ever becoming a champion. You can't put a roof on a faulty foundation." So, deeply chastened, I agreed to go back to square one.'

Gus Lussi's aim was to teach his students how to achieve elevation without a lengthy run-up. He worked on a small portion of ice, twenty by thirty feet, and stressed the importance of muscular co-ordination to give lift and suspension to a jump. It was a completely new approach for John.

'I was used to the usual idea of building up speed in order to get enough height for a jump. It was a rather unattractive method, but

49

I had no idea there was an aesthetically pleasing alternative. The only problem was that I simply couldn't do it. I fell all day long, even on the easiest jumps, and I was covered from head to toe in huge bruises. It was an embarrassing process for me – I was one of the top skaters in the world at the time, and people would come to the rink to watch me practise, only to see me slithering and crashing around, often ending in a heap against the barriers. I was mortified.'

In the evenings, John would climb into bed early and lie huddled underneath his bedclothes. He despaired of ever being able to conquer Mr Lussi's techniques and wondered yet again if perhaps his skating days were over. His misery was not helped by those who sought to counsel him, members of the rink's élite who urged him to abandon his futile efforts. He was far too old at twenty-four, they warned him, to change.

'I have to admit that I thought perhaps they were right. Perhaps my quest was beyond me and I was just too stubborn to see it. About half-way through my tenure with Mr Lussi, I made my mind up to tell him that I thought I shouldn't waste any more of his valuable time. I went early to the rink, so as to catch him before the session began, and while I was waiting for him to appear I decided to have one last try at a double toe loop jump, something that had eluded me completely. There was no one around and I focused totally on what I was about to do. Suddenly I felt myself rise into the air and turn; I seemed to hang in space for a moment before completing the second revolution and landing cleanly. I had done it! I let out a whoop of triumph, and then I heard the sound of clapping behind me. I turned to see Mr Lussi leaning on the barrier, watching me with just the suggestion of a smile at the corners of his normally stern mouth. "Good," he said simply. "Now we can begin."'

John's jumps came together quickly after that, salchow, axel, toe, single, double and triple, and by the end of his six weeks in Lake Placid he felt elated with his progress. As he left, he thanked Gus Lussi for his patience and his help. 'I could never have done this without you,' he said. 'Wrong,' was the reply. '*You* were the only thing standing in your way.'

The next stop on John's re-education agenda was a much longer sojourn in Colorado Springs, high in the Rocky Mountains. This was the nerve centre of American figure skating, home of many major international events and a base for Winter Olympic training.

50

The World Arena, set against a spectacular backdrop of mountain scenery, was run by a husband-and-wife team, Carlo and Christa Fassi, and they had achieved an amazing level of success with many of the top Olympic competitors. The most notable of these was the ethereal Peggy Fleming, who had won the Olympic gold medal in 1968 at the age of sixteen.

'I loved working with the Fassis. They were a fantastic combination, each complementing the other. I felt a warmth and gentle good humour from Mr Fassi, who tended to indulge me slightly, and in Mrs Fassi I found a taste and idealism which closely matched my own. It was she who would demand that I do a figure yet again, even after Mr Fassi had declared it to be "Hextraordinary!" I felt as though everything I had done up to this point had been leading here, to the rink in Colorado Springs, and to the Fassis. I was finally in the right place at the right time, and I was ecstatically happy.'

John was able to rent a small apartment in Colorado Springs, a fact which added to his sense of peace and serenity. Almost next door to him were some friends, a Dr and Mrs Graham, and he would often indulge in snowball fights with their children, or help them to build a snowman or an igloo. Out of respect for the Fassis, he did not indulge his passion for skiing or toboganning, but he liked to sit in the warm mountain sunshine, drinking coffee and watching the colourful array of people passing by.

'How I loved it all! It was as close to heaven as I ever expected to get. I was learning so much, so rapidly on the ice, and the atmosphere at the rink was congenial and warm and completely unlike the critical, resentful environment I had always been used to. I blossomed under the Fassis' guidance, and I can say without any doubt at all that Carlo Fassi is the very best teacher in the world. Not just technically – because many coaches excel in that department – but in his unique ability to understand his skaters and their individual reactions. He, unlike anyone before or since, knew instinctively what I needed, when I should be pushed and when I should be allowed to slow down, how to settle my nerves and how to make me feel good about myself, something no one else had ever been able to do for me. He was an extraordinary teacher, a gifted and inspiring mentor, and he never compromised under any circumstances. Carlo Fassi gave one hundred per cent of himself, and to him skating was a vocation.'

John made phenomenal progress and in the winter he flew to

Copenhagen to take part in the European Championships. He was well-prepared and calm, and looked forward to the event. He was no longer bothered by the sidelong glances of his army of detractors.

'I was actually quite amused by them. Their looks were so obviously incredulous – they couldn't believe that I would have the effrontery to come back after my dismal showing of the year before.'

The championships were held in Copenhagen, and John sailed through the all-important school figures with Christa hovering over him, quietly encouraging him.

'She watched over me like the proverbial hawk, but her presence gave me strength. I did well in the figures, and in the compulsory segment I managed to land the difficult combination jump. I was sixth going into the free-skating section, but before it took place I had a visit from the International Skating Union officials. I was warned that the costume I had worn for the compulsories – an electric-blue leotard and pants with a white vapour trail encircling the body – had upset the judges, and that I should not wear such a controversial outfit again as it had caused me to lose marks. I was amazed – it seemed that the supposedly conservative judges much preferred the sequins, circus spangles and gaudy beads that were the current vogue amongst the male skaters.'

Accordingly, John switched to a plain black costume for the free-skating and dazzled the audience with a lyrical programme full of difficult jumps. He finished ahead of his rivals, and ended up winning the silver medal.

'It was a sweet moment for me. In some ways it meant more to me than any other result in my career, because I had done what everyone told me was impossible – I had managed to claw my way back from obscurity and was once again in the front rank of international contenders.'

The World Championships in 1975 were in Colorado Springs, which meant that John could live in his own apartment while he was competing. This was important to him and helped him to maintain his equilibrium in the midst of the events. It also afforded him the luxury of skating on his home ice.

'Carlo had made me promise that I would avoid my fellow-skaters as much as possible so that I could concentrate fully on my own performance. This particularly bothered Toller, because we had become friends. I had been so impressed by his *Pagliacci* programme in Munich that I had started a correspondence with him, and he had been looking forward to spending time with me. But his flamboyant style and his avant-garde approach had the power to unnerve me – it's difficult to explain why, but for some reason it undermined my confidence and made me doubt my own direction. So I stayed in my own home and spoke to no one except the Fassis.'

John's period of isolation worked well for him. He placed well in the figures and then won the compulsory segment, skating to *The Rite of Spring*. Just before the final phase, the free-skating, he had a call from a friend of Toller Cranston's. 'Toller is terribly upset that you won't speak to him,' they said. 'He wonders what on earth he has done.'

'I knew that Toller was upset, but I dared not risk breaking my concentration at this stage of the competition. I knew it would be fatal and with the free-skating the next day I wanted to keep going with my vigil.'

The ploy paid off. John took the bronze medal and for the first time was invited to take part in the annual Tour of Champions exhibition circuit.

'The truth is, I didn't really approve of this tour. I felt it was an abuse of the amateur skaters who took part, and we were all made to feel that it was an obligation we were not at liberty to decline. It consisted of the top skaters in each category, plus some special local favourites, trailing around on a gruelling succession of one-night stands, being paid a minuscule honorarium and raising funds for the various skating associations, little of which seemed to find its way back to needy skaters. Carlo, however, insisted that it would be political suicide to refuse to go the year before the Olympics, and Christa echoed this opinion. It seemed I had no choice, so off I went, dressed in my sober little black outfits and trying to persuade Toller that I was still his friend.'

John did not enjoy the Tour of Champions. He was exhausted by the constant travelling and demoralized by the partisan reactions of the American audiences. Although John was received with polite and respectful interest, most of the applause was reserved for the US Ladies' Champion, Dorothy Hamill, and for ice dancers Jim Millns and Colleen O'Connor.

'Jim and Colleen were comparative newcomers, and had skated brilliantly in the Worlds. With ice dance set to be an official category in the Olympics for the first time in 1976, they were hot favourites to win a medal. There was also much speculation in the press as to whether or not they were romantically linked off the ice, and this had further fuelled the imagination of the public. They were the Torvill and Dean of the Seventies.'

In Vancouver, British Columbia, the emphasis changed completely. Here the crowds had come to cheer the six-times Canadian champion, Toller Cranston. The exhibition appearances were arranged strictly in order of merit – with the fourth-place skaters appearing first, third-place second, and so on until the gold-medallists came out to finish the show. Accordingly, Toller skated in the first flight of performances, and when he left the ice the crowd screamed for more.

'They kept calling for him throughout the next few exhibitions, and when it was my turn to skate the clamour grew to a crescendo. I stood in the centre of the ice, waiting for my music to begin, and all I could hear were catcalls and boos. Then they started a steady chant and began to bang their feet on the floor and I could stand it no longer. As I left the ice, an empty Coca-Cola can was hurled at me, and I went to the dressing room, took off my skates and left for the airport. Even if it meant I would not be acceptable to the Olympic Committee, I had no intention of staying any longer. I swore I would never set foot in Canada again.'

12

Deeply hurt and disillusioned, John flew to New York to stay with the Streeters. He brooded about his future and about the humiliation he had endured in Vancouver. It seemed that every time he managed to get ahead, something would happen to knock him right back again.

'I tried hard to get the scene out of my mind, but it was hard to understand what I had done to merit the reaction of that crowd.

The organizers of the tour were furious with me for leaving, but I just couldn't contemplate going back.'

One day, at the Sky Rink, John began a conversation with one of the resident coaches. Brian Grant was about the same age as John, but he had long since dropped out of the competitive world. He supplemented his earnings at the rink by working as a model, and he was also trying to raise the money to produce his own ice show. He and John had a lot in common.

'Brian Grant had no track record as a competitor, yet his skating had a beautiful, lyrical quality which was quite mesmerizing to watch. I found myself telling him about my problems with the ISU tour, and within a very short time he had me laughing about it all. I felt better immediately. I told him that when I turned professional I intended to start my own company, and that when that happened I would be in touch with him to see if he would like to join. He seemed surprised that I would ask, yet he was exactly the kind of skater I wanted to nurture.'

John went back to Colorado Springs, the incident in Vancouver behind him, and started work again. He found that he had been joined in the Fassi stable by Dorothy Hamill, who was now living in their house.

'I was so delighted to find that Dorothy and I were to work together. Of all the current competitors, Dorothy was the one I most admired. She had the perfect skating body, ideally proportioned and muscular without the slightest hint of fat. She had a very distinctive style, open and bold, and a unique ability to relate to an audience. I thought she was quite dazzling.'

That winter, the Fassis took their students to Garmisch, in the German Alps. They stayed together, in a small hotel, and worked every day on the outdoor rink.

'The difference in Garmisch was that Mr Fassi understood my dislike of the cold. Unlike Davos, where I had been frozen for most of the time, here I was allowed to leave the ice to get warm whenever it became too chilly. It was such a wonderful period – we laughed continuously, or so it seemed to me. I thrived in the close, family atmosphere where everything was beautifully organized and predictable. During the day we worked very hard, and in the evenings we would all sit round in front of a log fire and drink hot cider punch. I was very, very happy.'

At the beginning of December, John flew to England to take part in the British Championships. He was a long way from reaching his Olympic peak and as a result he almost lost the British title to a young skater called Robin Cousins.

'I was very lucky to hang on to the championship. I fell early in my free-skating programme and had great difficulty in recovering. Robin, who was just emerging as a front-runner, skated a thrilling performance to win the segment. His exuberant, open style captured the crowd and he had a superb mastery of jumps, soaring high into the air and seeming to hover for a moment before landing with an elegant flourish. I was bowled over by him.'

John flew into New York on his way back to Colorado. He had been shaken badly by his narrow victory in the British Championships and found himself once again suffering from nerves.

'I was terribly depressed again. I just couldn't shake it off. It wasn't that anything specific was wrong with my life, but I was lonely all the time, even though I was surrounded by kind and loving friends. One evening, I phoned Brian Grant and asked if he would like to have supper with me, and he offered to cook a meal for us at his flat. I wondered if I had finally found someone who would understand the way I felt.'

Brian cooked a delicious pasta dish with crusty Italian bread and salad. For once John was able to relax and talk freely of all the things he had been suppressing. Brian was a good listener and the conversation continued until well past three in the morning.

'Brian made me face the problem I was having with my nerves. He told me about Erhard Seminar Training, a treatment intended to help people towards psychological growth. He had friends who had gone through EST because they had been unable to cope with the stress of their everyday lives. I had also known someone – a very good dancer – who had suffered from stage fright, and had attended an EST seminar in an effort to overcome it, but it had entailed many hours in a large group, deprived of food and water, and hectored by stewards. I was sceptical about its relevance to my own situation. "You're suffering from stage fright too," Brian told me. "You should give EST a try. You have nothing to lose."'

Brian phoned John the next morning to tell him there was to be a guest seminar in a New York hotel that weekend. Why didn't John go, just to see what it was all about?

'I thought about it for a very long time. I knew all the criticisms of the EST methods, about the mind control and the demoralization technique. But there was something inexplicable that drove me towards it. I decided to go and see for myself. If I didn't like it, then I wouldn't have to continue.'

The seminar was held in the New York Hilton, a modern sky-scraper on Sixth Avenue. Immediately John arrived, he was irritated by the over-friendly reception and the requirement to address every-one by their first names.

'They gushed. Beaming faces with wide, plastic smiles kept leering at me. I was treated like a naughty, repentant child and told to sit on a hard chair and I was not allowed to go to the lavatory until it was over. I thought it was grotesque and I knew there was no way I could ever subscribe to it.'

By the end of the seminar, however, John was in the grip of a strange compulsion. He had no liking whatsoever for what had just taken place, yet he found himself signing up to take the full two-weekend course.

'I thought the whole thing was dreadful, yet I was convinced that I should do it. I didn't seem to have any choice at all and in a way that was a huge relief to me. It was very expensive, but for once I didn't even consider the cost. All I knew was that something very powerful was pulling me towards it.'

John had been due to return to Colorado for the all-important preparatory period leading up to the Europeans and the Olympics. Now he would be staying in New York for two extra weeks – weeks he knew to be vital to his training.

'It was impossible to explain to Mr Fassi why I had chosen to do this. He wasn't at all angry, but he was deeply concerned about my judgement. I think he had visions of me being swept into the clutches of a cult. And on a practical level he was worried about the loss of valuable training time. He finally realized that I was not to be dis-suaded, however, and he sighed deeply. "Just be careful," he said. "You got a busy time ahead of you."'

John felt a metamorphosis over the next two weeks. In the bare room with the hard chairs, he allowed himself to be initiated into a new way of handling his life.

'At first I was humiliated. I was made to drag up things that had long been buried inside me. I cried a great deal, but that was encouraged. I came to realize that it was actually all right to cry. I felt as though my being had been ripped inside-out and my most private thoughts were scattered across the floor for everyone to see. But out of all this emotional rubble, a central core of strength emerged and it took root and flourished as the days progressed. I felt curiously light and energy flooded through me with startling force. I felt I could do anything.'

John flew back to Colorado and went immediately to the World Arena. He greeted a startled Carlo Fassi with the announcement that he had already put together his Olympic free-skating programme, set to the music of *Don Quixote*. 'I thought you didn't skate all these days!' Carlo said. 'Where did you do it?'

'In my head,' was the reply.

'I insisted that Mr Fassi watch me run through the programme then and there. He was astonished, because normally it took me several days to adjust to the high altitude. What was even more amazing was that, although I had never actually skated it before, I was able to go through it immediately without any mistakes. It was as though my feet were being guided by an unseen hand, and whenever I did that programme it was always the same. I was inspired.'

A close friend of John's flew to Colorado Springs to spend a few days with him. He had known John at the time of the Richmond bedsitter, and he thought his new environment was splendid. That evening, as they ate dinner together, he looked at John strangely. 'Are you sure you're all right?' he asked. 'It's a bit odd, but I sometimes get the feeling I'm talking to a stranger.' John laughed. 'I'm not a stranger – I'm the same person with a new approach to life. Don't you think it's an improvement?' The friend shook his head. 'I rather liked you the way you were,' he said.

'Whatever anyone liked to say, EST had brought me a new kind of freedom. I was no longer plagued by nerves, wondering if I would be able to get through the competitions without falling. I was buoyant, eager to do my programmes and very sure of myself. And even more important for me was the fact that I was no longer lonely. I felt high all the time.'

In January, John and Carlo flew back across the Atlantic to take part in the European Championships in Geneva. It was going to be a very tough event, with the former World Champion, Jan Hoffman, making a dramatic comeback, and Kovalev and Volkov, the two great Russians, in top form. It would be a powerful prelude to the Olympics.

'I discovered at that competition the advantage of being coached by someone who is not only a brilliant and inspiring teacher, but also a politically active member of the skating fraternity. Mr Fassi took care of his students in every possible way.'

The compulsory programme, the middle phase of the Men's competition, consisted of set elements – jumps, spins and footwork – which had to be performed to a piece of music of no more than two minutes' duration. The elements were marked twice – once for technical merit, and once for artistic interpretation.

'I was skating to a piece of music by Rachmaninov, and I felt that the inclusion of a spread-eagle to lead me into the required double axel would add tremendously to the dramatic impression. Some of the Russian judges were watching my practice sessions, and Carlo overheard a discussion between two of them in which they pointed out the spread-eagle as an illegal move. They were apparently excited because they felt I could be penalized on this basis. After the practice, Carlo took me aside and explained the situation to me. "They will use any excuse they can to mark you down, but we are going to fool them. You continue to do the spread-eagle in practice, but in the competition you leave it out! It will destroy their plans."'

John did well in the school figures, finishing in second place. He was well positioned going into the compulsory segment, and felt confident that he could hold his advantage.

'It became clear to me, that day in Geneva, that I was not supposed to win a major championship. John Curry, for some reason that escaped me, had already been written off by the powers that be. I skated a clean programme, completing all the required moves without mistakes and leaving out the controversial spread-eagle. I felt I had done a good performance, and was terribly depressed when all I got was a raft of average marks. I was left just hanging on to my second position.'

Carlo had been observing the judges during John's programme, and he was clearly annoyed. 'They didn't even see you skate,' he fumed. 'How could they know how to mark you? They were too busy discussing where your spread-eagle had gone, and most of them weren't even watching your performance. These marks are too low.'

John wondered if they should lodge an objection, but Carlo shook his head. 'No, no, no. This would just make everything worse. You can't win that way. You will just have to skate twice as well in the long programme. You can do it!'

'I was disillusioned, to say the least. It seemed that no matter how well I skated I would never be able to win. I appeared to be a political pariah. I had always thought that competitions were about evolution and excellence. A way to encourage and reward effort and achievement. But that wasn't the case: it was about greed and control and prejudice. Events were decided before they took place, and only in extreme circumstances could this be overturned.'

John took the ice for the free-skating segment, and called on all his powers of concentration. He stood, waiting for his music to start, and closed out everything around him. He skated a flawless programme which, as it ended, had the audience on their feet screaming their approval.

'The judges seemed to take for ever. They were having some kind of frantic discussion, and finally my marks came up. They were still average, and I was suddenly weary of the whole thing. I didn't see how I could possibly win, because the best skaters were still to come. I sat in the backstage area, feeling empty, and waited for what seemed an eternity for the competition to finish. When the last skater came off the ice, I started to pack up my things and leave, but I stopped when I heard Mr Fassi shouting for me. He ran towards me, puffing and panting, and waving a piece of paper. "You got it! You got it!" he squeaked. "You won!" It was hard to take it in, but it was true. I was the new European Champion.'

13

John was hugely relieved at the outcome of the European Championship. He had fully expected to finish third or, if he was very lucky, second. He had assumed that the Eastern judging block, which always supported Eastern skaters, would be far too partisan to allow the possibility of a Western skater taking the title.

'In a nutshell, the whole thing was usually fixed in advance. The Eastern Europeans were always on top, and the judging was always weighted in their favour. This pattern had never been broken until Geneva, but a Czechoslovakian judge had actually flown in their faces and placed me first! It was a breakthrough, and it tipped the scale just enough to allow me to win. I met the judge later, and he told me that he had been in serious trouble for his decision, but that he knew it was the right thing to do. "I would do the same thing again," he said. So it took one honest man to send me to the Olympics as the European Champion. Had I *not* won in Geneva, then I am fully convinced that I would not have won the Olympics either. Such is the stuff of politics.'

Although John had always insisted on skating in a way that he found aesthetically pleasing, in the Olympic year he decided to take a different approach. He studied carefully the winning programmes of the past four years and tried to analyse them from the judges' point of view.

'The judges responded to athletic exhibitionism and seemed to care little for grace and elegance. The gold-medal programmes were almost invariably filled with difficult jumps preceded by physical drum-rolls, unnecessary flourishes and tricks. The music would be put together by the coaches, who would just pick out the famous bits or the pretty bits and slap them on to a tape – chop, chop, splice here, that'll do. Choreography meant moving around as fast as possible and jumping as often as possible. I despaired for the future of skating, because the competitors of today were the teachers of tomorrow, and this awful tradition would be self-perpetuating. I promised myself that if I won the Olympics I would do everything in my power to change things – to create a viable alternative for skaters who looked upon skating as an art form.'

John's *Don Quixote* programme was exquisitely moulded to a flaw-lessly edited version of the music, but instead of his usual seamless choreography, with the movements flowing effortlessly into each other, he added obvious preparatory steps which would announce the most difficult elements. His credo had always been to make everything look as easy as possible, but now he deliberately made things look hard.

'I realized that, depressing as it was, this was what the judges were looking for. A thrill a second. To turn in the air as often as possible without crashing. It was all quite horrifying really – there would come a day when skaters would need a runway to take off and a parachute to land. But for now I had no choice. I had to conform if I wanted to be in contention for the title. I don't think I actually compromised myself, but I certainly made everything look difficult and added a few extra gestures.'

John prepared diligently for the Olympics and was careful to avoid any situation which might distract him. He developed an astonishing ability to focus totally, both on and off the ice, and kept rigidly to his self-devised health and fitness routine. By the time he left for Innsbruck, he felt he had done everything he could possibly do to prepare.

'I had an uncanny premonition that I would win the gold medal. It wasn't arrogance, nor did it have anything to do with my actual abilities. It was just part of a peculiar feeling of being swept along on a current so powerful that all I could hope to do was hang on tight and try not to fall off. It wasn't an unpleasant sensation at all, but rather afforded me a strange sense of peace.'

John was selected as the British team leader and as such he was to carry the flag in the opening ceremony. He had an enormous respect for the Olympic tradition and he was delighted at the prospect.

'As an ideal, I thought the Olympic Games was a superb opportunity for nations to interact at the highest level. Working together as teams, each team saluting the other, a striving for excellence and an environment where taking part was itself a kind of winning. When I entered the stadium with the British flag held proudly in my hands, I marched not only for my own country, but for all that is best in mankind. It's impossible to explain, because so many people nowadays ridicule the Olympic spirit – not least the competitors themselves – but it is the same inspiration that drives any good impulse, any great endeavour in a just cause. It is a force that, in its purest form, is capable of uniting the world. The tragedy is that the Olympic Games has now become a commercial farce, where medals are worth millions of pounds and are traded as such. The wolves have arrived at the gates of Eden.'

John had a number of serious opponents in the Men's Championship: the two leading Russians; Jan Hoffman, the German champion who was rapidly regaining his World Championship status; and the Canadian challenger, Toller Cranston. The unknown quantity in the group was Toller, who had been practising away from the eyes of his rivals.

'If anyone was going to beat me in the Olympics, it had to be Toller. He was a brilliant innovator, with a very strong technique and an unconventional approach to choreography. I was consistent, as was Jan Hoffman, but on a good day Toller was capable of passing us all. His biggest problem was similar to my own – the judges tended to mark him down, possibly punishing him for his flamboyance and his complete disregard for convention. He was advised to tone down his performance to fit in with the mainstream of the competitors, but he refused to compromise. The decision cost him the championship.'

The first event was the figures, and John felt calm and confident as he waited his turn to skate. He laid down each figure carefully, taking great care not to make eye contact with anyone except Carlo or Christa.

'I focused on the ice immediately beneath my skates. I shut out the noise around me and emptied my mind of everything except the tracings made by my blades. When it was over I was in second position, right behind a boy who was not a particularly strong figure skater. Mr Fassi told me that I was now in a better situation than I had been after the figures in Geneva. He warned me to keep quiet, eat properly and try not to think about the other competitors. I had no difficulty following his advice. I ate a very light meal, had a hot bath and spent the evening reading *Bleak House*. I was ready for "phase two".'

The compulsory short programme provided John with his biggest challenge in the championship. Although he was thoroughly pre-pared, the heavy emphasis on the technical aspects afforded a slight advantage to some of the more athletic skaters.

'For some reason, I was never very comfortable with my Olympic short programme. It was set to Rachmaninov and it was one of the few times when I was unhappy with the quality of my presentation. I had deliberately omitted everything except the required elements and the linking footwork, and I felt the result was rather uninspiring. However, the judges saw it differently, and they awarded me a very strong set of marks. I won the segment and emerged as the clear leader going into the final phase. All that stood between me and the gold medal was the free-skating.'

Dorothy Hamill, the American Ladies' Champion, had been following John's progress eagerly. They both trained in the Fassi stable, and were both strongly favoured to win medals. The day after the short programme was a free day for them both, and Dorothy invited John to have lunch with her.

'If anyone could understand how I felt at that particular moment in time, it was Dorothy. I made no secret of my admiration for her, both on and off the ice, and she seemed to feel the same way about me. We spent three hours in a coffee shop, laughing and sharing confidences. It was important for me, because it gave me a sense of perspective, and I also realized that I was not alone in the world of ice. She, too, had endured a political backlash and survived. We felt like two fugitives who were about to be granted amnesty.'

Late in the afternoon, John went back to his room to prepare for the free-skating. He sat in a lotus position, the curtains drawn and the lights out. He focused his mind completely on his programme, going through every step and every jump in his mind, 'seeing' the whole sequence as though he were watching himself skate.

'I had learnt the visualization technique and it worked well for me. I would run through the programme until I could see myself skate a perfect performance and then I would freeze the image. After that I would continue to sit quietly, and consciously relaxed every part of my being. It was like switching on lights in dark rooms. I lit up one part after another until I felt completely alive. Then I got up slowly, stretched thoroughly and carefully, and went down to the arena to warm up.'

The order of skating is decided by a draw, and John had drawn to skate first in the second half of the free-skating segment. This is regarded by most skaters as the least desirable place to skate, like running a race without a pacemaker. John, however, welcomed the positioning.

'I know all the conventional reasons why it is better to skate last, but I have always preferred that first position. It cocooned me, and meant that I could warm up and remain on the ice for my performance, while everyone else had to leave and try to keep limber. My muscles were loose, my energy fresh and my concentration undiminished. Even more important was the fact that I had no time to develop stage fright. I had prepared for this moment for so many years, and now that it was here I was going to make it count. In retrospect I suppose it sounds melodramatic, but to me everything hinged on the next few minutes. Not only my own future was at stake, but also the future of skating as an art form.'

John circled near the barriers, waiting for his name to be called. Finally he was announced, and he glided to centre-ice and took up his opening position. The first strains of *Don Quixote* filled the arena and he began to skate.

'It was as though the building disappeared. The music enclosed me and I was skating inside the walls of sound, more at peace than I could ever remember. I was not aware of the judges at all. I seemed to be borne along on a cushion of energy, each step falling effortlessly into place without any danger of a fall. My blades had become part of the ice and I was supported by some kind of invisible thread from above. It was one of those rare times when every aspect of my being fused together, mind, body and spirit working in total harmony.'

John skated a virtually flawless programme, landing all three triple jumps and producing a dazzling display of footwork, spins and spirals. The five minutes ended with a grand flourish, one knee on the ice and a hand curved elegantly in the air above his head.

'I knew in that moment that I had won the Olympic gold medal, and yet I felt strangely calm. The noise of the arena came flooding back to me and I could hear the crowd erupting. Flowers were everywhere, so thick on the ice that I had difficulty in moving through them. People were straining over the barriers, calling to me, but I couldn't respond. I was in a kind of stupor, and all I could do was move blindly towards Mr and Mrs Fassi, who were waiting for me in the competitors' area. I knew from the look on their faces that they were pleased, but we just hugged each other quietly and sat down to wait for the marks. When they came up, they were consistently high and I had taken an almost unassailable lead. "You got to wait for the other boys to skate," Mr Fassi said. "Then we will know."'

The scene backstage was chaotic, and the television reporters and journalists crowded towards John, thrusting microphones into his face and asking him how it felt to be the new Olympic champion.

'It was so unfair. The remaining competitors were there, trying hard to keep their concentration, and all they could hear was the babble of that media zoo. It must have been devastating for them. I pushed through it all and went into my dressing room to be alone and started to unlace my boots. I couldn't feel anything at all. Then our team leader came in and hugged me and when I saw tears running down her face something broke inside of me. I felt all the pent-up emotion push up into my throat and flow out of me. I cried too, but they were tears of joy. The struggle was over and the years of heart-ache and frustration were all behind me. I had no idea, that day in Innsbruck, that it was only just beginning.'

14

At the medal ceremony, John stood at the top of the podium with silver-medallist, Vladimir Kovalev, on his right. On his left was Toller Cranston, who had skated a dramatic rendition of Prokofiev's *Cinderella* to take the bronze medal for Canada.

'It is difficult to describe exactly how I felt as the British flag was raised and the anthem began to play. There was a tightness in my chest and no matter how hard I tried to stop it my lip insisted on quivering. I'm not certain what was making me so emotional – per-haps a dormant feeling of nationalism coming to the surface, or just the realization that I was being publicly acknowledged after so many years of being told I was a failure. At any rate, whatever it was, it was an extraordinarily proud moment for me.'

John's mother and brother were in Innsbruck for the Games, and John went back with them to their hotel for a celebratory supper. They toasted each other and talked about the people who had helped John make the long climb up the Olympic ladder. Finally, Rita raised her glass and said, 'Let's drink a toast to your father, John. He would have been so proud of you today.'

'We had avoided any mention of my father for so long that I was shocked when Mother said those words. I experienced a confusion of emotions – anger, sorrow, hurt, regret, and even what I thought to be the beginnings of compassion. It would have meant so much to me to have my father there when I skated my Olympic-medal performance, and suddenly I realized, perhaps for the first time, that he would never be with us again. He was gone. I raised my glass slowly and clicked it against Mother's. "Wherever he is now," I said, "I hope he is finally at peace."'

John left his family, promising to spend the next day sightseeing with them. He made his way down to the hotel lobby, smiling wearily in acknowledgement of the many handshakes and congratulations. Just as he was about to leave, he spotted a young English journalist he had befriended in Geneva and walked over to greet him.

'We decided to share a bottle of wine in the hotel bar. I wasn't in the habit of drinking, but I decided it would help me to unwind. He was very good company and I found myself confiding in him, telling him things I had deliberately suppressed for years. He was careful to reassure me that we were there as friends, and therefore whatever I told him would be confidential. He asked me if I was happy and I said no, I didn't think so. I lived in a homophobic world and I was homosexual, which made it very difficult to be relaxed and self-assured. I had to keep my preference a secret, which meant that I was obliged to live a rather lonely life. He told me that he understood completely, and I felt a sense of relief to have discovered such a warm and sympathetic confidant.'

The next morning John joined Rita and Andrew for a trip to a nearby resort. They went for a sleigh ride through the snow and ate lunch in a little Alpine hotel. It was almost four o'clock before they got back to Innsbruck.

'I left Mother and Andrew and walked back to the Village. I was aware of strange looks from people as I passed, and, in sharp contrast to the night before, no one spoke to me. I thought it was all rather peculiar. When I got to my room, the phone was ringing. It was a reporter from the *News of the World* and he offered me a hundred thousand pounds for the exclusive rights to my story. I was astonished. I told him I was very flattered, but I didn't think the *News of the World's* readers would really be interested to read about me. He snorted down the phone. "Oh, I think they would be very interested indeed," he said. "The stories in today's papers have only just whetted their appetites." I froze. I hung up the phone without speaking, and reached for the unopened newspaper lying on my bed. There, on the front page, was the story of the unhappy Olympic champion who was forced to hide his homosexuality from the world. I had been betrayed and I felt sick to the pit of my stomach. I knew that I would never, ever, as long as I lived, be able to trust anyone again.'

John read through the pile of messages and telegrams lying on the bedside table. Most of them were connected to the revelations in the morning papers. He telephoned Carlo to ask what he should do, and to apologize for any embarrassment he might have caused them.

'Mr Fassi was wonderfully supportive and practical. He brushed aside any suggestion that I should be ashamed or that I should worry about other people's feelings. "Is just life," he said. "They will soon forget about it." He told me a press conference had been arranged for later, and that I should go there and spend half an hour talking to the reporters. "Just be honest," he told me. "Tell them something – not too much – and then they will go away. Better do it all at once."'

John spent a long time dressing for the conference. He tried to rehearse what he would say, but he couldn't seem to focus. When he arrived at the press room it was filled to overflowing, with batteries of microphones and cameras everywhere.

'It was terrifying. I was never that nervous waiting for my turn to skate in a competition. My throat was dry and my heart pounded so hard against my ribs that I was sure people could see it. I sat at a table, feeling terribly exposed, and began to answer questions. The journalists were relentless, asking questions about my personal life, my beliefs, how long I had known I was gay, and who my lovers might be. I tried not to be offended and to answer as simply and as honestly as I could. After half an hour, Mr Fassi motioned to me and I stood up and thanked them all for coming. Then I walked quickly from the room, trying to hide the fact that my knees were shaking. It was only then that I remembered I had not yet told Mother.'

John telephoned Rita's room and knew immediately from the tone of her voice that she was unaware of the furore surrounding him. He asked if he could see her alone.

'She had been planning to have dinner with friends, but she asked them to go without her. When I got into her room, I took two miniature brandies from her mini-bar, poured them both out and handed one to her. Since it was unusual for either of us to drink, she knew that something was terribly wrong. I took a big gulp, then said in a rush, "Mother, you are going to find this out from the newspapers and it was important to me that I tell you myself. I'm sorry not to have told you before, but the fact is that I am a homosexual and the news will be all over England by now. I wish there was some way I could have saved you this embarrassment, but it's already out of my hands." I stopped to see what she would say, relieved that I had finally told her. She came over to me and put her arms around me. After a moment she said, "There is nothing to be embarrassed about. I understand completely, and it will all be forgotten in a few days. You've got so much to be thankful for and you've made us all very proud of you. Now, let's go down and have some dinner."'

The next morning John had breakfast with Carlo and Ed Mosler. Nothing was said about the stories in the newspapers, but all three seemed in very low spirits. Carlo wanted John to quit, even though he had planned to go on to the Worlds. 'There is no reason,' he said. 'Nobody cares anything about it. If you lose, it damages your Olympic reputation. If you win, it adds nothing. It's better you stop now.'

'I wanted very much to try to prove the Olympic win hadn't been a fluke, but Mr Fassi was so adamant about it that I finally agreed not to go to Göteborg. Part of me thought what a relief it would be not to have to practise figures any more, but another part of me felt an enormous depression at the thought that it was all over. Mr Mosler told me I must do what I thought best, and I thanked him for his support over the past few years. I told him that without his help many fine skaters could not have completed their training and that in the years to come I hoped to help others in my turn. He smiled. "Nothing would please me more," he said. "I won't be around for ever and I would like to know that someone will be there to carry the torch."'

The last event of the Olympics was the Ladies' Free-Skating competition. Dorothy Hamill was in an identical position to John's at the same point in the Men's event. All she needed to do was skate a clean programme, and she would be the new champion. John went to the arena before the final warm-up and found her backstage.

'She was shaking. Very few people would have appreciated exactly what she was going through at that moment, but she knew, without my saying a word, that I understood. She looked at me as I came up to her and flashed the famous Hamill smile at me. It was a dazzling smile that hid a deep well of doubts and insecurities, and its brilliance unnerved her competitors. She hugged me. "I was hoping you'd come," she said. "It makes me feel stronger, knowing you're there."'

Dorothy skated an inspired performance, and when it was all over Carlo had a second Olympic champion in his stable. He beamed happily and thumped John on the back.

'Mr Fassi's delight was not just for the boost this victory gave his own reputation. It was also because, for once, the right person had won. In the history of skating, only a tiny handful have left a permanent stamp on the sport, and Dorothy is one of them. She has a unique relationship with the ice, and she skates with a strength and beauty that mesmerizes people. Dorothy is one of the few skaters who truly understand the medium.'

All the medallists were expected to perform in an exhibition during the closing ceremony of the Games. John had elected to do one of his favourite pieces, set to the music of *Scheherazade*, but he began to have serious doubts about it.

'I had been deeply affected by all the wild stories I had read about myself during the preceding days. Few of them were true, but this didn't stop them from making me paranoid. How would I be perceived in full stage make-up? What reaction would the choreography get? What about the costume? I questioned it all. I was caught like a rabbit in headlights, unable to make up my mind about anything. I decided I couldn't skate at all. I couldn't face it. I would tell them that I was ill and just go home.'

About an hour before the performance, John changed his mind. He raced around getting ready, throwing his things into a bag, and then he headed for the arena.

'I had finally come to my senses. That intrinsic style that was so much a part of me had almost been obliterated by doubt. I had always been so sure of myself on the ice, presenting myself in a way that was a true reflection of how I felt inside. It was the very thing that had carried me all the way to the Olympic podium and now, because of the scandal surrounding me, I had almost betrayed it. In a nutshell, I had forgotten who I was. I went out on to the ice that afternoon and healed myself. I skated with a passion that startled me, and I felt it was perhaps the best performance of my life. I never again contemplated any kind of compromise.'

15

While he was in Innsbruck, John had received several telephone calls from a man called Warwick Charlton. He was organizing a luncheon in London's Guildhall, to honour those who had made outstanding contributions to the sporting ideal, in terms of honour or courage. It was known as Valour in Sport, and he wanted John to be the guest of honour.

'I had not returned Mr Charlton's calls, because I assumed the recent scandals would have rendered my appearance at such a function impossible. I planned to write him a polite note thanking him for his interest. As I left the closing ceremony, however, I was approached by a young, red-haired woman who said she was a journalist. "I'm a friend of Warwick Charlton's," she announced. "I've come to take you back to London, and I don't want to hear any nonsense about all this media coverage. It just makes it all the more important that you agree to appear at Warwick's lunch." She held out her hand to me. "By the way, my name's Samantha Ward. You can call me Sam." We both burst out laughing, because she knew that I would agree to come. She took me back to my room, helped me pack and bundled me off to the airport. By the time we reached London I realized that I had found a friend who was able to cut straight to the core of my life without any of the usual preliminaries. I liked her enormously.'

Back in England, John was shocked at the extent of the media interest he was generating. Everywhere he went people stopped to congratulate him, shake his hand or ask him for autographs. They would lean out of buses and taxis to shout to him, reach out to touch him as he passed, or even follow him down the street. The avalanche of publicity had only served to endear him to the British public, and he received nothing but warmth and support.

'Sam was a tremendous help to me during all of this attention. She was a journalist herself and she made me put it all into perspective."People don't really believe what they read in the press," she assured me. "Remember that today's papers are tomorrow's garbage. You have to learn to laugh, especially at yourself." She took me shopping for new clothes ("You need some colour in your wardrobe. You're not going to a funeral") and helped me write my speech for the Guildhall awards. ("It has to be strong, because we're trying to get across to the public what absolute shits the British government are when it comes to supporting their sportsmen. They want all the credit, but they don't want to pay for it.") Finally she bore me off to Fortnum and Mason's for tea. As we munched cucumber sandwiches, she stared at me critically. "The face is smashing," she said, "but we need to do something about those bloody awful curls."'

The day of the luncheon, John had an attack of nerves. He had never spoken in public before, except to thank people for medals, and the responsibility terrified him. The event was to be televised, and he knew it was a vital opportunity to call attention to the lack of facilities and financial aid in all areas of sport.

'My knees shook all through the luncheon. I listened to extraordinary stories of endurance and courage and wondered what on earth qualified me to be present at such a gathering. When I finally spoke, I delivered my treatise with a passion and conviction that surprised me, and found myself adding a postscript: "Until today I thought I had retired from amateur competition. But I have some unfinished business to attend to – I need to take part in the World Championships in Göteborg and face again the possibility of defeat. If I can do this with humility and sportsmanship, then, no matter what the result, I will feel I have scored an important victory."'

John immediately telephoned Carlo at his training base in Helsinki. Carlo was horrified to hear his decision, and tried desperately to dissuade him. 'You are mad,' he said. 'You've stopped training. You can't do it.'

John was adamant. 'I'm arriving tomorrow morning. Are you telling me that you won't work with me?'

Carlo spluttered on the other end of the line. 'No, no, no, no, no! But you better just remember what I told you. You are a crazy boy!'

'The training week in Helsinki was disastrous. In the days since the Olympics I seemed to have lost any ability to skate a clean programme. I fell continuously, and Mr Fassi was almost hysterical. "Go home," he pleaded with me. "What are you trying to do? You look like a beginner." But I stubbornly refused to leave, and at the end of the week I set off with everyone else for Göteborg. I was determined to take part in the World Championships.'

From the moment the team arrived in Sweden, John found himself once more the centre of the media's attention. Unscrupulous journalists tried all manner of tricks to get him to talk to them, but when these failed they would simply invent stories, each one more shocking than the last. He found the barriers had been bugged at the practice sessions. 'Can't we sue somebody?' he asked Carlo. Carlo shrugged. 'What for? Just try to ignore it. You have to concentrate on the competition.'

'Finally the day of the school figures arrived. I was in terrible shape, worried about the effect the publicity was having on Mother and worried about the wisdom of my own actions. I thought perhaps Mr Fassi was right – maybe I *was* crazy. But it was too late to turn back now, and I went out on to the ice to lay down my first figure. It was a bracket, which was normally an easy figure for me, but this time it went horribly wrong and I ended up fifth. Mr Fassi begged me to withdraw. "Say you are ill. Just promise me you won't go on." I thought about it for a few moments, sitting in the bleachers surrounding the rink. Then all my resolve came back to me – this time with the energy of conviction. I had let the media affect my ability to concentrate, and I needed to focus again. I had a job to do, and I intended to do it.'

At the end of the Compulsory Figures, John had pulled up into second position. Carlo was still agitated, but had now accepted that John could not be persuaded to retire.

'Mr Fassi was inconsolable. He walked around looking mournful and muttering about "hidiots". The practice for the short free-skating programme was at seven the following morning, and he wisely suggested that Mrs Fassi take me to it – I was not famous for my disposition during early practices, and he felt she was better able to handle me. Poor Mrs Fassi – no matter how hard she tried, I simply couldn't seem to get anything right. I fell over and over again on the big triple combination and in the end I suggested we stop.

"We both know I can do this," I told her. "It'll be up to me to pull it off this afternoon."'

Although John skated well in the short programme, he put his foot down on the ice at the end of his triple combination, before he had completed the jump, rendering it invalid. For one split second he had allowed his mind to wander, and instead of capturing the lead he remained in second place.

'I was still in with a strong chance of winning. Toller had finished well ahead of me in the short programme, but was so far behind overall that he had no chance of taking the gold medal. My main rival was Kovalev, who had an uninspiring free-skating programme and who rarely performed well under pressure. I knew that, above everything, I must keep myself calm.'

Dorothy Hamill had arrived in Göteborg, much to Carlo's consternation. He had advised her to quit after the Olympics, believing that, like John, she should leave well alone. But Dorothy had decided to continue and nothing anyone could say would persuade her otherwise. 'Now there are two of them!' Carlo wailed. 'How am I supposed to stand the pressure?'

Before the final free-skating phase, John invoked his visualization technique. He 'saw' his programme, without a fault, without a fall, and when he went out on to the ice to compete he was as confident as he had ever been. He made no mistakes, and when it was all over he was the new World Champion.

'On the podium, as the medal was hung round my neck, I felt the tears come. I knew then that my competitive career *was* finally over, and that I had achieved everything I could have hoped for. Part of me wept in relief that I would no longer have to endure the trials and tribulations of the amateur world, but another part of me was weeping because for so long this had been the only life I had known. The door was closing for the last time, and I would never be able to go through it again. It felt like a kind of death.'

16

After the Olympics, John was inundated with offers from all over the world: ice shows, agents, managers, talk shows, television specials, endorsements, galas and charity benefits. For several months he divided his time between America and Britain, trying to sort it all out. Eventually he responded to a call from London impresario Larry Parnes, who was intrigued by John's desire to turn skating into a form of theatre.

'Larry Parnes was an old-fashioned West End man, with a bit of the dreamer still left in his soul. When he met me I had already considered – and rejected – the idea of joining one of the established shows. I have to admit that the money was very tempting, because after so many years of poverty I couldn't help thinking, Why not do it for a while, and then do what you want afterwards? But in the end I decided against it. Perhaps I made a silly mistake, but I don't think so. The moment for me to do what I had chosen to do was in front of me. If I wasted it, in any way, it would never be there again. I sought to take skating into a new realm, and I needed to keep the momentum. I told Mr Parnes I would be happy for him to produce a show for me, providing it was a show of my own design.'

Larry Parnes announced to the press how 'proud and privileged' he was to be John's sole personal manager and business representative. John could, he enthused, earn in excess of £350,000 next year. 'The future looks bright for us, because we get along very well. We are both Virgos.' Larry and John agreed to a six-month trial period to see if it was possible for them to work together. It was a difficult time for both of them. Larry discovered the full extent of John's idealism and his complete refusal to compromise; John discovered the pragmatic aspect of Larry's approach to showbusiness and his penchant for established theatrical formats. At times it seemed impossible that they could ever find common ground.

'It was horribly frustrating. He just didn't seem to understand what I wanted to do, and I'm sure he thought I was being unreasonable, but I couldn't bring myself to abandon my dreams. I would rather have stacked boxes in Sainsbury's than take part in a traditional ice show.'

In June, John was awarded the OBE for his services to ice. Later

in the summer he recorded a television special for Christmas trans-
mission; this was an opportunity to put some of his ideas to the test,
although these ideas did not always meet with the agreement of the
producer, John Scoffield.

'In retrospect, John was extremely considerate of my wishes, but
at the time I'm afraid I became rather irritated by him. He insisted
on including my Olympic programme, which I reluctantly agreed to
do – after all, everyone had already seen it a million times and there
was no way I could do it as well as I had done it in Innsbruck. I felt
we should leave well alone, but he prevailed.'

Larry Parnes approached one of Britain's most respected
choreographers, Norman Maen, who agreed to create a piece for
the special, built around a deep blues composition called 'I got it
bad and that ain't good'. John was excited at the prospect of working
with an established dance choreographer for the first time, but was
bitterly disappointed when Norman elected to use an ice surface of
twelve by fifteen feet.

'I couldn't imagine what he was thinking of. It meant we were
severely limited for no apparent reason. He explained that he was
deliberately harnessing the potential of movement into a tiny fraction
of its natural space. I was dubious about it, to say the least, but
everyone seemed to think it had worked very well. Later I was to
become a devoted fan of moving against the established choreo-
graphic progression of skating (I liked to refer to it as "inner boundaries"), but at that point I had not yet gained sufficient insight into
that thought process.'

The central piece of the programme was to be *L'Après-Midi d'un
Faune*, the ballet originally made famous by Nijinsky. John invited
Peggy Fleming to partner him. They had skated together before, in
charity galas, but this would be their first professional collaboration.

'Peggy Fleming was the most ethereal of all the skaters. She had
a beautiful bone structure, like a ballerina, huge expressive eyes and
long dark hair. She reminded me of Margot Fonteyn, and she moved
with the same mixture of strength and grace. When I first skated
with her, I was almost afraid to touch her in case she broke! But I
became used to partnering her and we developed an uncanny empathy between us which translated on to the ice. It was a wonderful
experience, and much more satisfying than skating on my own.'

When the taping was finished, John flew to New York to spend some time with the Streeters. He was suffering from a deep depression, and felt his dreams were as unattainable as they had seemed before he won the Olympics.

'All my plans had gone awry. Larry and I had reached an impasse and were barely speaking; I had just heard that another producer who had promised to back an ice company for me had dropped the idea; and I had no professional work on the horizon at all. The Olympic victory now had a hollow ring – I had thought of it as a way to achieve my own goals, but instead it appeared that it was looked on as a way for other people to achieve *their* goals. It seemed that the only way to function in such a world was to effect a constant state of compromise between idealism and practicality. As I sat in the Streeters' living room that summer, I wondered again if I should give up skating altogether.'

Sam Ward was in New York on business, and invited John to lunch. They met in the Mayflower Hotel on 61st and Central Park West, in the Palm Restaurant. John talked about his disillusionment and his thoughts of retirement. She listened quietly for a while, then said, 'You're stark raving mad! You spend most of your life working to get an Olympic gold medal and as soon as you get it you can't wait to throw it away again. You looked on the Olympics as the end of your competitive career, but in some ways it was only the begin-ning. The truth is, you were protected as an amateur – you really didn't have to think about anything except the skating itself. Now you have to face all kinds of tough situations, and it's absolutely no good running away because a bunch of bureaucrats are playing silly buggers. You're a pioneer, John, and that's never easy.' She grinned at him. 'Anyway, you can always join *Holiday on Ice!*'

'Sam had a way of making me laugh at myself. I suppose I *had* been feeling rather victimized, but by the time we finished lunch I had a different slant on things. She was right, of course. I couldn't just give it all up. I went back to the Streeters' and wrote a long letter to Larry Parnes, explaining in minute detail how we could do a show which was both artistic and inexpensive. I had no idea how he would react, but at least I felt I had set something in motion.'

To John's surprise, Larry called him as soon as he received the letter. He told him he thought it a very workable plan, and that he would be willing to go ahead with it. The only drawback was the lack of available theatres – the Cambridge was open, but it would give them a very narrow ice surface. However, he insisted that it was important he present the show before the Olympic year was over. 'You need to take advantage of all the publicity, and get people to come and see you while they are still curious.'

'I wasn't sure I liked being thought of as a curiosity, but I agreed to consider the possibility. I marked out an area of equivalent size on the ice at the Sky Rink, and spent several days experimenting. The result was rather depressing, but I discussed it with Nancy Streeter, and she convinced me that I should go ahead and take the chance. It would, after all, give me a West End forum to try out my ideas, and at least it would be a step in the right direction. I telephoned Larry and told him I thought it could work. A week later, he had booked the Cambridge and we were set for a December opening.'

Each year, Ed Mosler organized a fund-raising gala for the US Olympic Committee. It was known as SuperSkates, and many of the leading Olympians took part in the exhibitions. In 1976, John felt a particular obligation to appear, especially in view of the support he himself had received from the Mosler Foundation.

'I really didn't have time to do it, but I hit on a plan that would make it possible. I suggested to Mr Mosler that I prepare one of my solo numbers for the Cambridge show and première it at Super-Skates. I would invite Twyla Tharp to create a piece for me, and this would hopefully bring dance fans into the event, as well as the usual skating crowd. [Twyla Tharp was America's leading contemporary-dance choreographer.] Mr Mosler thought it an excellent idea, and was delighted at the extra publicity it would bring. I approached Twyla and she came to the Sky Rink late one evening to watch me practise and weigh the potential. She said very little, except to keep asking me what else I could show her. I went through everything, from basic figures to the most difficult tricks I knew. At last she said, "I'll go home and think about it." I was desperate for her to say yes – I wasn't sure I could handle a rejection at this point! However, the next morning she telephoned to say she would do it, and we arranged to spend three weeks working together.'

What evolved as they developed the piece was something entirely new to skating. Twyla had chosen to work with the Albinoni Trumpet Concerto in B Flat, and had edited seven minutes from it. Although John had taught her the entire vocabulary of skating elements to prepare her for the project, she essentially threw it away and gave him completely new ways of moving on the ice. He found it an exciting and challenging procedure.

'I had such fun working with Twyla. In three weeks she restored all my faith in the ice medium. She showed me that potential has no horizons, and forbade me ever to question the intrinsic artistic qualities of skating. "You mustn't compare it to dance," she said. "It's a different, and wonderful, medium in its own right. Skaters can do things that dancers could never hope to do, and vice versa. Ice can be as beautiful, moving and meaningful as you want to make it. It's up to you." I was so inspired by her words that I almost cried – I think for a while I had actually lost sight of my own convictions, and when I performed the piece in Madison Square Garden, in front of fourteen thousand die-hard traditionalists, it was received with rapturous applause. I knew then that I was not alone in the world.'

17

John decided to call the Cambridge show *Theatre of Skating*. He liked the simplicity of the title, and felt that it accurately summed up what he was trying to achieve. He invited Peter Darrell, of the Scottish Ballet, to direct it and decided to approach Norman Maen once more to do some choreography.

'I liked Peter enormously, but it was very difficult to work with him at first. This was not, I hasten to add, his fault in any way. It was entirely my own. I had very strong ideas about how I wanted to be presented in the show, and by insisting on sticking to them I'm afraid I rather spoilt the balance of the performance. I had always had a horror of "star" images – I suppose you could say I was anti-star. I disliked the way ice shows traditionally built up to the big star entrance, and I wanted to become just one of the company of skaters. So I entered almost anonymously, right at the top of the show, and people were left trying to decide if it was me or not. It was a silly thing to do, but at the time I thought I was right. Had I been a dancer, Peter would undoubtedly have insisted on his own way of doing things, but he was intimidated by working in a foreign medium and this made him insecure.'

The weeks before opening were fraught with problems. The ice engineer was having terrible difficulty with the unit, trying to create an ice configuration to conform to the shape of the stage. It refused to set, and the company had nowhere to rehearse the show.

'I was frantic. We were having to do all our work on the floor, in the hope that we would be able to transfer it later. This meant I had no idea how it would actually *look* on the stage. I became very tense and irritable and I wasn't an easy person to be around. So much depended on the outcome of this show, and I felt it was not being given the proper attention.'

Several leading choreographers had been invited to create pieces for the show. John was particularly excited about working with Sir Kenneth MacMillan, who was the Director of the Royal Ballet. He had chosen a piece of music which was extraordinarily difficult to skate to – *Feux Follets*, Study No. 5, by Franz Liszt.

'Mr MacMillan asked me over and over again if I found it all too difficult to sustain. I think he must have suspected that I was having a hard time with it, but I absolutely refused to admit it. I loved the piece passionately, because it was challenging and inventive. It almost killed me, but somehow I managed to pull it off and by the end of the Cambridge engagement I actually think I had it right! Opening night, though, was another matter.'

Although the critics were unanimous in their praise for *Theatre of Skating*, and the public stood and cheered every night, John became increasingly despondent over the show. He listened only to the handful of people whose opinions he trusted, and most of them offered him some measure of criticism.

'Sam came to several performances and one night we went out for dinner after the show. I knew she was concerned about the production and I wanted very much to find out why. "It's not you, John, and it's not your concept. But I'm going to tell you exactly what I think and I hope you won't be offended. First of all, the costumes are ghastly. I know the budget was small, but surely you could have done better than that? Secondly, what you have out there on the ice is not the company you say you've dreamt of, but a collection of ill-matched skaters, some of whom are bordering on fat and some of whom don't seem to be able to skate very well. You've tried to melt in among them, and in so doing you've robbed the public of the very thing they came to see – an extraordinary artist in an extraordinary show." I was shocked by her words, and yet I knew she was right. I suddenly felt very tired.'

John arranged a meeting with Larry Parnes shortly after Christmas. He thanked him politely for all his help, but told him that as soon as the Cambridge run was finished he would terminate *Theatre of Skating*.

'Larry seemed stunned by what I was saying. He just stared at me, and then he said, "Well, of course that's out of the question. I've put a lot of money into this show and I intend to get it back. I'm not sure what your problem is, but everyone I've talked to thinks it is a marvellous production. We're bringing it to the Bristol Hippodrome and then back to the West End for another season." My heart sank. I seemed to be trapped.'

John's spirits had been further diminished by his appearance at the Sportsman of the Year Awards. He was the 1976 winner, and was guest of honour at the dinner. On the way to the venue, his taxi was involved in a minor collision and he arrived late.

'I had been looking forward to that dinner. Sam was to be there as well, in her own capacity as a sports journalist, and she was sitting near several of the leading rugby players. She had been engaged in a heated discussion with them about skating – they were scathing about it, and felt it did not qualify as a legitimate sport. Sam, of course, had quite another opinion and was expressing it in very colourful terms. Just as I arrived in the doorway, one of them could be heard to say, "Why hasn't the Christmas tree got a fairy on the top?" and to my acute embarrassment another one answered loudly, "Oh, here it comes now. It just walked in."'

Sam was furious. She tried to reassure John that he should not be upset by the words of someone who 'should have stayed in the trees where he belonged', but for once her attempts to make him laugh had no effect.

'I think that incident was one of the most hurtful of my life. It made me realize what a terrifying gulf there was between me and that segment of the heterosexual community that liked to be referred to as sportsmen. I thought it unlikely that it could ever be bridged.'

The atmosphere between Larry Parnes and John grew so hostile that it began to affect the morale of the company. John felt he was unable to continue to perform in a show that fell so far short of his expectations, and so he went to Larry with a compromise.

'I suggested that he allow me to create a new version of the show, hopefully one that would correct the mistakes we had made in the first one. In this way we might both be satisfied – I would have a better show, and Larry could try to recoup his investment. He agreed, and I set about making the changes.'

One of the major criticisms of the first show was that it was too serious. It had no contrasts. John went to Ronald Hynd and asked him to create something light-hearted to open the second version – something that would give the audience a few fireworks and a smile or two before they were introduced to the more artistic offerings.

'I remembered hearing somewhere that Sir John Barbirolli, the conductor of the Hallé Orchestra, had introduced his audiences to unfamiliar and avant-garde compositions by creating a musical sandwich. He would open with Chopin, put Bartók in the middle, and close with a Beethoven. I thought we could apply this concept to skating, and so we created something called "Valse Glace" for the opening number, which Ronald filled with tricks and sunshine. He then set about creating a closing number, one in which the whole company could take part and which would leave the audience happy. For this we chose some Gilbert and Sullivan music and created a living postcard called "Winter, 1895" – a wonderful, witty romp in which I played a Cockney pearly prince, delivering newspapers. It made a memorable ending to the show, and as a result the whole production was much stronger than the original.'

The show was to have a two-week trial in the Bristol Hippodrome before moving to the London Palladium. John had commissioned John Butler, an American choreographer with experience of ice, to create a dramatic narrative for him. This piece – an account of the Icarus legend – was one of the most difficult John had ever attempted. It was full of movements which leant against the natural skating momentum, and stretched the accepted parameters of ice to the limit. Larry Parnes made no secret of his feeling for the work, and demanded that it be cut. 'I'm not going to pay for it,' he said; but he had reckoned without John's determination. For the first – but by no means the last – time in his career, John opted to finance the piece himself.

'Under no circumstances was I going to cut "Icarus" from the programme. It was very much the direction I intended to follow, and I wanted to get an audience reaction. So I commissioned it, and nobody could argue with me after that.'

John had assembled a larger company for the second version of the show, with only four skaters being held over from the first. One of the new skaters was a Canadian, Ron Alexander, who had befriended John during his amateur days.

'"Icarus" called for two skaters, the second acting as a dominant partner, lifting and throwing me around. I cast Ron Alexander in the role, over the objections of just about everybody involved. He was a tall and (I thought) handsome boy, and I felt he fitted the requirements. John Butler was not pleased, but seemed too weary to argue with me. Sam, however, came down to a rehearsal and cut straight to the core of the matter. "Darling," she said, "I don't care if he's Adonis himself. He can't bloody well skate." I was offended for the first and only time in our relationship and refused to discuss it further. The fact is that I had promised Ron the role and I was not about to disappoint him.'

On opening night in Bristol, John was horrified to hear catcalls and boos during the performance of 'Icarus'. This was repeated on several other nights and at best the work only received lukewarm applause. One reviewer described the costume as a chamois-leather nappy, and Larry Parnes begged John to take the number out. He refused.

'It was something to do with the number of people who were against it. Somehow it ended up pushing me the other way. I believed in it, and I wanted to stick to my guns. I promised Larry that if the London audiences hated it then I would withdraw it without further discussion. London, however, loved it, and the reviewers were full of praise. On opening night, Ron and I shared a bottle of champagne and for the first time I tried some marijuana. I felt intensely happy and was at a loss to understand why everyone was warning me to stay away from Ron. I liked him enormously and he seemed to understand me.'

The Palladium show was a hit. It became the hot ticket in London and celebrities flocked to see it and offer congratulations to John.

He was courted by every columnist and invited to appear on every television and radio interview show in the country. One that he accepted was *Wogan*.

'Some journalists had described me as the Nureyev of ice, and Terry Wogan thought it a good idea to get both Rudolf Nureyev and myself on the same show. I was delighted with the prospect, being an admirer of the great dancer, but no one had told Rudolf that we were both to be on at the same time. When he was informed, he stormed out of the green-room and refused to appear at all. Apparently he thought ice skating was a very poor excuse for an art form!'

It seemed that with the Palladium season John had finally reached the goal that had eluded him for so long. He had made a powerful artistic statement – ice had been accepted by the critics and the public as a legitimate theatrical medium – and he was no longer lonely, having embarked on a relationship with Ron Alexander.

'It was very strange, but I had become like the boy in the Icarus legend, who wanted desperately to reach the sun, but when he managed to fly close to it it melted his wings. Events were set in motion, in the summer of 1977, which would ultimately shatter my dreams and threaten my survival. At that time I thought myself to be happy and fulfilled and I had no inkling of disaster.'

18

As soon as the Palladium show was open, John and Larry Parnes began to have arguments about the future. They had sharply differing views on how to proceed with *Theatre of Skating* once the London season was finished.

'The truth is that Larry and I had absolutely nothing in common. This wasn't his fault, and I'm not blaming him, but I was becoming increasingly frustrated at being thought of as his property. He was holding all kinds of meetings with American impresarios and arena

Left: John with Rita at Acock's Green *(courtesy of John Beaumont)*

Above: John, Rita and Andrew *(courtesy of John Beaumont)*

Below: *(courtesy of John Beaumont)*

John and Toller Cranston, winners of the gold and bronze medals respectively, on the podium at the 1976 Olympic Games *(courtesy of John Beaumont)*

John with Peggy Fleming, skating *L'Après-Midi d'un Faune* *(courtesy of John Beaumont)*

Pro Skate: 'La Habanera'
from *Carmen* *(Celine McDonald)*

John receives the Skater of
the Year Award, 1984
(Christie Jenkins)

David Spungen

Bill Judd

John and JoJo returning from a skiing trip at Vail *(David Lokey)*

Keith Davies and Shelley Winters
(Trevor Spinnet)

Janet Lynn skating to
the *Blue Danube*
(Terry Hancey)

John with Dorothy Hamill
(David Spungen)

John as teacher, coach and critic, with Dita Dotson *(David Spungen)*

Twyla Tharp *(Kenn Duncan)*

Eliot Feld *(David Spungen)*

Laura Dean
(Judy Hammond)

Lar Lubovitch
working with JoJo
Starbuck
(David Spungen)

The company performing Ravel's *Valse*, 1983 Canadian tour *(Trevor Spinnet)*

managers, and they were all sitting around discussing my future as though I had nothing to do with it. I was never once asked for my opinion. Perhaps they thought I didn't have one. Whatever the reason, I knew that this couldn't continue. I would have to find an alternative.'

One evening, after the show, John was approached by two young New York dance producers, Charlotte Kirk and David Singer. They told him they would like to bring his work to the USA. They would have to raise the funding, but if John would give them the opportunity, they felt confident that they could do it.

'I liked Charlotte and David. They were such an enthusiastic team and their optimism was infectious. They had entered my life at exactly the right moment, and I told them I would be very happy to have them as producers. The only provision was that they would have to work things out with Larry.'

Larry Parnes agreed to a meeting with Charlotte and David, but he was not impressed by their credentials. 'They've never done anything like this before. They have no funds available,' he told John. 'There are far more experienced producers who would present you, not only in New York but all over North America.'

John shook his head. 'I don't think you understand. They *are* going to produce my show – it's just a matter of working out the details.'

'I heard nothing further from Charlotte and David for several weeks, and I became severely depressed because I saw the future as a choice between continuing with Larry Parnes or giving up altogether. I couldn't concentrate on anything and I resented having to go to the Palladium every night. I found myself irritated by everyone around me, and I snapped at the skaters, often reducing them to tears. I wanted to stop, but I couldn't. I had so much to be thankful for, yet this terrible black anger had invaded me and blocked out everything positive.'

John began to frequent some of the more notorious London night spots. Sometimes he would go alone, but more often than not he was with Ron Alexander. He was introduced to the sadomasochist scene, and started to experiment with cocaine and mescalin. The effect on his skating was alarming.

'I had always been a very secure performer, but now I found myself falling. No one except Ron knew about my nightly excursions, so my deterioration was put down to depression and fatigue. I knew I was on a dangerous course, but I needed desperately the measure of escape it afforded me. It gave me a kind of happiness and, if there was a price to pay, then I would just have to pay it. I couldn't stop.'

One warm night, John was making his way back from a club in the Soho area. He was wide awake and full of energy, so he opted to walk. As he made his way down a quiet Chelsea street, he heard the unmistakable sound of footsteps following him.

'I had never felt fear in London. It was one of the things I liked best about the city. But that night I felt a cold shiver go down my spine. I didn't turn around, but I knew that someone was stalking me. I tried to quicken my pace, but as soon as I did so the steps caught up with me, and the next thing I knew I was lying on the ground, being kicked viciously. I struggled hard, but it seemed that more than one pair of arms was pinning me down. All I can remember is the putrid smell of bad breath and a voice filled with hatred. "Bastard poofter!" it hissed. "You're sick!" I was kicked again. "Are you listening, scumbag?" Then I received a blow to my head and everything went black. When I came round I was in the hospital.'

John was reluctant to discuss the incident with anyone. It put him out of action for a week, and some performances had to be cancelled. Although there were no permanent injuries from the attack, the bruising was severe and the doctors were concerned about the psychological scars it might leave. John, however, seemed peculiarly calm about the whole affair.

'It was difficult to explain to anyone how I felt at that time. Part of me was relieved that I had an excuse to stop performing for a while, but another part of me was horrified to think that I had allowed myself to become involved in such demoralizing activities. On an impulse, I called Sam and asked her to come and see me.'

Sam arrived bearing armfuls of gifts – fruit, flowers, books, magazines and champagne. She took two crystal flutes from her handbag, popped the cork, poured two measures and handed one to John. 'Here,' she said. 'It's terribly expensive, darling, so don't waste it.' John laughed, and took a cautious sip. 'I don't think the nurses will like it,' he said. 'Sod the nurses,' Sam answered. 'They're not getting any.'

'Sam sat there that afternoon and gave me a lecture. She knew, without being told, that something had gone wrong with my life since we had last seen each other. "I don't know what kind of hanky-panky you've been up to," she said, "but whatever it is, it doesn't suit you. You look awful." She pressed more champagne on me, told me some outrageous stories and made me laugh. I was beginning to feel better. As she got up to leave she said, "You get out of here on Friday. On Saturday morning I'm coming to pick you up and I'm taking you away for the weekend. No arguments." And she left. I found myself looking forward to the prospect.'

The weekend was an unqualified success. Sam drove John to a castle in the New Forest. 'My father lives here,' she explained before they got out of the car. 'But you don't need to worry. He's away, so we'll have the place to ourselves.' They ate a large lunch, went for a long walk, took a nap and lit a fire in the inglenook fireplace. After dinner, which Sam cooked, they sat talking on the hearthrug, sipping at two snifters of vintage brandy.

'I was as relaxed as I could ever remember. I felt as though I had known Sam all my life and it seemed the most natural thing in the world that we should share the same bed that night. In the morning, I woke up to find her smiling at me. "You've never done that before, have you?" she said. "I don't know about you, but I thought we were rather good together. With a bit of practice, I think we could be fantastic!" We often went away for weekends after that, and I stopped going to clubs altogether. I no longer felt the need for stimulants, and we seemed to laugh all the time. One evening, as we sat over dinner in her apartment, she said, "If I wasn't already married, I think I might propose to you!" I smiled at her. "If you weren't already married, I think I might accept!"'

Charlotte Kirk and David Singer came back to England and told John they had now managed to arrange a New York season for him, and had found the necessary financing. The only problem was that they were unable to come to terms with Larry Parnes.

'Larry owned *Theatre of Skating*, and therefore it could not be transferred to the USA without his permission. If he refused to sell the rights to Charlotte and David, then the only alternative was to start from scratch and create a new show for them. I thought about it overnight, and the next day I presented my concept to them. They loved it, and *Ice Dancing* was born.'

The atmosphere at the Palladium became very strained. Larry

Parnes considered legal action against John, but decided it was not worth the aggravation. He was deeply hurt and felt he had been treated poorly, but he realized that there was little he could do other than accept the situation. John worked swiftly to implement the new plan, and contacted several choreographers to see if they would be interested in working with him. Peter Martins, from the New York City Ballet, agreed immediately, and so did Donald Saddler. Later John got acceptances from Jean-Pierre Bonnefous and Douglas Norwick and – to his delight – from Robert Cohan, the *enfant terrible* of the contemporary-dance world.

'I asked Mr MacMillan's permission to use *Feux Follets* in New York, and he agreed. I also asked Norman Maen if I could take *L'Après-Midi d'un Faune* and he seemed pleased that I intended to include it. Finally I approached Twyla Tharp to ask her to revamp my SuperSkates number, "After All", for me, and once again I received a yes. I felt that I would finally have a totally integrated programme to offer, and I was both excited and nervous about the potential.'

John invited three members of the London company to join him in New York, and these included Ron Alexander. He ignored Sam's pleas for him to drop Ron ('What on earth do you want him there for? He's a mediocre skater and he looks scruffy'), feeling that he needed to have an ally with him. He also telephoned his old friend Brian Grant, and invited him to join.

'We were set for a 21 November opening at the Felt Forum in Madison Square Garden. I can't say that it was my ideal venue, but I was persuaded that it would be a good place to try out the show. I flew to New York, and settled in with the Streeters, and the hard work started again. I was told by my producers that I needed a female "name" to partner me in the production, someone who might help to sell tickets. I was not at all happy about this – Cathy Foulkes had been in all my companies to date, and in my opinion she was the ideal leading lady. I felt it would be insulting to bring in someone else and bill them above Cathy. However, I seemed to have no choice, and once again I had to compromise my own values in order to accommodate the box office. The Olympic pair skater JoJo Starbuck was brought in, and the publicists had a field day with the information. Poor JoJo – it took me quite a long time to warm to her.'

John had stopped using drugs at this point, but he was still feeling the effects of them. He suffered from insomnia, and was once again vomiting after every meal.

'Sometimes I felt as though I was in an emotional blender. I felt tremendous pressure to succeed with the new show; I missed Sam; I was lonely; and, above all, I was desperately insecure. Nothing seemed to change that. Critics could write wonderful reviews, audiences could give standing ovations, people could tell me how much they loved me (or hated me), but I still had this dark, empty place inside me that refused to be pacified. I thought perhaps I would never truly understand what it was to be happy.'

The Felt Forum was a tremendous success, attracting an eclectic audience who responded enthusiastically to the performance. The dance critics praised the work and singled out several of the skaters for special mention. One criticism, however, that cropped up several times concerned the uneven nature of the company. 'It is quite extraordinary to see a group of skaters,' wrote one critic, 'some of whom are breathtaking in their beauty of presentation, and others who are barely able to stand up, let alone move around gracefully.' John was hurt by these comments, and blamed the short rehearsal period for the ragged appearance of the troupe.

'It amazed me that anyone could imagine a random group of skaters could become a legitimate corps without a very long time to prepare for that – to integrate. We certainly didn't have the luxury of a protracted rehearsal schedule. Far from it. Skaters are not even trained to work together in a group – they spend their competitive lives in relative isolation. So I wanted people to look at them and say how well they had done under the circumstances, rather than point out their rather minor shortcomings.'

Shortly before Christmas, David Singer managed to secure the Minskoff Theater, on Broadway, for a post-Christmas run. *Ice Dancing* would be transferred intact, but it would require some adjusting to the completely different configuration of the stage.

At the end of the Felt Forum run, John went to Maine for a long weekend with Brian Grant. He had borrowed a small cottage right on the edge of a lake, and the two had a happy and very relaxing time.

'I liked Brian. He was gentle and sweet, and quite unlike anyone else I knew. He was also very intelligent and knew a great deal about music, so we had some wonderful conversations. We talked about the possibility of doing an ice version of *Cinderella* one day – very romantic, with gorgeous costumes. Brian and I became lovers that weekend, but it was very different from the tempestuous kind of relationship I had experienced with Ron. Brian was kind and considerate and made me feel safe. I returned to New York in a very good mood.'

As the Minskoff opening approached, John became nervous and jittery. He was not skating particularly well and felt the whole idea was a mistake. Twyla Tharp came down to the theatre to restage 'After All', and for the first time since they met they began to have problems.

'I seemed to have lost my nerve. Twyla kept asking me to skate right into the front corners of the stage, but I would chicken out before I got there. She was incensed, telling me that I was going to ruin the piece. Finally, I lost my temper and deliberately skated right off the edge into the orchestra pit. "Is that what you wanted?" I demanded. Twyla stared in disbelief, gathered her things and turned to leave the auditorium. "I don't work with children," she said. It was several days before we calmed down sufficiently to complete the changes.'

The opening night was a huge success, filled with celebrities from the theatrical community. Afterwards there was a glittering party, and late in the evening Charlotte and David sat down with John. They were exhausted.

'We were all excited because we felt the opening had gone very well indeed. We toasted each other and I thanked them for all their hard work. Charlotte beamed at me. "We are a great team," she said. "You'll never have to compromise again – we're going to create a company for you on a year-round basis. *Ice Dancing* is only just the beginning!" I wanted so badly to believe her, because to have such a company was the thing I wanted more than anything else in the world. But somewhere in the back of my mind I couldn't help remembering Larry Parnes' words: "You're going to do yourself in, John. One of these days you'll wake up and realize that artistic skating is a contradiction in terms. You'll be an old man before you prove your point."'

John became the darling of the glitterati, sought after for charity luncheons, galas, parties and openings. Celebrities flocked to see his show, and came backstage to meet the new golden boy. Lloyd

Bridges, Katharine Hepburn, Sylvester Stallone, Ted Kennedy – they all fell in love with the new art form. One evening Joni Mitchell, the Canadian folk singer, came to see him. She invited him to dinner at her loft in Greenwich Village and told him she would like him to meet a few friends.

'That was about the only invitation I accepted. I had been a fan of Joni's for a long time, and I loved the originality of her music. I wanted to get to know the person behind it. When I got to her loft, it was an absolutely stunning space – all glass and white pillars and paintings. The paintings were her own, because she was a gifted artist as well as a composer. I realized as soon as I got inside that the "few friends" were like a *Who's Who* of the music world. Stephen Stills, Grahame Nash, Paul Simon, Jimmy Webb and, in one of the back rooms, Bob Dylan in heavy dark glasses and an afro wig. When I went into the kitchen to get a glass of milk, there was Jack Nicholson, leaning against the sink. What do you say to Jack Nicholson when there's no one to introduce you? I loved *Five Easy Pieces*? I didn't have to say anything in the end, because he grinned at me and said, "How's your new record doing?" Since I wasn't a film star, he assumed I must be in the music business. I didn't disillusion him.'

John offered Joni tickets to the show and she brought several people to see it. They were to go out for dinner afterwards. During the first half of the performance, John fell heavily and had to leave the stage. Humiliated, he refused to continue, and one of the other skaters had to fill in for him. Joni and her friends left the show at intermission and she sent him a message asking him to join them at Elaine's Restaurant afterwards.

'I couldn't face them. I was too miserable and felt I had nothing to say to them anyway. I had started using cocaine again, believing that I could control my intake. I told myself that it was only until the show ended, just to enable me to cope with all the tension. I thought no one would know, but it began to affect my skating again, and I became shockingly thin. Brian guessed what was happening and begged me to stop. "You'll ruin yourself," he said. "You don't need it." But I did need it – I felt I would collapse entirely without it.'

Ice Dancing was a massive critical success, but it failed to attract the established theatre crowd. After four weeks, Charlotte and David told John that they would have to post notice. They could only run for two more weeks. No one had come forward to take it on tour, and Kirk/Singer Productions had no money available. *Ice Dancing* was finished.

'I was devastated. I had somehow convinced myself that Charlotte and David would be able to create an ongoing company for me, but instead we had lasted only six weeks. Bunny Olnick, a producer from PBS TV in Boston, made a recording of the show which was broadcast on the public television network. It was very well received, and we made a little money from it, plus it gave us a permanent record of *Ice Dancing*. After that, however, I saw no point in wasting any more time. I disbanded the skaters and enrolled in acting and dance classes. I had decided to retire from the ice and, even if it took me years, I was determined to create a new life for myself in the theatre.'

Part Two

As the ferry approached Fire Island, I could see the outline of a figure sitting on the docks, legs dangling over the sides and head bowed forward. Even from that distance, it was obviously someone deep in thought. It wasn't until the boat pulled alongside, however, that I saw it was John Curry.

I walked over quietly and stood watching him. There were tears on his cheeks and his knuckles were white where they gripped the boards. He looked up then and saw me, and he smiled briefly. 'Hello, Elva,' he said. 'I was just sitting here wondering what it would be like to drown.'

19

I had known about John Curry long before I met him, because I managed and produced his Canadian rival, Toller Cranston. Initially they had been friends, and they would write long letters to each other and exchange telephone calls. Later, without any apparent warning, John stopped speaking to Toller. This was in 1975, and we had just arrived in Colorado Springs for the World Championships.

Toller was hurt by this sudden rejection, and asked me to go and speak to John for him. 'Find out why he's being so piggy to me,' he pleaded. John, however, was polite and dismissive. 'I can't discuss it,' he told me firmly. Two days later, *Vogue* asked me to interview John for a personality profile, and so I approached him again. This time we got on very well together, and talked for many hours about his dreams, his art, his loneliness and his experiences with Erhard Seminar Training. As we parted he said, 'It's too bad you're already working with Toller. I think we would have made a very good team.'

After Colorado Springs, I returned to my home in Toronto and Toller and John both set off on the ISU Tour of Champions. One day my phone rang and John was on the line. He said he was calling from New York, and told me he had left the tour in Vancouver. He couldn't face another year of amateur competition and was seriously considering dropping out of skating altogether. 'If I work very hard,' he said, 'I think it's not too late to make a career as a dancer.'

I wasn't sure why he had chosen to call me, nor was I sure if he expected me to react to his announcement. Whatever the case, I told him that I was appalled to hear him speaking that way and he should on no account give up competing just because some Canadian rednecks had been rude enough to throw a Coke can at him. 'You are one of the world's finest skaters,' I said. 'If you go into ballet, you can only hope to be a good member of a troupe. You are not Nureyev – you are John Curry, and you are both at the same level in your own disciplines. Don't throw it all away.' He thanked me politely and hung up. It was to be nine months before I saw him again.

I did not go with Toller to Innsbruck for the Olympics. I was busy with the show he planned to launch in the summer. But I did go to Göteborg, and saw John shortly after he won the World Championship there. I hugged him and told him how pleased I was. 'You made the right decision,' I said.

'Did I?' he answered. 'I wonder.' It was strange, but even though he had just won the long-coveted World and Olympic titles, he still did not seem to be happy.

Toller and I were engrossed in the business of his own ice show and for several months we heard nothing of John. Then we read that he was opening *Theatre of Skating* in London in December, and Toller asked me to send him a good-luck telegram. John did not acknowledge this and Toller was somewhat offended. Early in the New Year, a reporter from the *New York Times* who was writing an article about the rise of artistic skating rang Toller for his thoughts on John.

'John Curry has been called the Nureyev of ice,' said the reporter. 'Do you agree with that?'

Toller thought for a moment, then he said, 'Yes. I think it's a very good description. They skate very similarly.'

After that I was not able to mention John's name in front of Toller. It wasn't until two years later, when Toller's show had closed, that I flew to London to see *Theatre of Skating* at the Palladium. I had spoken to Larry Parnes and told him I would be interested in bringing the show to New York.

I sat through two performances before I went to talk to John. I had already agreed a deal with Larry and I assumed the meeting with John would be a formality and an opportunity to discuss a possible change of format. I thought some of his skaters were weak, and I also felt that the show needed a director. As it turned out, however, none of this was relevant because John had already committed to the two New York dance producers Kirk and Singer and the show was not available. I took him to lunch before I left, and I couldn't help noticing how sad he looked. 'What's wrong?' I asked. 'You're not happy, are you?'

He shook his head. 'One day we'll discuss it all. Now is not the time. I have a feeling we will work together one day, you and I, and then there'll be plenty of time for talking.'

When John came to New York to open *Ice Dancing*, he invited me to the first-night party. I was shocked at how gaunt he looked, and felt his gaiety to be forced and unconvincing. He came over to me at one point and looked at me hard. 'Why don't you meet me for lunch?' he said. 'You're the only person in this room who sees right through me, and it would be nice to have someone to talk to about it all.'

We met in the Village, and wandered around in the winter sunshine, looking in shop windows and making small talk. When we had eaten lunch, he started to tell me about his childhood and his competitive career. He told me of his constant depressions, his frustration, his bitterness and his sexual ambivalence. 'The funny thing is, I'm surrounded by people who like me, yet none of them really knows who I am. That makes me feel very lonely.'

After that we often lunched together, or took a morning coffee. Sometimes he would call me to come and watch him rehearse. He didn't feel well, but refused to go to a doctor. 'There's nothing they can do for me,' he said glumly. 'They'll just fill me up with pills.'

John was beginning to doubt his producers. As the run at the Minskoff progressed, the talk of further tours began to die down. The show was losing money, and it was becoming obvious that it would have to close. 'I don't blame them,' he told me; 'I'm sure they've done the best they can. I can't go through all this again, however, and I've made up my mind to retire.'

I stared at him for a moment. 'Are you sure you mean that?' I asked him. 'Don't forget we've had this conversation before. Perhaps you just need a rest – remember Disraeli's words: "I will sit down for now, but the day will come when you will hear me!"'

He smiled sadly. 'No – I'm afraid that day will never come, but at least I tried.'

John did give up skating, as he had threatened to do, and he studied acting and dance with a determination that surprised everyone. In the summer of 1979 he was cast in the Broadway revival of *Brigadoon*, and I went down to watch rehearsals. The great Agnes de Mille, who was reviving her original choreography for the show, was not at all impressed by the champion skater in her cast. 'There are no blades in *Brigadoon*,' she told him sharply. Although John was an accomplished dancer, she refused to work with him and a young client of mine, William Shenston, was brought in to coach him. 'She's being horrible to John,' William told me. 'She refuses to see that he is a good dancer in his own right. She can't seem to forgive him for being an Olympic champion.' The reviews were respectable, but no further offers of this kind came to John. He grew increasingly despondent and disappeared. When I tried to reach him I was told he'd left no forwarding number.

One day, towards the end of the summer, I took the boat to Fire Island, the summer haunt of Manhattan's artistic community. As we approached the pier I caught sight of a lonely figure sitting on the dock, and when we drew closer I realized it was John. 'Hello, Elva,' he said quietly. 'I was just sitting here wondering what it would be like to drown.' I sat down beside him and put my arm around his shoulders. 'Come on,' I told him. 'Nothing is that bad. Why don't we have one of our lunches, and talk about it?'

He smiled at me. 'What sent you along at exactly this moment?' he asked.

I laughed. 'I was hungry, and you know how I hate eating alone!'

We talked the rest of the day away, and by the time I left for New York John had promised me that he would come into the city the following week and see if we could figure out something for him to do. I wasn't at all sure he would turn up, so I was pleased when I saw him walk through my office doorway.

I had three suggestions for him that day, but I was careful to explain to him that they were still conceptual and that no funding was yet in place. 'If you like any of them,' I told him, 'I will find the funding. But I would want your commitment first.'

He listened quietly while I told him that I wanted to create an ice ensemble company that could skate to live symphony orchestras. I also wanted to put together the first head-to-head professional championships, which would be designed and run by skaters, and which would lean heavily towards the artistic and performance values of the skating. Thirdly, we wanted to establish a school, where skaters like John could live and train at the same time as they pursued their academic careers. They would start at the age of ten, and would be exposed to all aspects of the arts – music, dance, mime, theatre, painting. It would be run along the lines of the Vaganova School in St Petersburg, which prepares dancers for the Kirov and Bolshoi

Ballets. When I had finished outlining my plans, I added: 'It is only fair to tell you that these things are still in the dreaming stage. I don't know how or when I will ever be able to make them happen, but that day will come.' I saw tears welling in his eyes.

'It doesn't matter how long it takes,' he said. 'These things are the stuff of my own visions. I want you to do it, and I want to be part of it. Just let me know when to start, and I'll be there. And don't ever let anything put you off.'

Several days later I received a note from him telling me that I had restored his desire to skate.

20

One day in the spring of 1981, my lawyer called me. I was writing for NBC Television at the time, and was not actively involved in skating. 'I want you to meet someone,' he told me. 'Can you come down to my office at two o'clock?'

When I arrived, I saw a very tall man with broad shoulders, extraordinarily white teeth and kind eyes. He was somewhere in his thirties and he was dressed in blue jeans and a denim jacket. 'This is David Spungen,' said my lawyer. 'I'm going to leave you two alone, because I think you'll find you have a lot in common.'

David and I talked all afternoon, discovering a mutual passion for quality skating and a shared sense of humour. By the end of the day we had decided to start an ice production company together.

David had been working for a company called Candid Productions, run by the two-time US Olympic skating champion Dick Button. Dick was involved in virtually all televised skating in the USA, and produced the majority of professional ice 'events'. David had been the co-ordinating producer for the hugely successful show *Challenge of Champions*, but had been greatly disturbed by the way Dick presented figure skating. 'He has it all sewn up. He just uses the same stars over and over again, and he won't even consider including skaters that the networks don't recognize. How is the sport supposed to develop? His stuff is just manufactured television specials.' I told him of my long-standing dreams for a professional circuit that would be designed by skaters themselves. 'Then why don't we make that our first project?' he said. 'You have the concept, and I have all the energy you could ask for. I think we'd make a great combination.'

Within a week, we had started the incorporation process. I had only just met David, but I knew instinctively that we had the right chemistry to make a partnership work. I felt I could trust him, and he seemed to feel the same way about me. (As far as I was concerned, this was the most vital ingredient in any professional relationship. Everything else could be worked out, but without an underlying trust there could be no real collaboration.)

I called John to tell him about David, and suggested he come into Manhattan to meet him. 'I've met him already,' he told me. 'I was in one of those dreadful Dick Button events and David was there. He was the best thing about it, and certainly the only one there with any artistic integrity. But I'd like to meet him again, and hear about your plans.'

We met in the Maestro, near Lincoln Center, and had a long and stimulating lunch. The three of us got on very well together, and we laughed constantly. As we were waiting for the bill, John hugged each of us in turn. 'I sense something momentous is happening. I'm not sure what it is, or when it will come into being, but I do know that it involves the three of us. We all three dream the same dreams for ice, and perhaps we need each other to make them come true. I think your idea to start a professional skating circuit is wonderful, and I want to help in any way I can. And when the time comes to do something in the artistic realm, then perhaps you can help me.' He picked up his glass of Perrier. 'Let's drink a toast – to us, the Triple Threat!'

David and I made a business plan and began to haunt potential investors. I had recently produced a roller-skating extravaganza with noted rock promoter and manager Steve Leber, and I thought he might be attracted to the concept. I went to see him seven times, bombarding him with reasons to become involved. He was dubious: 'I'm not jumping up and down about it,' he said. 'But I'll see what my Canadian partner thinks about it.' He called Michael Cohl, the impresario responsible for touring the Stones, and got an enthusiastic response. 'It's a great idea,' he said. 'Find out more about it.' I explained to Steve that amateur skating was a closed shop, where skaters' careers hung on the whims of partisan judges and a marking system that defied reason. I told him that we wanted to create a pro circuit where top skaters from different generations could compete against each other for prize money. They would be judged by a mixture of skating experts and top professionals from the arts world, and the rules would be devised by the skaters themselves. There would also be input from the audience, who would become the public judge and have a say in the outcome. It would be a kind of grand-prix circuit, much as in tennis or golf. Steve began to warm to the idea.

By Christmas we had the first year's events lined up. The inaugural competitions would take place in Canada, with Men's and Ladies' singles, and Pairs and Ice Dance categories. John spent a great deal of time with us, helping us to work out the details and suggesting skaters he felt we should include in the roster of competitors. Robin Cousins was the reigning Olympic champion, having won the gold medal in Lake Placid the year before, and he showed extraordinary courage by agreeing to participate. 'It's the future of skating,' he said. 'If I don't put my medal where my mouth is, then I'm not worth much.' His involvement lured in many other top skaters, and we were able to assemble a dazzling field. We decided to call it Pro Skate.

I wanted to create a special slot in the events for John, and I arranged to meet him at a café one bitterly cold January morning. 'It reminds me of Davos,' John shuddered. 'How I hate this weather!' We warmed our hands round steaming cups of cappuccino, and I came straight to the point.

'We have the green light for the first year of Pro Skate,' I told him. 'There will be five events on the Canadian circuit, followed by a championship event at Madison Square Garden in December. That will be televised on ABC TV's *Wide World of Sports*, and they have already agreed to our judging format. We have just about every major skater in the world taking part, and we've also included a number of the unknowns suggested by you. If we do our job properly, this project will cause quite a stir and will reach a very large segment of the population. I want you to take the opportunity to skate artistic exhibitions in front of this captive audience. I know you don't like arenas, but this is different, I promise you. You won't have to worry about box office, and you will be able to make your own personal statement in a uniquely beneficial setting.'

He put out his hand to stop me. 'I accept! You don't have to tell me what a fantastic showcase Pro Skate will be. But I do have to ask a very crass question.' He paused, looking somewhat embarrassed. 'Will I be paid anything? You see, I have very little money at the moment and it would be nice to think I could give some to my mother.'

I laughed. 'Paid? You'll be the highlight of the whole circuit. I intend to see to it that you are very well paid indeed.'

I knew that John's agreement was only valid if we could negotiate an acceptable deal with his agent. I suspected that Dick Button had already put a rival bid on the table, as he had expressed his displeasure at our intrusion into what he considered to be his exclusive territory. He wasn't going to allow Pro Skate to take off without putting up a fight, and he had started bidding wars over several of the top skaters. I thought the important thing would be to get Steve and Michael committed first.

This proved easier than I had anticipated. Michael had always been a fan of John's, but Steve had taken longer to recognize his true worth. He was persuaded now, however, that John had an invaluable role to play in Pro Skate as the *éminence grise* of the circuit. His presence would attract the established skaters and inspire the younger ones; he would add enormously to the credibility of the production. Steve was convinced of John's value, but felt that he should compete. 'We can't pay huge amounts of money just for someone to exhibit,' he said firmly.

David and I agonized over the situation. ABC had made a very good deal with Pro Skate, giving us a total of just over $5,000,000 for a three-year contract. For this, however, they were demanding that the Olympic gold-medallists should all compete; they were not at all interested in exhibitions. Reluctantly we agreed to include a team competition, in which John, Peggy and Dorothy could take part. They were the skaters who refused to compete head to head, but they accepted the team concept because the individual scores would not be released, and only the team totals would be displayed. ABC, however, could advertise the event as having all the Olympians participating. In this way, everyone seemed to be satisfied. We made one condition on our own side – and that was that they must agree to show all of John's exhibitions as well.

I was depressed by the reversion to team competition. It had been done for years, and was nothing new. I saw it as an appalling compromise, and felt that as long as it remained as an alternative we would never truly break down the resistance to pro competitions. This resistance came both from the skaters themselves, who were conditioned to believe that once they had won a World or Olympic medal they must never again put their reputations on the line; and from the amateur ice-skating establishment, which stood to lose control of competitors (and therefore income). I went to discuss the team concept with John, to see how he would react to it.

'Because I know Pro Skate will handle it very well, I have no problem with it,' he told me. 'If it is the price you have to pay in order to develop the real professional competitions, then I think it is worth it. After all, let's face it – I don't think I can really hope to beat Robin at this point in my career! I could never begin to jump as well as he can. I think this is for the best, and it might actually turn out to be fun. What's important is that we all get behind Pro Skate and make sure that it succeeds – if it does, it will provide a forum for all those excellent skaters who are pulverized by the amateur machine.'

John's business affairs were handled by the Robert Lantz Agency in New York, and the next step was to meet with his personal agent, Irv Schwartz. He told me that John had expressed a very strong desire to sign with us, but that he already had an offer on the table from Dick Button. 'It's for a great deal of money,' he told us. 'I don't think you can afford to match it. It would take a firm offer of a hundred thousand dollars a year, with a three-year guarantee. No out clauses.' I tried hard not to gasp. It was almost double the amount we had anticipated, but I was determined we would work something out. I told Irv we would get back to him the next day.

Michael and Steve were anxious not to lose the top skaters to Dick Button, and they felt John was a key player in this tussle. They came up with a solution they felt would work – they would guarantee the $100,000 a year for three years, if $40,000 a year could become John's fee for a television special, which Pro Skate would produce. In addition, John would become an official spokesperson for Pro Skate and would become exclusive to us in the New York geographical area and in the field of competitive skating. There would be no out clauses on either side, and John would have 'favoured-nations' status with any other skater in the event (this meant that any perks given to other top competitors would automatically be granted to John). I was delighted with this, because I knew that Dorothy Hamill already had two first-class return air fares, a suite in a hotel for each night of the competitions, and $100 *per diem*. Three days later, Irv told us that they were willing to accept the deal. The only condition would be that John must have conceptual control of the TV special.

I took John to meet Steve and the three of us went out to lunch. John outlined his ideas for the first television show, to be based on Hans Christian Andersen, and Steve thought it a very good idea. He was captivated by John and found him to be articulate, intelligent, charming and well-mannered. 'He's a gentleman!' he enthused. He was used to handling heavy-metal rock groups and having to grapple with the likes of Aerosmith, AC/DC and Ted Nugent, and he found John a refreshing contrast. 'He actually offered to pay for the lunch!' he marvelled.

John signed the Pro Skate deal and we all celebrated by having tea at the Plaza Hotel. 'You do know you won't be allowed to skate for Dick Button for the next three years?' I teased him.

'I suspect that will suit both Dick and me equally well,' he answered. 'The last time I had the misfortune to work with him, I decided to leave before the end of the event and I seem to remember being forcibly returned to the arena. I have no wish to repeat that experience, believe me!'

The Canadian circuit took place in March and early April, and covered five cities – Montreal, Vancouver, Edmonton, Calgary and Toronto. The first event, in Montreal, was a memorable occasion. It was the first time in skating history that top professionals had competed against each other on a head-to-head basis, and skating's élite flew in from all over the world to witness the happening. The Montreal Forum was sold out – 17,500 spectators jammed the stands and the air crackled with excitement.

Backstage, John was nervous – not just for himself, but also for the other skaters. He walked around, trying to reassure them. Robin Cousins was hot favourite to win the Men's event, but Toller was the one the locals were cheering for. When John saw him he hesitated, uncertain of the reception he would receive, but Toller seemed genuinely pleased to see him. John held out his hand. 'I wish you luck,' he said. 'You've got more courage than I have!'

Toller grinned. 'I'm just sorry you're not competing,' he said. 'I wanted the chance to have one last crack at you!'

Janet Lynn, who had not skated for several years, had trained very hard to prepare for the Ladies' competition. John had flown to Denver in February to choreograph a special piece for her, set to the music of the *Blue Danube*. As she waited now to go on to the ice, John hugged her. 'You've always been my inspiration, right from the first time I saw you skate. Go out there today and show everyone what true joy is all about!'

Janet won the Ladies' event by a wide margin, and went on to be the unbeaten Ladies' Champion of the circuit. The *Toronto Star* spoke glowingly of her abilities and said, 'She is the rarest of skaters, and John Curry's choreography is perfectly attuned to her talents.'

Besides skating solo exhibitions on the tour, John was also skating pair exhibitions with JoJo Starbuck. JoJo was one of the most popular figures in the skating world, and had won the bronze medal at the 1972 Olympics with her partner, Ken Shelley. John choreographed a charming *pas de deux* for them, set to the *Skaters' Waltz*, and the audience responded warmly to their obvious delight in each other.

Right before the final event – the Men's Championship – John skated his solo exhibition. He had chosen Ravel's *La Valse*, and wore a simple ink-blue costume. For five minutes he mesmerized the crowd, moving around the huge ice surface with such grace and elegance that the only sound to be heard was the swishing of the skate blades. It was a dramatic, poignant display of artistry that reduced many of the spectators to tears. As he finished, the arena erupted in wild applause and people ran down to the barriers to offer him flowers. He came off the ice and walked across to Michael and Steve. 'Was it all right?' he asked anxiously.

They couldn't help laughing. 'It was more than all right,' Michael told him. 'It was fucking sensational!'

The Men's event was the most-awaited of the championship. The field was incredibly strong, and Toller skated a brilliant programme to *Tosca*. The response was electric, and he received a very high score. The last up was Robin Cousins, the skater most people had come to see. He was visibly nervous as he waited to take the ice, watching the tiny flower-girls scurry around picking up the dozens of bouquets that had been tossed out for Toller. At last they had finished, and he moved to centre-ice, waiting for his music to begin. As the first notes sounded, he seemed to sail into his choreography, spinning with dazzling speed and soaring into the air without any apparent effort. His jumps were so high, and so feather-light, that they produced audible gasps from the spectators. He finished his performance with his famous lay-out back flip, and the audience leapt to their feet. When the marks came in, Robin had beaten Toller by a narrow margin. It was a thrilling end to the first event.

The next stop on the route was Vancouver, and John was sick with nerves at the prospect of appearing at the Pacific Coliseum. 'I swore I'd never do it again!' he moaned. 'I don't know why I agreed. They hate me here.' Dorothy, Peggy Fleming and JoJo Starbuck were also skating exhibitions on the tour, and they took pity on him. They decided to look after him for the day, and took him sightseeing, thoroughly spoiling him. Two hours before the event they marched him up to his hotel room and deposited him there. 'We're coming back for you in ninety minutes, so be ready!' warned Peggy.

The Coliseum was full. The Japanese champion, Fumio Igarashi, had now joined the circuit and there was tremendous anticipation of the Men's event. The fact that he had to skate right beforehand made John very nervous. He paced up and down, trying to keep himself focused, going over his programme in his head. He had decided to skate to Beethoven's Moonlight Sonata, and he wore a simple white costume with white boot covers. The music started and he glided out into the middle of the vast arena, head bowed, body held motionless. He seemed to be floating above the ice, without apparent traction. For the next five minutes he held the capacity crowd in thrall, moving with seamless elegance in a performance which was part skating, part dance and part mime. As the final bars of music sounded, he travelled slowly across the ice, his body perfectly still, his head thrown back, his hands turned palm upwards in supplication. He came to a stop and there was silence. Nobody moved. Then, from somewhere in the back of the auditorium, someone began to applaud. Gradually the entire audience joined in, rising to their feet, cheering and stamping loudly. John remained in the middle of the ice, overwhelmed by the reception. This was more than an enthusiastic reaction to his work – it was a vindication of everything that he stood for.

21

With the Vancouver performance behind him, John was able to relax and enjoy the remainder of the Canadian tour. He experimented with a different solo programme and skated pair numbers with JoJo. Everything was well received and the critics wrote rapturously about the little-known English champion's talent. He was, one wrote, 'the quintessential creative skater, bringing ice into another dimension'.

In Toronto, the last stop on the tour, the competitors were housed in the luxurious Harbour Hotel. This was Michael Cohl's home territory, and he treated them all like rock stars. Backstage at the Maple Leaf Gardens, the drab dressing rooms were transformed into luxury accommodation – the tables were laden with bowls of fruit, nuts and raisins, juices and salads. Japanese chefs had been brought in to cook fresh dishes to order, and huge vats of chilled spring water were everywhere. 'It was never like this at the Olympics!' said Dorothy.

Toronto was a cosmopolitan city with a tremendous appreciation of dance in all its forms. Because of this, John had chosen to perform 'After All' as his final exhibition on the tour. It was brilliantly skated and brought the audience to their feet for a ten-minute ovation. As the applause died down, he crossed to the referee's stand and asked for a microphone. He waited until everyone was quiet, then said:

'We have just completed a tour of Canada, which has been a revelation to us all. Pro Skate is a brave new concept – one which is rich in promise. It has afforded top skaters from several generations an opportunity to compete against each other on an equal basis, and it has brought out the best in everybody. I would like to offer, on behalf of all the skaters, a vote of thanks to the four people who made this possible – David Spungen and Elva Oglanby, who conceived and developed it, and Steve Leber and Michael Cohl, who took that concept and made it into a reality. They risked their money as we risked our reputations, and together we have created something that epitomizes the true meaning of sportsmanship.' John paused, and looked slowly round the arena. Then he added: 'There was a time when I feared for the future of skating, but from where I stand tonight it has never looked more positive.'

Only the Men's competition remained, and a buzz of excitement ran round the stadium. It was to be carried live on national television, and Canada was rooting for Toller to win. Unfortunately, Robin had been obliged to cut short his own involvement in the tour after Vancouver, due to a long-standing professional commitment in Britain. Fumio Igarashi, who had won the Vancouver competition, was still on the circuit however, along with several other world champions. It was a very powerful field.

Olympic silver-medallist David Santee, one of three American men in the category, skated a dazzling performance to the theme from *Rocky*, and the crowd responded enthusiastically. Fumio Igarashi pulled off three triple jumps in a row, in a superb samurai number, and seemed set to win the medal. Last up was Toller, who entered the arena dressed in a dramatic black costume. He was performing his signature piece, to *Pagliacci*, and as the opening chords rang round the building, the audience became absolutely still. He had never skated as well – he seemed to be possessed by the music, and his unique style, his body twisting and turning in strange, abstract shapes, gave the choreography an eerie, surrealistic quality. As the music ended, he fell to the ice in one seamless movement, his hand still grasping empty air where he had hoped to find life. The sad clown was dead, and Toller had won the title. It was a hugely popular victory with Toller's home-town crowd, and a magnificent comeback for the ex-Olympian.

There was a big party that evening, in the revolving restaurant on top of the Harbour Castle. It was thrown by Labatt's, the circuit sponsors, and no expense was spared. Peggy, JoJo and Dorothy all insisted on dancing with John, who was in high spirits. Much to Michael Cohl's pleasure, John made a point of thanking the representatives of Labatt's, and told them: 'You have done a very important thing in supporting this tour, and I only wish corporations in my country would follow suit. I want you to know how much your generosity was appreciated by us all.'

Before he left the party, John came over to sit with David and me. 'This has been one of the happiest periods of my life,' he told us. 'It has been such a wonderful experience for me, in more ways than you can possibly imagine. Now – I have a favour to ask of you.' He paused, and I wondered what was coming. 'I am going to stay in Toronto for an extra week, to work with Davies and Winters. I think they have exceptional promise, and I want to help them. If they do as well as I think they will, can you find a way to include them in the Madison Square Garden event in December?'

Something about the request disturbed me. It wasn't that I questioned John's judgement, but rather his motives. Keith Davies and Shelley Winters were a talented young pair of skaters and, as Canadians, had been a popular ingredient in the Pro Skate tour. But they were not yet world-class contenders, and I had a strange feeling that John's interest was too intense to be professional. Keith Davies was a handsome, well-built boy, with a shock of blond hair and clear blue eyes. He was also deeply entrenched in a monogamous relationship with a boy from Ontario. I had a strange premonition that this attraction – if that's what it was – would end in disaster.

John spent the early part of the summer in England, taking acting classes and appearing in a production of *A Midsummer Night's Dream* in the role of Puck. He received some enthusiastic reviews and returned to New York in a buoyant frame of mind.

He decided to accept an invitation to stay with some friends on Fire Island, and occasionally we would visit him there. He seemed to be totally relaxed, enjoying a casual, bohemian lifestyle among the artists and intellectuals who made it their summer home. 'I really wouldn't mind if I spent the rest of my days here,' he said one afternoon, lying amongst the sand dunes. 'I feel at peace.'

Once or twice he came into New York to visit Steve, who had taken a tremendous liking to him. 'He's the only skater I've met so far', he announced bluntly, 'who's got anything at all between the ears. I like him!' It was a golden time for us. We were in the honeymoon period of our projects and so far we had encountered no real problems.

22

The Madison Square Garden events were set for 9 and 10 December 1982. David was handling the liaison with ABC TV and I was overseeing the actual competition. We were both involved in the daily business of running the circuit itself and in the myriad details that surrounded such a complex undertaking. We had received very strong support from potential celebrity judges and had been fortunate enough to secure an excellent referee in Bruce Hyland, a Canadian ex-champion and coach who enjoyed the respect of the skating community. As the prize money totalled over $1 million, the media were taking a keen interest in the event. The press conference to launch the box office was set for mid-November.

John called one day and invited us to lunch. Steve was in Washington, but David and I met him at the Dorset Hotel. I was immediately struck by the change in him since we had last seen him on Fire Island eight weeks earlier. He looked drawn and tired, and his face was deathly pale. He was also extremely nervous. He fiddled with the cutlery and picked at his food, then he asked if he could have a glass of red wine. I was surprised, because he rarely drank at lunchtime. Conversation was unusually strained, and finally David stood up and said, 'If you all will excuse me, I need to get back to the office.' He smiled at John. 'You take care of yourself, my friend.'

'I hope David didn't think me rude?' John said anxiously. 'I have something on my mind and I'm not sure how to tell you about it. Elva, something terrible is happening to me.' I was alarmed. I ordered two more glasses of wine and waited for him to go on. When he did, it all came out in a rush. 'My agent has arranged for me to appear in a show in Radio City Music Hall, starting in February. It will be called *Ice* and will star Toller and Peggy as well as me. It's to be produced by Bob Shipstad, and I've agreed to go to California to meet with them all and see what I think about it.'

I was surprised. 'It would have been nice if your agent had asked us if we minded,' I told him. 'After all, we do have a geographical exclusion clause for New York. But other than that, how do you feel about it yourself?'

He looked miserable. 'I hate the whole idea, but they insist it would be good for me. What do you think?'

This was a very difficult question for me to answer. I didn't want to undermine his confidence in his agents, but I did want to be honest with him. His long-term career was too important for him to make a mistake at this stage. 'John, Bob Shipstad is a very nice man, but he produced *Ice Follies*. This doesn't seem like a natural marriage to me, but perhaps you should wait until you hear what they have in mind before you decide anything.'

He flew to California for three days of discussions, but was back within twenty-four hours. When he came to the office, he was depressed. 'It was untenable,' he said. 'The idea of being the third string on a vaudeville bow was grotesque, to say the least. I'm disappointed that Peggy has agreed to do it, but Toller doesn't surprise me. He seems to be way over the top at the moment. Someone in Canada wrote that he's the "Liberace of the ice", and that just about sums it up.' I disagreed with his assessment of Toller, but didn't feel this was the moment to say so. 'The thing is,' he finished miserably, 'my people are making the most tremendous fuss about it all. I've told them I won't do it, but they won't leave it alone.'

Ice was forgotten in the excitement of the press conference for Pro Skate. John acted as the chief spokesperson for the event and was eloquent and persuasive. When the box office opened, ticket sales were brisk and from the early signs it looked set to be a hit.

John went to England to see his mother and to start preparing his new exhibition programmes. While he was gone, a full-page advertisement appeared in the *New York Times*, announcing *Ice* at Radio City Music Hall. It was to star Peggy Fleming, Toller Cranston and John Curry. Before I had time to digest it, Steve came bursting through our office doorway, waving the newspaper. 'What the fuck is this?' he demanded. 'You told me he'd turned it down!'

'He did,' I said. 'He was adamant about it.'

Steve shook his head. 'This advertisement cost twenty-five thousand dollars – Bob Shipstad wouldn't put John's name on it without his agreement. He's not a total moron.'

I rang John and told him how shocked we were. '*You're* shocked!' he said. 'What do you think I feel like? I'm absolutely livid about it. I'll have to come back and sort it out.' He arrived the next day and went to see his agent. Afterwards he came to the office, looking tired and dejected. We went in to see Steve, and John sat down heavily. 'It seems that I must do this awful show,' he told Steve. 'If I refuse, then apparently it will cause my agent and Mr Shipstad terminal embarrassment. I can't think how I came to be in the middle of such a mess, but Robert and Shirley Lantz have been very good to me and I have agreed to go forward for their sake.' He stopped for a minute and sighed. 'My name was included in this show without my knowledge or permission, but I think it is now best if I just do it. I know you must be very disappointed in me, and I'm very, very sorry for upsetting you all like this. I hope you can understand.'

'What I understand,' Steve said, 'is that you are being railroaded into doing something you don't want to do. But if you have decided to go forward, then I respect your reasons and we will support you. There'll be no legal repercussions.'

Steve was impressed by John's straightforward attitude. He watched him through the window, walking slowly down 55th Street. 'If he was my client, I wouldn't have let him anywhere near that show,' he said. 'The boy is a fucking genius if ever there was one. He's in a league of his own and they don't seem to understand his potential.' I realized John had a powerful new champion.

We managed to persuade Steve and Michael to include Keith and Shelley in the Pro Skate Pairs event in December, on the basis that there were not enough Canadians. I rang John to let him know, and he was delighted. 'You won't regret it,' he assured me. 'Wait and see.' They came down to work with John at the Sky Rink for a few days, and he invited us to watch them rehearse. I was absolutely astonished by what I saw. John had managed to transform them into a fast, co-ordinated, confident team with a new air of maturity. I watched him work, perched on top of the barriers, monitoring their every move, and I realized what a truly gifted teacher he was. He was tireless in his attention to detail and he instilled in his students an elegance and a sense of self-worth that made them glow. My respect for him deepened, and I was sorry I had ever questioned his reasons for becoming involved with Keith and Shelley.

Madison Square Garden sold out two weeks before the event, and Manhattan was gripped with ice fever. David and I worked late into the night on 8 December, to make sure no detail had been missed: airport cars, practice sessions, buses, skate-sharpening, judges, seat allocations, flowers, prizes, medals – not to mention the closing-night party at the exquisite Chinese restaurant Dish of Salt. Every major star in the figure skating world had flown in to take part in the competitions, and expectations were running high.

This championship event was important for John in a number of ways. He was to captain one of the competing teams, and this gave him a stature within the established professional skating hierarchy. In addition, he was to perform two exhibitions which would be carried on the ABC TV network – one solo, to music by Grieg, and the other in partnership with Peggy Fleming, to the Pachelbel Canon. This combined exposure would bring him to the attention of a wide American audience.

On the first day John skated the Grieg piece right after the Ice Dance competition. He was rapturously received by the sophisticated New York audience, and he was delighted with the response. Many people came backstage to see him and told him they had followed him ever since seeing him skate 'After All' at the SuperSkates gala. 'It's hard to take it all in,' he said happily. 'I'm afraid to say anything, in case it all goes wrong again.' Later in the day, Janet Lynn performed his *Blue Danube* choreography and won the Ladies' event by an overwhelming margin. This was to be Janet's swansong as a performer and her three small children sat in the stands, watching her. Afterwards, John hugged her and both of them were weeping uncontrollably. 'Please don't retire,' he pleaded, but she shook her head.

'It's time to go,' she told him sadly.

David and I had created a Skater of the Year award, to be presented during the Madison Square Garden championships each year. It was designed to honour those skaters who had made a unique, individual contribution to the sport and the art of ice, and the first recipient was to be Janet Lynn. She was not aware of her selection, but had been carefully positioned in the stands to watch the Teams event. John had been asked to make the presentation immediately after the end of the competition, and he had hidden the trophy – a beautiful crystal prism from Tiffany's – in his skate bag.

The Team Championship was fun for skaters and audience alike. John's team included Peggy and Toller, and he had also selected Keith and Shelley, who had given a very good performance that morning to finish third in the Pairs. In the end, John's team won by the narrowest of margins, and all the participants hugged and shook hands. The audience rose, thinking the evening was over, but John took the microphone and asked if they would sit down again for a few minutes.

'I want you to pay tribute to a very special lady, a unique artist who has, in my opinion, brought more beauty and inspiration to skating than anyone in my lifetime. She has always skated with a joy and freedom which transcend the normal boundaries of ice. Her performances are born of pure love, and she radiates a kind of incandescence which uplifts everyone who sees it. Sadly, she has today announced her retirement, but the memories she leaves will stay with us for ever.' The ABC cameras were now close in on Janet's astonished face, and her children were jumping up and down in excitement. 'Mummy! Mummy! It's you!' they shrieked. John turned to face Janet, and held his hand out towards her. 'Ladies and gentlemen,' he said proudly, 'I want you to welcome Janet Lynn, Skater of the Year for 1982.'

Janet, always shy and retiring, came down on to the ice to join John, her face pink with embarrassment. John hugged her, kissed her cheek, and handed her the trophy. 'I am so glad to be the one to give you this,' he told her. 'No one deserves it more.'

At the Dish of Salt, John sparkled. He was more gregarious than I had ever seen him, and he was laughing and joking with everyone there. He thanked Michael, Steve, David and me and made a special point of praising the sponsors. Steve was impressed by his sincerity and sensitivity. 'He's sensational!' he enthused. 'Look at the sponsors – they're lapping it up!'

On Monday morning John rang to say he was going down to Radio City Music Hall with his agent, to discuss the creative aspects of *Ice*. 'Wish me luck,' he said. 'I have a horrible feeling I'm going to need it.' It was to be an all-day session, and Toller and Peggy had stayed over from Pro Skate to be there too. About two in the afternoon, the office door opened and John walked in. He was smiling broadly. 'It must have been a fantastic meeting,' I teased him. He shook his head. 'No – it was dire. But I've got a Christmas present for you that I think you'll be pleased with.' He paused for a second, then he said happily: 'I quit! I don't care what anyone says, I simply cannot do it. They will all have to just manage without me.'

I looked across at David. 'Do we have any champagne?' I asked.

David brought three flutes from Steve's cabinet, and a dusty bottle of Dom Perignon. 'What happened there today?' I said.

John took a deep gulp of champagne. 'It turned out to be a glorified version of *Ice Follies*. I left as they were describing how I was supposed to jump around on top of a piano while mirror balls whirled overhead.'

Once the initial euphoria had worn off, John became despondent. 'It's going to be very difficult,' he said. 'They won't like it. I wonder if they'll even speak to me again? I can't help feeling I've let them all down.'

'John,' I said, 'you've let nobody down. You've done the only thing you could do, and it was the right thing. You have to stop worrying about it.'

He sighed. 'I seem to be rather tired. It would be nice to be able to go away somewhere for a few days, to get away from it all.'

I thought quickly. 'Stay here for a minute and talk to David,' I said. 'I won't be a moment.'

I went down the corridor to Steve's office. He was delighted when I told him that John had decided not to do *Ice*. 'He's made the right decision,' he said.

'Yes – well, I'm glad you're pleased. The thing is, John desperately needs to get away for a few days. To have a rest and recover. He only used one of his Pro Skate air tickets – he was entitled to two – and he hasn't used any of his hotel entitlement. If he could convert that into a package deal, he could go somewhere warm for Christmas.'

Steve spluttered. 'What two air fares? He fucking lives here! He's a ten-dollar cab ride across the park!'

'No, he doesn't live here,' I explained. 'He stays with friends, but he could have chosen a hotel. Steve, please be a good person, and just for once do something that doesn't really make any sense to you. John is such a good advocate for Pro Skate, I think we should do this for him.'

Steve laughed suddenly. 'You should have gone into politics,' he said. 'Oh all right – if it's in the budget, you can do it.' As I was leaving, he called out: 'By the way, he should go to St John's in the Caribbean. It'd be perfect for him.'

John left the next day for St John's, a small island community. It was an idyllic setting, with no motor traffic, no television or radio and one hotel set deep among the palm trees. Coral reefs were visible beneath the clear turquoise water, and tropical fish in rainbow colours swam everywhere. John spent two wonderful weeks relaxing, reading, sleeping and walking. 'I thought it was paradise,' he said later. 'There was a complete absence of pressure that I had never experienced before. I was incredibly happy there.'

While John was sunning himself in southern climes, David and I were battling the New York elements. It had turned bitterly cold and the streets were covered in frost. There was a great deal of work to do following the Madison Square Garden event, and we barely had time to think about what we might do for John when he came back. He had begged us to find a project that 'might be suitable' for him, since he now had a ten-week gap in his schedule. On Boxing Day I went to visit my old mentor, Bill Judd, to see if he had any wisdom to offer me.

Bill Judd was a tall, regal, silver-maned man of seventy. He came from a distinguished theatrical family and straight from college had gone to work for Columbia Artists Management, who handled all manner of classical performers. Bill had created a division of CAMI that came to be known as Columbia Festivals, and under that banner had toured the Boys' Choir and the Spanish Riding School from Vienna, and the Royal Tournament from Britain. He now ran a prestigious small company called the Judd Concert Bureau, which handled the pianists Rudolph Serkin and André Watts, and tenor John Aler. We had known one another for several years, and we had dreamt of having a touring ice show which married beautiful skating to live symphony orchestra. It was to be known as *Symphony on Ice*. That day, as we sat together having lunch, Bill said to me: 'Perhaps now is the time for you to produce this project? It would be ideal for John.'

I thought about it carefully for several days. I agreed that the concept was perfect for John, and that it could accommodate his wish to have a permanent company. I called Bill and asked him if he thought a tour would be possible, to enable us to finance it. 'It's a bit of a Catch-22,' he told me. 'We need to know what the programme would be, and who the skaters are, before we could sell it.' I told him I would think about it some more, and get back to him.

When John returned, refreshed, after his vacation in St John's, he contacted me to see when we could meet. 'Let's have lunch today,' I suggested. 'I'll meet you at Columbus Circle at twelve, and we can walk across the park to the Agora.'

It was one of those magical New York days, when the winter sunshine made everything sparkle, and people walked around smiling, with their jackets open. John was full of his trip, anxious to move on to the next phase of his life. He had received his December Pro Skate cheque and was planning how he would spend it on renovating the cottage he had recently purchased for Rita. 'Mother loves it,' he told me. 'But it only has an outside loo at the moment. It gets a bit nippy for her at this time of year. It's very pretty, though. Only a short way from Stratford. And it has the most amazing garden. Did I ever tell you how much I love gardens?'

Over lunch, he began to talk about the things he felt he must accomplish before he retired. 'It's funny,' he said, 'but I feel this sense of urgency nowadays. I don't have time to waste on anything I don't want to do.'

I looked at him. 'What *do* you want to do?'

'My dreams are very similar to your own. They will sound too grandiose, I expect, but I'll tell you anyway. I want a permanent, year-round ice repertory company, like the ballet companies; I would like a school, where I can teach people to skate beautifully; and I want an opportunity to combine top artistic talents from all the major creative fields.'

I laughed aloud, and he stopped. He looked offended. 'Why are you laughing?' he demanded.

I took a small notebook from my pocket and handed it to him. 'These are my suggestions for you. Read the first page,' I instructed. 'You will see that I have written down exactly the same things in that book.'

As John read, a smile spread across his face. 'I see there's more than that written here!' he said. 'What's all this about the Metropolitan Opera House?'

'It's where your company will make its US debut,' I said. 'It's exactly the right place.'

John laughed. 'Now I *know* you're mad!' he said. 'A skater could never play the Met.'

I smiled at him. 'You're wrong, you know. But you'll find out sooner than you think.'

117

When we got back to the office, everyone was out at lunch. We made coffee and sat at the Pro Skate desk, John on one side and me on the other. 'Now,' I said seriously, 'the moment of no return. If David and I make this commitment to you, it will have to become a way of life. We can't do it unless you are also prepared to make a commitment. It will take all three of us to make this company happen, each in our own way. David and I have no money of our own, and we will have to keep Pro Skate going because that's how we earn a living. If that's all right with you, then we would both be willing to give it our best try.'

John had tears in his eyes. 'I'd already given up hope,' he said quietly. 'But I believe in the three of us, and I think we can make this work if we stick together. I am prepared to make one last attempt, if you and David will join forces with me. It won't be easy, but I believe it will be worth it.'

23

On 3 January 1983 John came to the office in the early afternoon. I took him into an empty room at the back of the complex, where I knew we wouldn't be disturbed, and took out a yellow pad. 'Now,' I said. 'Tell me what you mean by a permanent repertory company.'

'A select group of excellent skaters who would be available to me on a year-round basis,' he began. 'And a lot of ice time in an arena where we felt welcome. The opportunity to put together programming, bringing in some external choreographers, and lots and lots of rehearsal time. The thing is, the skaters would have to be moulded into an ensemble – that wouldn't happen overnight. We'd need costumes, an ice engineer, a conductor, a company manager and someone to oversee the costumes. The important thing would be to create this kind of family, all bound together in a common purpose.'

I took a deep breath. 'What skaters are you talking about?' I asked.

'Because I have to tell you that you had some skaters in your other shows who were very much below standard, and I was rather shocked by that. It didn't fit in with your stated ideals at all.'

He looked embarrassed. 'I know who you're talking about, and I admit those people were there for personal reasons. It's hard to explain, but it was important to me at the time.'

'John,' I said, 'if we are to make this enormous project work, then that kind of thinking has to go out of the window. If you are to have a company, then you must assemble the finest group of skaters available to you. Otherwise it won't merit all the other ingredients. There'd be no point.'

I told John about *Symphony on Ice*, and suggested that we marry it to his own concept of a repertory company. 'It would work wonderfully together, and it would all look so much better if we have live symphony music.' John was enthusiastic, and we began to talk about the make-up of the company.

'Everyone will have to be versatile,' he said. 'That's paramount. For some reason skaters are trained only to jump in one direction, usually to the right, but in this company they are going to have to jump both ways, like dancers. We need one strong pair and one strong dance team. But everyone will have to be able to partner with everyone. Again, like dancers.' He took out his address book and began to leaf through it. 'How many can we have?' he asked.

'How many do you want?' I countered. John thought for a moment, then said, 'Ideally, I would like twelve. That's always been my magic number.' He started to make notes. 'Keith and Shelley could be the pair. And for dancers, Jim Bowser and Nancy Berghoff.' Keith and Shelley were obvious choices, and Jim and Nancy were US ice-dance champions of great charm and ability. 'Cathy Foulkes, because she has been with me for all my shows, and she is the most like me; Patricia Dodd, who is extraordinarily artistic, with a beautiful style. She's a bit difficult on a personal level, and she's relatively old for a skater, but I still think she'd be a good choice. Mark Hominuke – he's a pain in the neck, but he's strong and good-looking and he's able to do pairs and singles. Do you know him?'

'I had him in Toller's company,' I answered. 'I think he's a very good idea.'

'Then we should have Tim Murphy; he's tremendously artistic –

a bit on the small side, but I don't think that really matters. And Jack Courtney – you produced a roller-skating show for him, didn't you? – he is equally good in either medium and I think he'd be fantastic. In addition, I'd like to ask JoJo Starbuck, because she really wants to do something like this and I think she and I have a good chemistry on the ice.'

I wrote down all the proposals and then I suggested that John start phoning everyone up. 'To do what?' he asked.

'To see if they would be interested, and if they could be ready to start by the end of this week.'

Within an hour, John had tentative acceptances from everyone on the list. 'What about Lorna Brown?' I asked. 'You had her in everything else.'

John sighed. 'Oh, yes, Lorna. She's wonderful, of course. In some ways, she's the best of all. But she can't be in this company because she's much too fat. Lorna simply *refuses* to be thin.'

The door opened and David came in. 'What are you guys up to?' he asked in surprise, seeing the address book and the lists of names.

'Remember *Symphony on Ice*?' I asked him. 'We're going to do it with John.'

David sat on the windowsill. 'I suppose I shouldn't be surprised, and I don't want to be the one to put a damper on things, but how are you proposing to pay for it?'

'I've got an idea about that,' I said. 'Wait here a minute – I need to go and talk to Steve.'

I walked down the corridor to Steve's office and went in. He was on the phone and motioned to me to sit down. 'What do you mean, Whitney Houston doesn't want to play Fanny Brice?' he roared. 'It's a fabulous idea! It would make her famous. Well, trust me, she'd be a superstar after this. So what if Fanny Brice was white – what difference does that make?' He slammed down the phone in disgust and immediately forgot about it. 'I need you for a minute,' I said. 'I want you to give John forty thousand dollars to start a repertory company. If you do it, then that will represent the amount of Pro Skate money that is owed to him for a TV special. You've spent your whole life dealing with rock and roll, and this will give you a chance to do something meaningful – you'll be the one person who made it possible for John Curry to create a company that will make skating history. You can be the benefactor of all that, without really having to give anything up at all!'

Steve stared at me in amazement. 'You're fucking mad!' he spluttered. 'You expect me to hand over forty grand just like that? I don't *do* things like that – it's the reason I'm rich and you're not.'

'You're the only one who can make it happen, Steve,' I told him. 'Think about it. I know you'll find some way.'

John and David were sitting in silence when I returned. 'Well?' David demanded. 'What did His Nibs say?'

I grinned. 'He'll do it,' I said.

'He said yes?' David whooped. 'I can't believe it!'

I shook my head. 'No – he hasn't said yes exactly, but he will. Trust me.' I told John that we needed another twenty-four hours to pull it all together, and that we would phone him as soon as we had a definite answer.

As soon as John had left, David and I went back to see Steve. He was making notes on a pad. 'I wanna see a budget,' he said, without looking up. I handed him a handwritten sheet of paper.

'It's all here – six weeks of rehearsal, ice time, salaries, everything. It comes to sixty thousand dollars.'

He looked up. 'Where's the rest of it coming from? I'm not pouring Pro Skate money down a black hole.'

Suddenly David stood up. 'I think I can raise ten thousand. The rest can go on my credit cards,' he said. I looked at him in astonishment. He had never been one to take risks before. 'If I do that, though, I need to know you'll put in the other forty thousand – and don't forget, while you're getting the credit for it, it's actually money that belongs to us all. It's Pro Skate money.'

Steve called Michael Cohl in Toronto. He explained the plan to him, and Michael immediately saw the potential of it. 'Let's do it,' he said. 'I'm not a fan of Elva's business acumen, but this idea makes sense from many points of view.' Steve hung up. 'Well, then, that's it I suppose. We'll do it.' He paused. 'Since we will have the television rights to whatever John puts together, we should also find out if there's any interest from the networks.'

David had many contacts within the television world, having spent his early professional years as a cameraman. He began to make enquiries, and the results were encouraging. By the end of the day he had telexes expressing strong interest from two cable companies and the ABC network. We showed them to Steve and he was impressed. 'Hold off on that for the moment,' he said. 'Michael might want to produce it out of Canada.'

David and I left the office and waited outside for a taxi. The wind was bitterly cold and there was a threat of snow. 'Where on earth are you going to get ten thousand dollars?' I sighed.

'Maybe I can,' David said, flagging down a speeding cab. 'I'm going to see my friend Lew Rappaport tonight.'

At eleven p.m. my phone rang. It was David. 'I did it!' he bellowed. 'I got it from Lew! Meet me at eight tomorrow morning at the office. We have a lot of work to do.' I wondered if I should ring John, but decided to wait until everything was finalized.

Next morning we met with Steve and drew up a letter of intent for Lewis Rappaport. Lew was an old family friend of David's, and he had agreed to put in the money in exchange for a ten per cent stake in *Symphony on Ice*. Steve called his lawyer and instructed him to start the incorporation procedure for *Symphony on Ice*, and we spent half an hour negotiating the share division. In the end, Steve agreed to take forty-five per cent; David, Bill Judd and I would share forty-five per cent; and Lewis would hold the other ten. It seemed fair. 'Let me go and call John,' I said.

Steve looked up from his notepad. 'You really think John Curry can do this thing?' he said.

'You know he can,' I told him. 'I'm surprised you even had to ask.'

John was delighted with the outcome, and came immediately to join us at the office. 'Before we start,' I said to him, 'I want to say something to you. David and I have talked about it, and we would like to split our shares in *Symphony on Ice* with you. It would make us happy if you would take them.'

He shook his head. 'No – thank you for offering, but it's not at all necessary. I just want to be able to run my company and have an opportunity to create beautiful skating. The one thing I would want, though, is to have creative control of the venture.'

I asked Steve to draw up a document reflecting John's request. 'He wants it in writing from you,' I said.

This made Steve nervous. 'I've never known any artist who didn't abuse that power at some point. It's too dangerous,' he said. In the end he agreed to it, but he warned me that, if his prophecy ever came true, it would be on my shoulders that it fell.

'Don't be depressing,' I said. 'John isn't like that.'

'They all are!' he said gloomily.

We decided that each person in the company would be paid $300 a week, an amount John felt they would accept. 'If I can live with that, then they should be able to,' he said. 'We must all be treated exactly the same, including me. Everyone will have the same travel and accommodation standards. Everyone will have to take off-ice training and dance, plus music appreciation and history of ice. In six weeks you will see a big difference in this group, I promise you. Oh, and I want everyone to get hot soup and sandwiches at rehearsals,' he said. 'That's important.'

He decided suddenly to see if Janet Lynn would be able to join in. He telephoned her in Denver, and her response was to cry. 'It's such a wonderful dream, John,' she told him, 'but I can't leave my family for six weeks.' John was not to be deterred. 'Then the mountain must come to Muhammad!' he declared. 'That settles where we will rehearse. It has to be in Denver.' The inclusion of Janet placed a strain on an already tight budget, but John had anticipated this. 'You can give Janet the money that was in the budget for me,' he said. 'I don't need it at the moment. It's enough that you're giving me the opportunity to do this.'

Within a week, David had booked an inexpensive hotel in the Denver area, found a rink with available ice time, and put thirteen plane fares on his American Express card. There was no formal contract between John, David and me. Our arrangement was one of mutual trust and it went far beyond the boundaries of a legal document. We were together on what we saw as the ultimate journey of our lives. None of us, at that pivotal time, could have possibly known that this beautiful dream would one day turn into a nightmare. In our naïvety, we thought the obstacles were all behind us and that only fulfilment lay ahead.

24

David and I discussed how we would handle the rehearsal period. We felt it was important not to leave John alone down in Denver, in case of any administrative problems. 'I think', said David, 'that I'd better go down with him and just stay there until it's over. I think you need to stay here and keep Steve motivated.' So David set off for Denver, with no idea that the anticipated six weeks would eventually stretch into two years.

He called me soon after they arrived. 'It's tentatively all right,' he said. 'John's not wild about the hotel – it's too far out of town for them to do much besides skate – but I think he'll be OK about it. Janet comes in tomorrow morning.'

The company was rehearsing at the South Suburban Ice Arena, Janet's home rink. We had arranged for six hours a day, five days a week, and this seemed to satisfy John. It was primarily a hockey rink, which meant that the ice was a little too hard for his liking (figure skaters prefer it much softer) but he accepted the fact that nothing could be done to alter it. The first few days passed without complaint, and John was happy when David arranged for hot soup to be sent in at lunchtimes.

Back in New York I had a visit from Hwisuke Taylor, David Santee's Korean manager. We went out for lunch and I asked her what David was doing. He had not performed well in Pro Skate in December, and she was concerned that he lacked motivation. 'What if he could go down to Denver and train with John's company?' I asked. 'I don't know if John would agree to it, but I know that it would be wonderful for David – he has all the technical stuff, but he could really do with the artistic help. Maybe he could even coach some of the other skaters in jumping technique.'

Hwisuke was intrigued by the idea. 'Ask John,' she said. 'And I ask David.'

I wasn't sure how John would react to the suggestion. He had so much to think about already, and David would just add to the workload. When I phoned him, however, he surprised me with his enthusiasm. 'I think it would be wonderful,' he said. 'I like David. He would be good for the others, and I think I could really help him. One condition, though – he can't be getting huge salaries. He must be on an equal basis.'

'He's not even getting that – we can't afford it,' I assured him. 'But David doesn't need it. He just wants to be part of your project. See how it works out. For now we'll just give him a hundred dollars a week and his room.'

The next two weeks were fruitful, and David Santee quickly settled into the routine. John was pleased with him. 'I want to make him a permanent member of the troupe,' he enthused. I didn't say anything at the moment, but I knew this was going to be difficult to arrange under John's democratic guidelines. David was an Olympic medallist and a box-office draw. Hwisuke had worked hard to promote him and she was unlikely to be happy with the established company salary. For now, I was able to placate Hwisuke on the basis that David was having a new number choreographed, which would be a great plus for him when it came to Pro Skate.

I met with Bill Judd to bring him up to date on the progress of the troupe. He was delighted, and told me he thought he might be able to arrange a tour of the Philippines. An old friend of his had good connections there. 'It's not what I would have thought of,' I said. 'But if it's work, I think everyone will be happy.' It would be in April, right after the Canadian Pro Skate tour.

I had a visit from Bunny Olnick, the Public Broadcasting producer who had put together John's two previous PBS television specials. She was a warm, energetic lady who appealed enormously to Steve. They laughed a lot and he promised that, if Bunny could bring in half of the financing for a special based on *Symphony on Ice*, then Michael Cohl would match it from a Canadian source. 'I'll certainly do my best,' Bunny said. 'I feel somewhat proprietorial about John now, so I'd hate for someone else to do this one.' She flew down to Denver to see the company at work, and came back full of enthusiasm. 'It's wonderful!' she told me. 'The best group John has ever had, and they're all beginning to look like him.'

John called me. 'Are we obliged to do a television special?' he demanded. 'I didn't realize that was part of the deal.'

'Do you have a problem with it?' I said carefully. 'We did discuss it, John. It's very expensive to do what you're doing, and it's a way of offsetting the costs.'

'I know,' he said irritably, 'but it feels like pressure all of a sudden.'

'Let's not make a decision yet,' I said. 'We'll talk about it when I come down there.' I asked David if he could manage to lay some groundwork, try to get John used to the idea. If he refused to do it, we would be in a very difficult position indeed.

Inevitably, rehearsal costs soared over the budgeted limits. David called me one morning and told me he had come up with an idea which might help to defray some of them. 'I thought we might sell tickets to a work-in-progress demonstration,' he said. 'What do you think?'

'Great idea,' I told him. 'It will help to acclimatize the skaters to performing together in front of an audience, and it will also drum up some good will in the local community.'

John responded enthusiastically to this idea, and David managed to sell two performances to the South Suburban Ice Arena for a cut of the ticket sales. The performances were set for late February, three weeks away. John called me late one night. 'I've been thinking that it would be good if we could have Jean-Pierre Bonnefous come down and make a piece for the company. Something that would give us some weight. Can you see if you can arrange that?' I agreed, of course, because it all made sense from a creative point of view. Ultimately it would even make sense from a business point of view. I just didn't know how we were going to pay for it.

Jean-Pierre was delighted with the idea and agreed immediately. He settled for a fee of $2,000 to do a twenty-minute company work based on Ravel's *La Valse*, and a *pas de deux* for Cathy and Mark, based on Massenet's 'Meditation' from *Thaïs*. He took David's hotel room and David managed to find a much cheaper one nearby. 'I just hope I'm getting Brownie points!' he laughed. Within two weeks, the new works were completed and everyone seemed to be pleased.

The next problem to tackle was the matter of costumes. We had none at all, and no time or money to commission them. David, John and Cathy went into Denver early one morning, and managed to assemble a complete set of costumes on David's credit card. The finale of the performance was to be a bright, comic company romp set to the *William Tell* overture. This had been Bill Judd's suggestion, and it was working very well. The costumes for this needed to match the spirit of the piece, and accordingly they bought bright red pants and skirts, white cable sweaters and red scarves. David found the whole lot in a sale, and the least expensive costumes in the show went on to last through the entire life of the company.

Michael Cohl was getting very strong interest from the First Choice network in Canada. He called Steve to tell him that he felt they would want to do the special on their own, with no input from PBS. 'Bunny won't like that,' I said. 'She'd set her heart on it.'

'Fuck Bunny Olnick,' Steve snorted. 'Why are you always so concerned about other people? Try looking after yourself for a change!' So First Choice got the rights to *Symphony on Ice*, and made two conditions. The first was that they would specify the location. The second was that it would include at least four Canadian skaters. 'We have three,' I told Michael: 'Keith, Shelley and Mark. We'll need to find another one.'

'Don't worry about it.' Michael was adamant. 'They'll probably be OK with three.'

Whenever I talked to John, he sounded tired but happy. He seemed nervous sometimes, perhaps because of the forthcoming public performances, but on the whole he was holding up very well. This equilibrium was rocked, however, one snowy night at the South Suburban Arena.

The company had reserved extra ice time to allow them to start their session with a full run-through of the repertoire. As they came into the arena, John saw that the ice was still being used by the hockey players. There was no sign of the game finishing, so he went to the office to complain. When the manager came out to clear the ice, the hockey players were reluctant to go and as they left the rink one remarked loudly: 'Hell, we gotta make way for a bunch of fucking nancies.' John turned white. He didn't respond, but marched outside to find David, who had just finished parking the minibus.

'This experiment is at an end!' he yelled. 'I might have known it wouldn't work. It was too much to ask that things could be arranged properly for once. This arena is horrible, and I will *never* skate in it again.' He hurled his overcoat into a pile of wet snow and began to stride away across the car park.

David was stunned, but he knew he had to react quickly. He jumped into the bus, started the engine and drove alongside John. 'Get in!' he bellowed. 'Just do it, or I'll have to come round and make you. We can talk about all this, but we're not doing it in a below-zero wind.' John climbed into the bus, and David drove to the arena and stopped outside. 'Wait here,' he told John. 'I'll be literally one minute.' He strode into the building and called Jim Bowser. 'Jim – you're in charge. John won't be coming to rehearsals tonight, but you guys can do the run-through as planned. I'll be back for you later.' He went back to the bus, got in and drove away without a word to John. When they arrived at the hotel, he parked the bus near the door. 'We're going to your room to talk this over,' he said. 'We need to get a few things straightened out.'

Once in the room, John broke down. He sobbed uncontrollably, and David called room service to ask for a bottle of brandy. When it came, he poured a stiff shot for John. 'Here,' he said. 'Drink this. You'll feel better.' John did as he was told, spluttering as the liquor burned his throat. 'Now,' said David, 'what's this all about? I can't believe you'd destroy your own future, just because a bunch of yobboes called you a name.'

John began to talk to David about his loneliness, his sense of isolation. 'I can't bear it,' he said miserably. 'Always being on my own. I always hope these things will change all that, but they don't. I tried to create a family this time, but it hasn't worked. They've all got each other and I'm the odd one out.' He began to cry again, and David crossed to him and put an arm around his shoulders.

'Come on, John,' he said kindly. 'It isn't as bad as you think. You're tired and it's a big responsibility. I can understand how you feel.' He poured another shot of brandy for him, and John swallowed it in one gulp. He blew his nose loudly, and tried to smile.

'You must think I'm terrible,' he said. 'It's not just the loneliness, of course. It's also the fear that it won't work out, that we'll fail after all this and I will have let everyone down.'

'You don't have to worry about that,' David assured him. 'The only person you'd be letting down is yourself. And I don't think you want to do that, do you?'

John shook his head. 'Can I tell you something else, without you being cross?'

David laughed. 'Try me!'

'Well, the truth is that I can't bear this arena, or the hotel. They're ugly and cold, and the people are horrid. It makes it almost imposs-ible to be creative.'

David sat quietly for a moment. 'If I do something about that, will you promise me that you'll try to settle down – no more talk of quitting?' John promised, and David got up to leave.

'One last thing,' John said. 'Janet. I do love her, and it's wonderful to have her as part of all this. But she isn't a proper member of the company the way the others are. I've been feeling guilty about it. I've made them all come to this awful place just to accommodate her, and I think perhaps it's not necessary. Do you understand what I mean?'

'Only too clearly,' David laughed. 'This particular area is depressing in winter – especially when we could be up in the Rockies.'

David started, early the next morning, to call round the resort areas. He was trying to find one that could offer comparable ice time, or perhaps present a works-in-progress performance. When he spoke to the Dobson Arena in Vail, he knew he had struck gold.

He called me in a state of excitement to tell me about his visit to Vail to meet with the arena manager, Pat Dobson. 'The place is unbelievably beautiful,' he told me. 'Fabulous arena, picture-book village, air like champagne. What's more, they want me to move the company up there, lock, stock and barrel. He can give us ice for fifteen dollars an hour, and I've negotiated a fantastic deal with the Marriott Mark Resort Hotel. You can't believe how fantastic it is.'

Within an hour, John was on the phone. 'David has pulled off a miracle,' he said. 'We're going to Vail, and we've managed to persuade Janet to come up there for the works in progress. She doesn't have to stay there: I've agreed to go back to Denver for one week before the end, to work with her. That'll be when we do the works in progress at the South Suburban. I guess we owe them that.'

In late February, I flew to Vail to see how things were going. I was immediately struck by how happy everyone seemed – they had become part of the fabric of the little mountain community. It was clear that Vail was proud of their resident company, and the tickets for the first works-in-progress evening had long ago sold out. John had blossomed in the new environment. He had become relaxed, positive and outgoing, and he exuded self-confidence. I watched the company take ballet class, followed by a work-out at the barre, then a session of lifts and throws, off ice. On the ice, the company now worked as an ensemble, gliding across the arena in breathtaking formation, using their upper bodies in a manner that had become the Curry hallmark – graceful movements, soft arms, everything working as an elegant whole. John turned to see my reaction, and his face was alight with pleasure. 'Do you see them?' he demanded. 'It's what I've been saying. It's only a beginning, but you can tell what it will be.'

In the afternoon, John and I took the chairlift up the mountainside, and sat in companionable silence as we rose high above the dark green pines. The air was cold and dry, filling our lungs, scented and pure. We got off on the top, and walked slowly along the snow-covered trail. I thought I had not seen John so happy before, and he spoke rapturously about Vail. 'I think it is the closest thing to heaven, the Dobson Arena. Can you imagine what it's like, to have flawless ice, to be warm, to be able to look up and see mountains and blue skies through the glass roof? And to have such a company – all dedicated to the same thing? And a community around us that welcomes and appreciates us? Elva, could you find a way for us to stay here? Could we make this our permanent home?'

I had no idea how we could accomplish this, but before I left for New York I had promised him that we would do everything we could to arrange it. Whatever it cost us, it had to be worth it. We were never likely to see John this happy anywhere else.

25

As soon as I got back, I told Steve how much the company had progressed and how well John was looking. 'Fantastic,' he said. 'But what about the television show? Did you talk to him about it?' I had to admit that I hadn't – I knew he was reluctant to do it, and had deliberately put off any discussion of it.

Bill Judd was also thrilled to hear about the progress of the company, and of John's pleasure in the Vail environment. 'Whatever you do, you must keep them there. You mustn't make them move their base again. John would see it as a step down, and it would demoralize him.' I agreed, though I had no idea at the time how on earth we could possibly pay for it. 'When are they due to finish?' Bill asked.

'Beginning of March, right before the next Canadian Pro Skate tour.'

'And after?' he persisted.

'After, they go to the Philippines. If that's still on. Oh, and then the Canadian television special.'

Bill looked thoughtful. 'I'm afraid they won't be going to the Philippines – my friend has let us down over the tour. Shall we say he was overly optimistic, and was unable to put it together. Not that it's a serious loss – I should have worried about those young skaters being in that dreadful place anyway. But I have some other ideas I want to talk to you about. I have dug up an old acquaintance who used to work with the Sol Hurok agency. He handled all the ballet tours, and other large musical extravaganzas. He's semi-retired now, living in the Midwest. His name is Sherman Pitluck – have you ever met him?' I shook my head. 'No matter,' Bill went on. 'Sherman is a very capable man. I would like to engage him as a consultant to the Judd Concert Bureau in order to book a Canadian tour for John's company. What do you think?'

Bill explained that he felt it was vital for the troupe to gain performing experience somewhere out of the media spotlight. Canada was ideal for that purpose. 'They need to work the kinks out without being scrutinized too much. And they need to get used to working together in front of different audiences.'

That night, I called John about the television special. 'We do owe it to Steve and Michael,' I told him. 'And it would give us a little bit more income to spend on the company. Why don't we just agree to it, and then we can get on with all our other plans?'

'All right,' he said reluctantly. 'If it's important, then I'll do it.'

The Vail works in progress were a huge success, and everyone was encouraged by the reaction of the audiences. With makeshift costumes, no lighting and music played over the arena's sound system, the performances still elicited a wildly enthusiastic response. The *Vail Trail* reviewed them, calling them 'Embryonic brilliance – one has the feeling that one has just witnessed the birth of a new art form.' The Mayor came to the second performance and made a point of congratulating every member of the company. He let it be known that he was delighted to have them in Vail.

Jack Courtney was now coming to Vail two or three days a week.

He was often accompanied by his girlfriend, top Canadian amateur Lori Nichol. Lori was a stunningly attractive girl, with a distinctive skating style. She was desperately anxious to turn professional and asked John if she could join his group. John studied her thoughtfully for a moment. 'You skate beautifully,' he told her. 'And I think you would be a wonderful addition to the group. The only worry I have – and I must be ruthlessly honest with you – is that you tend to be a bit heavy. Do you think you could do something about that?' Lori promised that she would get ten pounds off if he would only let her start working with the company, and he agreed to have her on a trial basis for a week. 'Let's just see how it goes,' he told her. 'There's no question of our being able to pay you anything yet, but if things work out then maybe we can talk about it.'

Lori's trial week was so successful that John asked David to see if we could induct her into the company officially. I looked at the budget in despair. We were desperately short of funds, and still had no foreseeable way to bring in any more. The only source of income was the works-in-progress project. I called Bill Judd to see how the plans for a 1983 Canadian tour were progressing. 'The guarantees will be small to non-existent,' he said, 'because the company has no track record. But in some cases we will be able to secure a small advance. Sherman is working very hard to put it all together.'

Jack Courtney decided to drop out of the company after the initial rehearsal period. He loved the work, but didn't want to leave his mountain home for a protracted period of time. This left a vacancy in the company which Lori could assume. Janet also decided, not unexpectedly, that she would retire at the end of the first session, so we were now back to the original number of twelve, and things began to look slightly more manageable.

First Choice had arranged to shoot their special right after the Pro Skate tour at the end of March. David had acquired a small video camera, and made tapes of the daily training sessions. He taped a run-through and sent this to Canada to show the scope of the work. It was well received, and a creative meeting was set between John and the producers. This would be held in Toronto, right after the conclusion of the final competition. There would then be a week of rehearsals, followed by the actual taping. The location had not yet been announced.

In early March, the company left Vail to spend a week in Denver.

This had been arranged to enable John to work with Janet, and prepare her for Pro Skate and the Canadian television special. It was now accepted that she was not a member of the ensemble as such, and she would perform only solo pieces and pair numbers with John. Half-way through the week, John failed to appear at rehearsals and David left Jim in charge while he went to look for him.

John was sitting in the deserted lounge of the Marriott, with a cold cup of coffee in front of him. He looked exceptionally tired and pale, and was staring glassily at a photograph in his hands. It was of a small boy skating on an open lake. David sat down quietly beside him and pointed to the photograph. 'Who's that?'

A tear slid slowly down John's cheek. 'Me,' he whispered. 'It was me when I thought skating would bring me happiness – if only I could win the Olympics, or have my own company, or skate in theatres. But I guess it was all an illusion. I've done all that, and I'm not at all happy. In fact, I'm seriously wondering if I have any reason to continue living.'

David stood up and held out his hand. 'Come on, John,' he said. 'Dry your eyes. We're going for a ride.' Without a word, John followed David out to the minibus and they sped off back to the arena. When John saw where they were going, he began to protest. 'I can't!' he said. 'Not today. I just can't face it all.'

David drove around to the back of the building and parked. 'You don't have to face anyone,' he said. 'Trust me. I just want you to come with me. No one will know we're in here.' They went in by the back door and climbed a narrow stairway. Two flights up, they walked round a corridor and eventually came out by another door. It opened into a glass-fronted box overlooking the ice surface. 'Sit down,' David said. 'You're in the manager's box. No one can see us. I want you to do something for me – just sit quietly here for a while and watch your company working. They don't know you can see them. I want you to have a look at this wonderful thing you've created. This *is* your family, John, but you can't seem to understand how much they need you.'

For an hour John sat quietly, visibly moved by the scene that was unfolding below. He watched as Jim conducted rehearsals, carefully overseeing the lines of the ensemble, the torsos, the arms, the positioning of the heads. Then he worked with Janet, helping her with a difficult segment of choreography. Finally she soared away and ran through all her pieces. For the solo, Jack Courtney stood in for John and it was immediately apparent that he knew every step by heart. Everyone on the ice was totally focused, giving Jim the respect that was normally reserved for John. No one questioned his authority: they were intent only on the business of skating.

At twelve the soup was brought in, and everyone left the ice. John turned to David with an expression of awe on his face. 'Thank you,' he said simply. 'I was so absorbed in my own problems that I had completely forgotten about my company.'

'They love you, John,' David said with a smile. 'You can't desert them – they aren't ready for that yet.'

'I suppose the truth is that I'm not a very good parent!' John said ruefully. 'But I've seen them through completely different eyes today, and it's made me so proud my chest hurts.' He looked at David. 'I'm sorry to be such a bother to you. I hope you can forgive me. I know I have to stick this out, and I have always said it would take about three years to bring a company to the point where it could stand alone. I'll do my very best to last the course, but I need to know that you and Elva will stay with me.'

David was touched by John's desperate sincerity. 'We'll certainly both be there for you,' he told John. 'But I think I must ask you an important question before we go any further. Elva is famous for talking people into doing things she feels they need to do; is it remotely possible that she's pushed you into this situation without your realizing the level of commitment it would take? If it is, then we would both understand completely if you wanted to give up at this juncture. You have to be honest about it, because so much depends on it. If we go forward, you will inevitably be the axis we all spin around, and that could be a very daunting prospect.'

John leant forward and hugged David. 'No one pushed me,' he said firmly. 'I do want to do this, more than anything else. It's what my life is all about. But I need someone in my corner when the going gets tough, because even though I'll try very hard to be good, there will be times when I fail.'

The performances at Denver went off smoothly and the houses were both sold out. After the box office was counted, the company made a profit of just over $3,000. David phoned me to tell me the news that we had been invited to return for two more performances in April. 'What's more,' he said, 'we have more performances in Vail as well. I think we'll just about be able to afford three or four more weeks of rehearsal at this rate.'

David went with the company to Canada; almost all of them were involved in the Pro Skate competitions, which made it very convenient for us. There was to be a two-week gap between Calgary and Toronto, and we arranged for them to fly back to Vail so that they could use the time for rehearsals, and to prepare for the television show.

Bill Judd had been appointed as the official adviser to the company – we had no money to pay him, but he was delighted with the title. He was passionate about the project, and talked of little else. I had dinner with him in early March and he had been giving some thought to the long-term outlook for the company. 'You want to put them into the Metropolitan Opera House?' he asked. 'Then we need to shape everything with that in mind. Your only opening would be the summer season, when external companies are presented there. Normally they are companies of international reputation, but perhaps they would make an exception in this case. John would have to prepare enough pieces for more than one evening – that would be essential. And the more well-known choreographers he can involve, the better. And with a live orchestra, you need to find a conductor who will devote himself to the company – you can't have someone coming into the mix at the last minute. The timing is crucial. I'll see if I can think of someone.'

Steve was concerned about the escalation of costs. 'You have to understand that, once the forty thousand dollars is gone, that's it. I'm not putting any more in, no matter what. You need to ease off a bit, do this more slowly. John can't expect to have everything he wants.'

'It's not just John,' I told him. 'It's all of us. We all want it. And we can't go more slowly. John is already thirty-four, and that's old for a skater. He only has three or four good years left to do this.'

Steve looked at me shrewdly. 'And what about you? How many good years do you have left to make some money for yourself? You won't make any out of this, believe me. You'll work yourselves into the ground and at the end of it John will walk away from you. He's an artist. They're made that way. Don't think he's going to be any different.'

'Why do you keep saying that?' I demanded. 'I thought you liked John?'

'I do,' he said. 'I like him and I respect him. But I would never in a million years, ever, dream of trusting him. It would be the worst thing I could do to him.'

Sherman Pitluck was softly spoken to the point of being inaudible, and he had a disconcerting toupee placed at an angle across his receding hairline. It seemed that he had made some considerable progress with the booking of our Canadian tour, and was confident that we would be able to get an advance from Vancouver. 'The same promoters want to take us to Seattle,' he told me. I was delighted: things were beginning to look up. 'Of course, there is one slight hitch – they're insisting that we have Dorothy Hamill as a guest star.'

My heart dropped. This was exactly what we were fighting to get away from. I sighed. 'Sherman,' I said, 'there is no way we can do this. John's company is an ensemble. There are no "stars", not even John. This is the way he wants it to be. I doubt Dorothy would even be willing to do it – it would mean she would have to rehearse with the company. And her agent is the toughest in the business. He'd charge so much we could never afford it.'

'Don't throw it out without a fight,' Sherman said. 'Perhaps the agent would see that this was a unique situation. At least ask him.'

I was ghost-writing Dorothy's autobiography at the time, and I had frequent dealings with her agent, Michael Rosenberg. He had always been very nice to me, and seemed pleased with the way we had handled his clients during the Pro Skate competitions. But much as he admired John, I doubted he would be willing to make financial concessions to his company. I telephoned him at his home in Palm Desert, California, and put the proposition to him. 'You should be down here,' he said. 'It's warm and sunny and I'm just off to play a round of golf. Seattle? Well, of course, Dorothy might agree to do it. You know how much she loves John. How much are you offering?'

'Nothing,' I told him frankly. 'It can't be for the money, Michael. You know we don't have it.'

'I might be able to let her do it for eight thousand,' he said cheerfully.

'Oh God, Michael, you're killing us.'

'For each performance. Plus first-class expenses.' I was silent.

There was nothing I could say. 'She normally charges twenty-five thousand dollars a gig,' he added. 'If anyone finds out I've made you an offer like this, I'll be dead in the water.' I told him I would be back to him the next day. I saw no way we could pull this one off.

Sherman, however, had other ideas. 'Take it!' he said excitedly. 'The promoter'll be thrilled. He can pay her separately.' I phoned Michael to let him know that we would accept the deal, and told him Dorothy would have to find a way to rehearse with the company before they went out.

'Why can't John come and stay with Dorothy for a while? They could work down here in Palm Springs.'

'No, Michael. She has to come to Vail. John has made it absolutely clear that if anyone comes in as a guest it's on condition they spend time working with the company and taking class.' He started to object, but I cut him off. 'Michael, I've had to agree to your terms, which are way outside of our limits. If Dorothy does this, then the condition is that she spends September in Vail, living and working with the company. You should encourage her to do it. She will get more out of that than you could ever dream of, and, after years of trailing around commercial shows, it will remind her why she became a skater in the first place. I think she'll thank you for it.'

'Perhaps you're right. How much will you pay her for rehearsals?'

'David Santee is working for a hundred dollars a week right now, and JoJo Starbuck gets three hundred. Why don't I split the difference and give Dorothy two hundred?'

'All right, I suppose that's better than nothing.'

'We'll deduct it from her fee,' I added.

Michael laughed out loud. 'You drive a hard bargain,' he chuckled. 'We have a deal. I'm sure Dorothy will agree to go to Vail.'

I didn't feel good about the conversation with Michael Rosenberg. I felt as though I had let the other skaters down. They had all thrown themselves into the company heart and soul, and were willing to take the conditions that were offered. Somehow it didn't seem right that we were now having to compromise in order to work. I decided to talk it over with John.

He was surprisingly philosophical about it. 'Well, I suppose I can't deny that Dorothy is valuable at the box office. If she's willing to come to Vail, then I think we should go along with it. But I don't think it would be fair to let the others know how much she's being paid. It would cause bad feeling, and I want to protect her from that. If she can be a part of the group for a few weeks, on an equal basis, I think it will change her life.'

Steve's efforts to book an American arena circuit for Pro Skate were being hampered by the exclusion clauses attached to Kenneth Feld's shows, such as the Ringling Brothers Circus and *Disney on Ice*. His muscle in the arenas was such that he could make it extremely difficult for any other family or ice events to tour, and this presented a major obstacle to Pro Skate's economic survival. In addition, the sponsors for the Canadian circuit, Molson, had just pulled out, leaving a sizeable hole in Michael's budget. It was a subdued Steve who greeted John in Montreal, and John listened sympathetically to his problems. Later he wrote to both Steve and Michael, expressing his support for their efforts and telling them how much he appreciated what they were trying to accomplish. 'You have done so much for skating,' he wrote. 'Please let me know if there is anything I can do to help you.'

In late March the company, including Janet Lynn, flew back to Canada for the final Pro Skate event in Toronto. Michael Cohl's spirits had lifted since the earlier phase, and he had produced the concluding competitions with his usual flair and style. All the skaters were invited to the closing party, given in the Harbour Hotel. It was a celebratory occasion, and everyone was optimistic about the future of the circuit. Molson and the Felds were felt to be temporary hiccups. Before he left the party, Michael reminded me that we were to meet the next morning in his office. 'We'll have a half-hour together before the First Choice people arrive, to go over the plans with John,' he said.

The next day was one of those brilliant, sunny April mornings that only Canada enjoys. The air was crisp and fragrant with the smell of woodsmoke, and everywhere clusters of snowdrops and primroses were thrusting up through the melting snow. David and I walked to Michael's offices, set in a charming old listed building on the edge of Cabbagetown. He was there with Griff, his right-hand man and general manager, and Billy Ballard, his partner. Billy's father, Harold, owned the Maple Leaf hockey team, and several of Canada's leading arenas. Billy, however, was something of a black sheep and was trying to establish himself outside his paternal circle.

John arrived and greeted everyone politely. He sat down and

waited. Billy made nervous small talk, none of which made very much sense, and John tried his best to be nice to him. Michael nodded to Griff. 'Tell John what the plans are,' he said. 'I want him to be prepared for the First Choice guys.' Griff looked at his notes. Billy, who now had his feet on the table, was swaying back and forth on his chair. Suddenly it plunged backwards and Billy fell off. He started laughing uncontrollably and John looked at Michael in disgust. 'Perhaps it would be better if your friend were to leave,' he suggested. Michael laughed. 'Billy's all right,' he said. 'Let's get on with this.'

Griff started to outline the arrangements for the TV special. 'We're going to shoot it in Banff, Alberta,' he began.

John stopped him. 'Banff? I didn't know there was a television studio there.'

'There isn't,' Griff said. 'We're not doing it in a studio. It'll be shot outdoors, on a glacier up on the Columbia icefields.'

John looked at Griff in horror. 'Are you mad?' he asked. 'Do you really think that I would allow my company to skate on glacier ice, in below-zero temperatures? I wouldn't even consider it.'

'John, it's all arranged,' Michael explained patiently. 'I'm sure you will be able to work it out.'

John glared at him. 'I think not! What a pity no one thought to discuss this with me beforehand. It might have saved us all a lot of trouble.'

Griff looked surprised. 'But Toller's already agreed to do it. I thought you'd like the idea.'

John stared at Griff in amazement. 'Toller?' he said carefully. 'I don't understand what Toller has to do with any of this.'

By this time, Billy had managed to scramble to his feet. 'He's the Canadian content,' he announced. 'First Choice won't do it without him.' John rose to his feet.

'Then they won't be doing it at all,' he said coldly. 'I'm sorry. We seem to have wasted each other's time.' With that he left. By the time David and I arrived at the hotel, John had already gone to the airport.

26

In New York, we were greeted by a very angry Steve. 'What the hell was that all about?' he demanded. 'Michael is really pissed off – you guys made him look like an idiot in front of the First Choice producers.'

'What did he expect?' I retorted. 'It was his own fault. He had no right to bring Toller in without discussing it with John. What was he thinking of? He wouldn't stick Alice Cooper into a Rolling Stones tour without telling them, would he?'

Steve sighed heavily. 'That's not the same thing,' he said.

'Steve, it's exactly the same thing. You know it is.'

Before we could become embroiled in an argument, the phone rang. It was John, and I put him on hold while I went back to our own office to speak to him. He sounded nervous, as though he was uncertain of his reception. 'I wanted to apologize to you for putting you into such a difficult position,' he said. 'But I couldn't stay in that room any longer. I had to leave.' I stopped him.

'John, please understand that we would have done exactly the same thing. David and I were furious about it – we hadn't been told either.'

'It didn't occur to me that you had,' he said. 'Elva, there's something very important that I need to speak to you both about; could you meet me at the Mayflower Hotel for coffee tomorrow morning, at eleven?'

The Mayflower was almost empty, and John was sitting at one of the window tables, overlooking Central Park. He was dressed in a grey suit and a maroon silk waistcoat, and he had a suitcase beside his chair. 'I'm going to England tonight, and I didn't want to leave without seeing you,' he said. 'Would you like some coffee?'

'John, why don't you tell us what's on your mind?' David reached for the coffee pot and poured two cups. He handed one to me, and John offered the cream jug. I wondered what he was about to say.

'I have spoken to everyone in the company,' he began. 'We have reached a unanimous decision that we no longer wish to work with Steve Leber and Michael Cohl. It's not that they're bad people – I'm sure they mean well – but they simply haven't the slightest idea what I am trying to achieve. If they remain involved, then I'm afraid I will have no choice but to disband the company. On the other hand,' he went on, 'if you and David would be willing to continue, then we would very much like to work with you. You two seem to be alone in understanding what we are all about.' He sat back and waited for us to say something.

I smiled at him. 'I think I can speak for us both,' I told him. 'We are one hundred per cent committed to you and to the company. Nothing will change that, as I think you know. This has become much more than a production to us. It is our vocation, as it is yours, and somewhere, somehow, we will find the money to continue.' I had no idea, as I spoke those words, what a monumental undertaking it would be.

Steve was livid. He marched up and down the office, hands clenched together so tightly that his knuckles turned white. 'How could he do this to me? After all I've fucking done for him! He wouldn't have a company without my help.' Suddenly the fight seemed to go out of him, and he sat down at his desk. 'I liked John Curry,' he said. 'I thought he was different, but it just goes to show you. I broke my own rule.' He looked up, the sentiment vanishing as quickly as it had come. 'I want my fucking money back!' he yelled. 'You guys better find some way to pay it, or I'll sue him for breach of contract. I oughta break his neck, and yours too.'

We sat in our office, racking our brains for inspiration. Suddenly David slammed his fist down on the desk. 'I know who'd do it!' he said. 'What about West Nally – they'd do just about anything to get back at Steve Leber.' West Nally was a world-wide organization which specialized in packaging sports and music events. West Nally Japan was run by a Japanese-American called Jack Sakazaki, and he had made a verbal deal with Steve to represent Pro Skate for Japan. Steve had reneged on this arrangement, and Jack was furious with him. It seemed like David might have hit on a solution.

There was an immediate response from Jack. He not only saw an opportunity to take something Steve had started, and make it succeed, but he also genuinely liked John's work. When he heard Janet Lynn was connected to the project, he became seriously interested in working out some kind of a deal. Janet had competed in the 1972 Sapporo Olympics and had won the hearts of the Japanese public. Her blond hair and sweet smile had made a lasting impression, and she was still known in Tokyo as 'the little angel'. We arranged a meeting with Jack and West Nally New York.

Bill Judd was disturbed by the turn of events. He had grave misgivings about our potential liaison with West Nally, and suggested an alternative solution. 'Forgive me,' he said, 'but it seems to me that to go from Steven Leber to West Nally is to jump from the rattlesnake to the tiger. It cannot possibly last. It will only be a matter of time before John decides they are commercial vultures. I don't criticize that – it's their business, after all – but it is not right for our young maestro. Let me make a suggestion.'

He made me wait until he had ordered another glass of white wine. Then he raised his glass and said: 'To you! You're a throwback to my days, when the artist reigned supreme. It's all about money now, but I think you can learn to deal with that and still manage to keep your flag flying. Here's to *Symphony on Ice* and all who glide in her!' Bill took another sip and cleared his throat. 'If John is to create a year-round company he needs a home for it. I know he loves Vail, but I'm not aware that they are offering any funding to make it possible for him to stay there. We need to be practical. I have very good connections at Fredonia College – it's part of the State University of New York – and an old client of mine, Harry John Brown, is the Music Professor there. I took the liberty of explaining our project to him and he had a word with the dean of the college. The response was inspired.'

I had to smile to myself, because Bill's eyes were shining with enthusiasm. Obviously John's welfare meant a great deal to him. I wondered what he was going to propose.

'Fredonia College', he announced triumphantly, 'would like to make Maestro Curry a professor of ice – a first in the world, I should imagine – and they are willing to take his entire company and feed and house them permanently, if he will in return conduct masterclasses at the college several times a year. They will work around his schedule, obviously, and over time they will make funding available to him so that he might create a permanent school as well.'

I was flabbergasted. I couldn't have imagined a more perfect situation for John. I couldn't wait to tell him about it.

I rang him in England that night. He was clearly in a deep depression, though he didn't offer any insight as to what was causing it. I told him of the Fredonia offer, and explained that they would build a special practice/performing centre for him, and would also find sponsorship for his company tours. His response was gloomy. 'It all sounds too ghastly,' he sighed. 'I don't think I would survive academia.'

'John, don't throw it all away without even thinking about it,' I pleaded. 'It would give you independence from the sort of commercial venture that you despise, and would provide the funding for you to develop your company without any external pressures. What could be so wrong with that?'

'It just feels bad,' he said. 'I don't want to belong to Fredonia. I want to work with you and David and my company. Why do we need anyone else?'

Eventually I persuaded him that he should at least go to Fredonia and meet the faculty. There would be no obligation, and if he didn't like it he could just say no. He agreed to fly back to New York the following Monday.

The morning we left for Buffalo, there was a snowstorm. John had brought Mark Hominuke and Patricia Dodd with him ('Since they will also be teaching, I would like their opinions'), and they all sat with Bill and me in the rear of the small plane. It tossed and pitched in the turbulent air, and Bill was sick. 'I haven't flown since 1962,' he told me. 'I vowed I never would again, but I thought this was important.' John sat with his eyes closed, whether sleeping or praying was not immediately apparent.

We were met at Buffalo Airport by Harry John Brown, and he drove us the sixty miles north to Fredonia. As we entered the town, we passed clusters of whitewashed houses with roses growing round the doors, and two beautiful small hotels with verandahs. The campus itself was built around an open stretch of emerald-green heathland, and the administrative building was set back from the road in the centre of a stand of pine trees.

John had refused to open his eyes at all on the way up. He sat hunched in the corner of the back seat, his arms clasped tightly around his chest. When we arrived I had to plead with him to get out and meet the dean and his wife. He was barely civil and Bill worked very hard to cover this up. The faculty had prepared a reception for us, and the dean made a speech about how excited he was, and how we would all make history together. We were taken on a tour of the town, and John was shown the house that had been earmarked for him. It was a picturesque cottage with an English-style garden and a pond. Mark and Patricia inspected the flats that would be allocated to the members of the company and told the dean's wife how much they liked them. They saw the site for the new rink, which would be built over the summer, and finally were driven to Harry John's house for dinner. John refused to get out of the car, pleading a headache.

After dinner I slipped out to see how he was. He was crying quietly. 'John, please don't,' I said. 'These people are not monsters. They just want to help you. Couldn't you just come in for a minute?' Reluctantly, he followed me inside and sat in a chair just inside the living room. Harry John had consumed a considerable amount of red wine by this time, and when John came in he stood up to make a speech. First of all he toasted John, then Patricia and Mark. Then he spoke emotionally about his love of music and how much he was looking forward to having such distinguished artists on his campus. What he was going to say next we never found out, because at that point he began to cry uncontrollably and had to sit down. The dean offered to drive us to the airport.

On the way, John thanked him for taking so much trouble to prepare for his visit. He told him how much he appreciated his offer, and what a wonderful opportunity it would have been had he not been committed to living and working in Vail. 'I hope you can understand,' he told him. 'Perhaps I'm being foolish to turn you down, but I hope you won't be offended.'

'I think I'm surprised, rather than offended,' the dean replied. 'But I respect your reasons and hope that if you ever change your mind you will let us know. We'll keep the door open for you.'

At the end of April, John left for England again. He was to spend the summer as Lysander in the Regent's Park Open Air Theatre production of *A Midsummer Night's Dream*, and wanted to spend time with his mother before the play opened. David and I drove him to the airport, and he said goodbye to us on an optimistic note. 'I know you'll find a way to make this all work out. I have complete faith in you,' he said. 'Call me when you have any news.' He hugged us both and disappeared through the passport checkpoint, leaving us to wonder what on earth we were going to do. It seemed that West Nally was now our only option.

27

Jack Sakazaki flew into New York to meet with us. We arrived at the West Nally offices at nine on a Tuesday morning and were shown into the boardroom. We had brought with us my lawyer, Bob Harley; his speciality was medical malpractice and product liability, but he had insisted on being present. He wanted to protect us in what he felt could be a treacherous negotiation.

We were introduced to a striking Italian woman called Rita Anichini, who was later to become a very close friend of ours, but at the time she was there as the New York account representative. We drank coffee and made small talk, and at half-past nine Rita said, 'Where the fuck are they? Oh, excuse my Italian!' Just then the door opened and Jack came into the room, followed by a worried-looking man in a dark blue suit. 'I'm Jack Sakazaki,' he said. 'And this is the president of the New York office, John Triggle. Sorry to keep you waiting. Shall we get started?'

By the end of the day, after much negotiating back and forth, West Nally had become our new partners. The deal we had made was complicated, but it seemed to suit our mutual purposes. West Nally would pay us $45,000, which we would use to buy out Steve Leber. West Nally would then own Steve's share of *Symphony on Ice*. Lewis Rappaport would leave his money in and retain his ten per cent, and David and I would share forty-five per cent, of which five per cent would go to Bob Harley in exchange for ongoing legal services and five to Bill Judd for his advisory services. In addition, West Nally Japan would pay *Symphony on Ice* $200,000 to present the show in their world première at the Yoyogi Stadium in Tokyo. There would be three performances, on 3 and 4 January 1984, and the skaters would be accompanied by the New Japan Philharmonic. The money would be used to pay for a rehearsal period in the autumn, plus costumes, lighting design and musical director. It would also have to cover the actual performing salaries for the company members and guest artists in Japan.

Afterwards we went for a coffee with Bob. 'You've got a very good deal,' he told us. 'But West Nally aren't going to play around. They have put a quarter of a million on the table and they'll want value for money. You need to put John and the company members under contract – you can't continue to operate on a handshake.'

'You're right, of course. But we feel it would not be fair to tie them in to the company when there is no guarantee of work and income.'

Steve was shocked when we handed him a cheque for $45,000. 'Where'd you guys get this kind of money from?' he demanded. We had been instructed by West Nally not to reveal their involvement to him, so I could only smile.

'From someone who knows that *Symphony on Ice* is a good investment,' I said.

He shook his head. 'Well, I have to hand it to you. You sure stick to what you believe in. I just hope it works out for you.' He had forgotten his previous anger. 'By the way,' he added, 'Robin Cousins is in town. He wants to see you guys.'

Robin wanted us to produce a show based on the music of Vangelis and Mike Oldfield, and I flew to London the next week, to see if I could find a British producer who would present the package in a West End theatre. I phoned John to tell him I would be over, and arranged to meet him for dinner.

At The Ark in Kensington, he looked relaxed and happy. 'I'm having a lovely summer so far,' he said. 'I've got this wonderful flat in Chelsea for ninety pounds a week, and the play's due to open soon. Shall we have some good wine?' I laughed, because I knew he was ordering it to please me. 'That would be lovely,' I told him.

We talked about West Nally for two hours, examining all the potential pros and cons of the relationship. I pointed out to him that, although the budget would be tight, it would enable us to prepare all the works needed for the Canadian tour in the autumn, and to buy costumes. 'How's the Canadian tour coming?' he asked. 'I'm surprised Bill Judd's still willing to work on it.'

'Then you don't understand Bill,' I told him. 'He only wants what's best for you. He understood about Fredonia. The tour's doing well at the moment, with three to four weeks booked.' I took a deep breath. 'John, I'm not sure you're going to like that tour and I'm nervous about that. I want to be honest with you.'

'Why wouldn't I like it?' he asked.

'Because it's mostly one-night stands in secondary towns. The music will be taped, we'll be in small arenas, and there will be hockey lines on the ice.' I stopped, and he laughed.

'I realize that,' he assured me. 'But it will give us an opportunity to get used to performing together and to work out any kinks. And, far more importantly, we will be exposing people to the company who might never have seen good skating otherwise. To me that's paramount, especially when it comes to the children.' I must have sighed, because he added: 'Don't worry – I'm not going to walk out on it!'

Since I was in London anyway, I decided to meet with the management of the Royal Albert Hall. I felt it to be the ideal venue for skating, and a wonderful place for John to make his comeback to Britain after a six-year absence. I received a very positive response from the hall, who suggested I talk to an impresario called Victor Hochhauser about presenting us there. I made an appointment to see him the next day, and I decided to ask John if he would come to the meeting.

I arrived early, and Victor approached me with his hand out. We were in the foyer of the Inn on the Park, and he introduced me to his wife, Lillian. I liked them immediately. Victor was a larger-than-life character who had spent his life presenting all manner of artists in Britain. He was a tall man with a wide smile and horn-rimmed glasses. He wore a cap at a rakish angle on top of his thinning hair, and he talked so quickly that it was difficult to catch everything he said. Lillian was a charming foil for him, with a much quieter approach and a reassuring manner. She handled Victor with a mixture of love, amusement and impatience, and they made a powerful combination.

John arrived on a huge Yamaha motor bike and parked it right outside the glass walls. I was horrified, but didn't think this the place to bring it up. He was wearing an all-white outfit and carried his helmet under one arm. Victor bowed to him. 'Maestro Curry,' he said, kissing his hand. John smiled and Lillian offered him a more conventional greeting. We had a wonderful meeting and we all got on extremely well. Victor agreed to present the company at the Royal Albert Hall, and had already secured the first week of April 1984. 'Will that be all right?' he asked. 'I think it's a good time, and I will be able to get a number of the performances as exclusives.' I asked what this meant, and he explained that the building of the hall had originally been financed through selling off a thousand seats to permanent boxholders, who were able to pass their seats down from generation to generation. However, a certain number of performances could be 'exclusive' of this, which meant that the presenter had the maximum number of seats available to sell. 'We'll probably use the Royal Philharmonic Orchestra,' Lillian told us. 'And Victor is keen to find a co-presenter to offset the costs.'

We said goodbye to the Hochhausers and I walked with John to the motor bike. 'I know what you're going to say!' he grinned. 'Believe me, Mother's already said it all. Yes, I am very, very careful – and no, I don't intend to stop riding it!' I was leaving the next evening, and we arranged to have a coffee in the morning. 'We can go over everything and make sure we're in agreement,' I said.

Robin's show meant that I would be spending a great deal of time in London over the summer, and this would afford me the opportunity to work with John. I told him about it when we met for coffee.

'Pro Skate is producing a show for Robin Cousins which will go into the Victoria Palace in August,' I told him. 'I will be here for a few weeks until it is off the ground, and then I will go back to New York to take care of our business. David will stay there throughout, and he will be able to handle anything that comes up. I want you to know that this show – which is to be called *Electric Ice* – will in no way take away from our commitment to your company. I don't want you to worry about that.'

John smiled. 'I'm not worried – actually, I'm rather pleased. It will give an opportunity to another group of young skaters, and will take ice yet another step forward. It all works together.'

I flew back to America and immediately put Robin's group on notice to start rehearsals the following week. David came up with an inspired idea of where to rehearse, and called Fredonia College. 'It won't be John's company, but at least it'll be something. Perhaps they'll forget about John now.' Fredonia were thrilled.

Sherman Pitluck seemed to have done a very good job on the Canadian tour. Dorothy was set for Seattle and Vancouver, and we had approximately four weeks of one-night stands across the country. The advances were small, but at least they were something. I met with West Nally and Rita told me that they wanted to create merchandising for the company: 'T-shirts and sweatshirts, that kind of thing.'

Back in London, I had discovered a promoter who had connections in the Middle East and I approached him to see if he would be interested in John. His name was Brian Miller and he was hugely enthusiastic, offering us a week in Dubai following the Albert Hall engagement. The fee was not large, but it would be an experience for the company and they would be accommodated in a five-star hotel. We signed a deal. John was dubious about it. 'It's work for the company, and I like that aspect of it, but do you really think it's safe to go there?'

We met with Victor and Lillian again, and Victor told John that he wanted him to meet a publicist called Kenneth Pitt. 'I know that name,' John said. 'I think he was something to do with David Bowie at one time.'

'He managed him, but David left him,' said Victor.

Kenneth Pitt was not an easy person to talk to and he seemed to make John uncomfortable. At the end of half an hour, John held out his hand. 'It was nice to meet you,' he said politely, and walked away down the stairs. I knew then that it wasn't going to work and I ended the meeting as tactfully as I could.

Later, John called me. 'I'm sorry, but that man gave me the creeps. I don't care if he's joined to David Bowie's hip, I couldn't possibly work with him. He's just another example of someone who doesn't understand what I'm trying to achieve.'

'John, I agree with you. You don't have to convince me. I'll call Victor and see if he can find us someone else.'

'Why do we need someone?' he asked irritably. 'You could do my publicity.'

I didn't argue at the time. I called Victor and explained John's misgivings about Kenneth Pitt. 'Lillian said John wouldn't like him. We'll put someone more conventional on to it in the morning.'

We had tea with Brian Miller one afternoon at his flat. Brian not only allayed John's fears about working in Dubai, but he also made him shake with laughter at some of the stories he told us. It seemed that an ice show was going to be a whole new experience in Dubai, and we would have to teach the company a new code of behaviour. 'You take just about everything you know and reverse it,' he said.

Dorothy Hamill arrived in London to stay at the Inn on the Park. She had recently married Dean Martin's son, Dino, and had flown over to attend a West End appearance by Dean. I moved into the hotel with her for three days to finish the interviews for her autobiography, and she told me how nervous she was about working with John. I was surprised. 'I thought you two got on so well?' I said.

'We do,' she answered. 'But when it comes to the artistic side of skating, I feel I have two left feet.'

I phoned John. 'Dorothy is here,' I told him. 'If I could rent ice at Queen's, would you work with her privately a couple of times? Just so she can get a feel for what you'll expect of her in the autumn?'

He understood immediately. 'Of course I will. You won't be able to get any daytime ice, but if you can get it from midnight, I don't mind that. We could do a couple of hours a night. That's all it would take.'

Dean lent Dorothy his limousine to take us over to the rink. It was a warm night, but Dorothy was shivering. 'I'm so nervous,' she told me. 'I don't know if I'm going to be able to do this.' The rink was deserted when we went in. The ice surface had been cleaned, and it gleamed under the harsh strip lighting. It was extremely cold and I could see our breath as we spoke. John arrived and hugged Dorothy warmly. Then he put on his skates. 'Why don't you go out and warm up for a bit, while I sort some music out?' he suggested.

It was one of those isolated occasions which stick in the memory, every sound, every movement playing back in the mind like a movie. John put a Chopin *étude* on the tape deck, and he began to work with Dorothy, creating steps and spins, praising and encouraging her, drawing out the artistry which was such a natural part of her make-up. She would approach each new movement cautiously, try and fail, try again until she got it right, clasp her arms together in delight. Each time she completed a new sequence, she would turn anxiously to see John's reaction. This was not two Olympic champions working together; this was teacher and pupil, each absorbed in their own role. It was fascinating to watch.

Electric Ice opened with all the attendant fanfare, and the audiences were wildly enthusiastic. The critics praised the music unanimously – the rock band was suspended over the ice in a cage that had once belonged to AC/DC – and for the most part they were positive about the cast. It was Robin himself who received some of the negative comments, however, and one of these was an unflattering and uncalled-for comparison with John.

John came with me to see *Electric Ice* a few days after the official opening. He had been invited to the actual première, but felt his presence would not be appropriate. Now he was deeply impressed by the show and by the talented young cast. 'Some of Robin's choreography is exceptionally inventive,' he said. 'It's so exciting to see this kind of thing happening. It's exactly what skating has always needed: a creative forum for experimentation.' He went backstage after the show, and made a point of congratulating the band members. Then he spoke to each of the skaters in turn, expressing his pleasure in their performances. Finally, he went to Robin's dressing room and hugged him. 'This is outstanding work,' he said. 'I'm very, very impressed. I wish you all the luck in the world with it.'

After the show, John went back to his flat and wrote a letter to the *Daily Mail*. It was never published, or even acknowledged, but it said at one point:

> your cruel and rather stupid attempt to belittle Robin Cousins through an inappropriate comparison to myself is not appreciated by me or anyone who has actually seen the show. Obviously you failed to watch it carefully, as I did, because if you had done so you could not have failed to respond well to this bold and exciting new approach to ice as theatre. Robin Cousins is one of the most gifted skaters in the history of the sport, and he at least deserves to be supported in his own land.

At the weekend John sent complimentary tickets to *A Midsummer Night's Dream* for everyone in *Electric Ice*. I had not yet seen his performance, so I went along with the group. It was a balmy, clear night and the theatre was set in the open air in Regent's Park. We sat in the middle of the bleachers sipping from plastic champagne flutes, and I realized that I was nervous. I knew how much acting meant to John, and I desperately wanted him to be good. He was: very good indeed. He had a charisma on stage which transcended the footlights, and he delivered his lines with authority and panache. I was very proud of him.

Towards the end of August, John and I had a long meeting to plot the strategy for the upcoming rehearsal period. We sat in his Chelsea flat drinking Earl Grey tea ('I do prefer the flavour to

English Breakfast, don't you?'), and made one of our eternal lists. Top priority was to find a suitable costume designer. 'We can't have one of the Broadway people,' I told him. 'It would be far too expensive. Do you have any ideas?'

'Yes,' he answered, leafing through his address book. 'Ann de Velder. She's wonderful and she does costumes for some of the good dance companies.' He found the number and called Ann immediately. 'Oh, sorry – did I wake you up?' he apologized. 'I need you to make some costumes for my company, and I'm wondering if you could come to England at once to spend some time with me? I'm sorry to spring this on you, but I do hope you'll say yes.' Ann arranged to fly over at the weekend. 'She can stay here with me,' John said. 'That will save on hotels.'

David called to tell me the Canadian tour was now set, and he had made all the arrangements to take the company to Vail in early September. 'I've found some ski lodges, divided into flats. Each one takes two people, and the skaters can decide who they would like to share with. See if John thinks it's a good idea.' He thought it was a wonderful idea, especially when he heard that he would have one all to himself. 'David says yours looks over the mountains,' I told him.

'The skaters will be so happy – they can have friends to stay and cook their own food,' he said. 'This is all beginning to shape up very nicely.'

We now needed extra skaters to round out the company. John really liked one of the girls in *Electric Ice*: Editha (Dita) Dotson, a tall, elegant American skater who was having problems dealing with the tempo of *Electric Ice*. I told John that I thought she would be very interested in joining our company. 'But I can't poach one of Robin's cast,' he protested.

'No, I understand that, but if she leaves anyway then I don't see why she can't join us. She has to work, and her whole background is classical. She's not suited to the rock idiom.' He suggested I talk to her about it, but cautioned me that he would want to ask Robin's permission before proceeding. 'I don't want to create any bad feeling,' he said.

John had noticed a young skater from Boston who was not from the established competitive circuit, but who he felt to be one of the most talented boys he had ever seen. 'His name's Nathan Birch,' he told me. 'We need to contact him to see if he would join us. He has the most amazing lines of any male skater, and he's only eighteen. I really think he could be prepared to take over the company from me.' Nathan accepted John's invitation to become a company member without any hesitation. 'It's a dream,' he told him. 'I never thought I would have this chance.'

Electric Ice was running smoothly, and my energies now needed to be channelled into John's troupe. Just before I returned to America I saw John, who was in an ebullient mood. 'I am so excited,' he told me. 'I can't wait until next week, to get back to rehearsals.' He looked serious suddenly. 'I have a question to ask you. I hope you won't mind me asking this, but it has occurred to me that what we are creating is something so substantial that it will be a full-time commitment from everyone concerned. I was wondering if you and David felt it would be worth your while to concentrate on it to the exclusion of all your other activities. You see, that's what I'm demanding from everybody involved. It would make me very happy if you two had the same approach. Then we'd truly be a family.'

I looked at him thoughtfully. 'John, I have just abandoned *Electric Ice* to the British producer. I have finished writing Dorothy's book. Our only other commitment is Pro Skate, and we can't afford to drop that because it pays us a small weekly salary. That's what we live on while we run your company. But I do promise you that our involvement in Pro Skate will be limited to a few weeks a year, just to produce the Madison Square Garden events. Is that all right?'

He hugged me. 'I know you're both totally committed, and I don't mind Pro Skate at all – in fact it's very good for our skaters, because you've invited so many of them to take part.' As I left, he ran after me. 'Elva – I've been trying to think of a name for the company, and only one seems right. What do you think if we call it the John Curry Skating Company?'

'I think it's elegant and totally appropriate,' I told him. 'I have a feeling it is destined to become one of the most revered names in the world of performing arts.'

28

The rehearsal period was enormously successful. The skaters were all glad to be back in the company, and they loved the new accommodation. Nathan had arrived and was already integrated into the fabric of the group, and Editha was set to join us in time for the Canadian tour.

John was anxious to involve new choreographers, and he invited young New Yorker Laura Dean to create a piece for the company. She came in late September and made an eleven-minute number to the music from Jean-Michel Jarre's *Oxygène*. She used her signature spinning movements, which worked to much greater effect on the ice than on the floor. John called me in a state of excitement. 'I can't wait for you to see this work,' he enthused. 'It's exactly what I was hoping for.'

It was arranged that David would go on tour with the company to oversee the box office and the promoters, but he needed someone else besides himself. John asked if I could locate a young company manager he'd met through Twyla Tharp. I tracked Richard Lenchner down and asked if he would like to do the tour, and the next morning he rang to say he had managed to clear his schedule. This just left the matter of costumes, and I approached a Broadway wardrobe mistress called Gayle Palmieri to see if she would do it. 'I'm used to having assistants,' she said dubiously.

'Well, you can have someone local in each place, but not someone to tour. We could never afford it,' I told her. 'All right, I'll do it,' she announced cheerfully. 'I'll send you a list of the things I'll need to have – trunks, a steamer, iron, ironing board, et cetera.' I liked Gayle; her aggressive professional manner was somehow reassuring.

David arranged three successive works-in-progress weekends, to raise some badly needed extra income. Costs continued to escalate, and we were fast accounting for the Japanese allowance. A great deal of it was to go to Dorothy Hamill, who had been requested by the promoters in Tokyo. They also demanded to have Janet Lynn, but we managed to persuade them that they would have to pay her separately.

Jack phoned one morning to tell me that he had now managed to add two performances in Hawaii right after the Japanese engagement. They would be in the Blaisdell Arena in Honolulu; the only drawback was that the building had no ice. We would have to make our own.

John recommended a celebrated Argentinian ice maker called Enrico Kossi, who was an ex-champion skater himself. David went to see him, and asked if he would be willing to handle the job for us. Enrico slapped him on the back. 'Don't worry about it! I been makin' ice for forty years, and I can put it anywhere. Just make the arrangements, and I'll do the rest.'

I flew down to Vail to watch rehearsals and talk to John about Japan. I felt it was important at this stage to keep him in constant touch with our plans. I met regularly with his lawyer, James Berry, to apprise him of developments, and we had engaged John's own accountant, Joe Concilio, to keep the company books. In this way, we felt he could be free of concern, since the people handling the company's financial affairs were his own representatives.

I was overwhelmed by the growth in the company. The ensemble had begun to gel, and skated with an authority and elegance not present at earlier rehearsals. Nathan was every bit as talented as John had described him, and had a breathtakingly eloquent line and an unerring sense of style. He had settled into a happy relationship with Timothy Murphy, and they shared a flat together. Timmy had been invited to choreograph some Gershwin pieces, and was happily planning his strategy.

John and I walked down into Vail and chose a small, cheerful restaurant for dinner. He was in a serious mood. 'Do you think we can make this work, financially?' he asked. I felt intuitively that I shouldn't worry him about the day-to-day financial struggles of the company. It was our job to solve those and John's to build the company. 'I don't think it will be easy,' I answered carefully, 'but I think we can make it work if we all stick together. I don't want you to worry about all that.'

'You know, if you ever do come to the point that something is in danger because you can't find the money for it, then I want you to promise that you'll ask me. I have money, and what I have can be put into the company. I'm aware of the financial sacrifices you and David have made, and I want to do my part – it's my company too.' As we walked back through the starlit mountain street, he brought the subject up again. 'I know you've allocated salary for me for this period, but I don't need to draw it. You aren't getting anything, so I would much rather I didn't. Put it into the company – it will do more good for me there.'

The Canadian tour was fraught with problems from the start. The John Curry Skating Company was unknown in Canada and the hoped-for ticket sales did not materialize. Promoters phoned in a panic to renegotiate their deals and many had to cancel dates. We were left with a choppy route and, in most cases, no advance guarantees. David came back to New York for the weekend, and we sat down in a gloomy bar on West 56th Street and wondered what we should do. If we cancelled the tour, the company would become demoralized and might disband. John would see it as yet another failure and might even give up skating. If we proceeded, we were facing a potential financial deficit and depressingly small audiences. I rang Bill Judd and asked him to join us. When he arrived he insisted on ordering a bottle of champagne and three flutes. 'I really don't care for champagne,' David protested. 'Nonsense!' Bill said firmly. 'Everyone likes good champagne, and when things are at a low ebb, it is always a good idea. It helps restore the morale.'

We talked at length about the tour and how we might be able to reshape it. I told Bill that I was concerned about John's reaction to the inevitably sparse audiences, and he held up his hand to stop me. 'I toured the great Pavlova,' he said, 'under Mr Diaghilev. The Ballet Russe was not well known outside of New York, and no one was willing to pay an advance to bring them. But she insisted on playing anywhere that she was invited. "If one person buys a ticket," she would say, "then I give the performance of my life for that person." She was the greatest dancer in the world, yet she would sit patiently on her suitcase on the station platform, waiting for the train to arrive. When it did, she would pick up her case and climb on board. There was no ego off the stage.' I understood what Bill was saying, and I hoped that I could somehow communicate this sentiment to John.

We rang Jack Sakazaki. He told us firmly that the Canadian tour was nothing to do with West Nally, and they had no wish to be involved on any level. I read into this that they were afraid it would lose money. We were on our own.

Finally, we made the decision to move forward. We decided to promote the tour energetically, and asked JoJo if she would be willing to do some PR for us. She agreed immediately and flew off for a six-city promotional blitz. Unlike the Canadian cities, Seattle had done exceptionally well, and had added a second show in its fourteen-thousand-seat arena. John flew down to appear on several chat shows, and spoke on two radio slots. He was articulate and eloquent and he must have revived interest in the performances.

Because of the cancellations, the tour began in the east, went all the way over to the west coast, then proceeded to zigzag back east again. Vancouver came after two weeks in the east, and I flew out to join the company for their performance there. The ticket sales were dismal, and John was in a gloomy mood. I didn't think it would be prudent to mention Pavlova.

The audience was dwarfed by the vast size of the arena, but when the show began they forgot their surroundings. The lighting was primitive, just a few follow-spots and a couple of coloured gels, but the skaters wove a magic that was mesmerizing. At the end, the audience stood and applauded for twenty minutes.

I thought John would be mollified by the reception, but he was not to be comforted. 'John, there were two thousand people in there. If Twyla Tharp got two thousand to come to one of her company performances she would be over the moon. But here they seem to disappear in the fifteen thousand other empty seats. It's all relative. Next time you're in Vancouver they'll come back and bring their friends. People were knocked out by the work.' John didn't answer. He seemed nervous and kept looking at the door. Just as I was about to leave, it opened and Ron Alexander walked in. John saw the shocked look on my face before I left.

The next day, he rang my hotel room at nine a.m. 'Can you please come down here? You can have breakfast with me. I'll order something.' I had lain awake the night before, worrying about Ron's presence. I had forgotten he lived in Vancouver and I knew from John's own admissions that he had been experimenting with hard drugs during his previous liaison with Ron. I was terrified that it would start all over again.

'Have a croissant. They're good,' John said as I sat down. He looked at me to see what mood I was in. I could see from his eyes that he had taken something. 'Are you disappointed in me?' he asked.

'I suppose I am a little,' I admitted. 'I do so want you to be all right. Happy.'

'I am happy,' he said. 'At the moment – but I am so lonely, Elva. You don't suffer from that, so you can't understand what it is to always feel alone. Sometimes I need to be with someone like Ron. I need something to help me get over this awful feeling.'

I sat in silence for a moment, then I took a deep breath. 'John,' I said, 'I have to tell you something. David and I have put a huge amount of effort into this company. It started off as your dream, but now it has become our common dream. You have a company of young, talented skaters who look up to you and rely on you. You have people's money at stake, as well as your own reputation. If you are going to continue to do drugs, then I don't want to have any further part in this company. I would rather leave now than go through that.'

He nodded. 'I do understand,' he said. 'I know it's stupid and I can give you my word that I will stop. I have no right to jeopardize everyone's lives this way.' He looked so crestfallen that I hugged him. 'I don't suppose Ron could travel with us?' he asked. 'He doesn't want to be paid and he could be very useful.'

'No,' I said. 'Especially not Ron. He is very bad news for you, John.'

He sighed. 'I knew you were going to say that but I thought I'd ask anyway. All right – I'll be good, I promise.'

Richard was down at the arena, supervising the packing-up of the equipment. 'Richard, do you know who Ron Alexander is?' I asked.

'Of course. He's been hanging around all tour,' he said.

'Well, if you see him again, I want you to make him leave. He is forbidden to be around this company from now on. Will you do that?'

Richard nodded. 'Be my pleasure,' he said. 'I'll keep an eye on John, too, if you like.' As I was leaving the auditorium, Richard called me back. 'Did you know that John has asked me to arrange for him to have an AIDS test?' he asked. I felt a stab of fear go through me.

'Oh God, Richard. Not AIDS. If he's having a test, he must feel he's at risk.'

'I'm sure he's only being cautious,' Richard said soothingly. 'After all, lots of people are paranoid about it nowadays. I wouldn't worry too much about it.'

That afternoon, a contingency of eighteen people arrived from

West Nally Japan. They had come to finalize the arrangements for the Tokyo engagement. Rita had flown out from New York to supervise their visit, and she told me she had booked a meeting room in the hotel. 'Will you let John know where it is?' she asked.

'John?' I said. 'I don't think he's going to feel like being there today.'

'He'd better be there! He's the reason they all came – they need to ask him questions about the show and the company. Just make sure he comes.'

John wasn't in his hotel room, nor was he in any of the restaurants or coffee bars. Just as I was about to give up, I saw him trudging up the hotel steps. He looked very, very tired and I suddenly remembered the HIV test. He must have been at the hospital. 'John,' I said carefully, 'there is a creative contingency here from Tokyo to talk to you about the New Year performances. I'm afraid you will have to spend a little time with them.'

He sighed. 'Can't I sleep for a while first?' he pleaded. 'I want so desperately to lie down.'

'I'm sorry, John. It can't wait. They only have this afternoon. I promise we'll get it over with as soon as we possibly can.'

It was a bizzare meeting. Everyone sat around the room holding expensive leather notebooks. None of the Japanese except Jack spoke any English, and every sentence had to be painstakingly translated by an elderly interpreter who sat in the middle. It made progress very slow. When John entered the room, everyone stood up and bowed to him. He was startled and bowed in return, which produced a fresh round of bows from the Japanese. 'Just sit down,' Rita hissed at him, 'or it will never end.'

The questions were endless. They wanted to know exactly which pieces would be skated, in which order, how long was each piece, who wrote the music, if it was still in copyright – it went on and on. John became very irritable and frustrated, because many of these details had not yet been decided. He wanted to settle the programme for Japan when he returned to Vail. 'Just tell them anything,' whispered Rita. 'It doesn't matter. They just want something to write in their notebooks.' This worked very well until John suddenly turned deathly white and asked if everyone would excuse him. The Japanese rose again to bow him out and gave him a round of applause. He had managed to make a very good impression.

David felt he should go after John to see if he was all right, so I stayed behind. When I heard what they had to say I was thankful that John had already gone. 'It's about the guest skaters,' Jack said. 'They want to know at which point in the programme they can skate.'

'You mean Dorothy and Janet?'

'No, no. Japanese guests. Two of our own skaters. Out of respect to our audience.'

I was horrified. 'What Japanese skaters?' I demanded. 'We didn't know anything about this!'

'Emi Watanabe and a young man, the Junior Champion.'

I froze. 'Jack – you do realize that this isn't possible? John will walk out, I'm warning you. It's outrageous. Emi is a chunky girl, to say the least, and as for a Junior champion, I'm appalled at the suggestion. There is no way they can skate in his company. It would be ludicrous.'

'It's imperative,' Jack told me. 'You will have to find a way to work it out. The sponsors are demanding it.'

I looked at him in surprise. 'Sponsors?'

'Yes,' he said. 'We have managed to get several.'

'How do you propose that will work? You aren't planning to have sponsor boards round the ice?'

Jack smiled. 'Of course. It has to be that way for them to have the proper television exposure.'

I almost choked. 'Television as well? We knew none of this. John will be absolutely furious when he hears.'

Jack took me aside and handed me a cup of black coffee. 'Here,' he said, 'drink this. You have to understand that we have taken very seriously the things that John has said he wants. A live orchestra – we have the best in Japan – gorgeous lighting, prestigious hotel. These things cost a fortune. Someone has to pay for them, and that has to be the sponsors. Now, the sponsors have asked for two things. Rink boards and Japanese guest skaters. Somehow, you must find a way to accommodate them. If you don't, then I'm not sure what will happen.'

When I told David about the Japanese situation he drew his breath in sharply. 'Jee-zuss! John'll never stand for it. If we don't tell him, he'll find out later and he'll quit. If we do tell him, he'll refuse to go to Japan and we won't have any income at all. What a bummer!'

'I have an idea,' I said. 'What if we had the Japanese skate in the intermission?'

He looked at me. 'They'd never go for that. It's rude.'

'It's better than losing the whole engagement,' I said.

'And what about the boards?'

'Those can wait until later. I have a feeling that when John sees the New Japan Philharmonic spread across the arena, he won't be so worried about the boards. But I will definitely suggest the intermission slot for the guests. It's at least worth a try.'

I had breakfast with Rita the next morning, and we got along very well. We managed to laugh about the guest-skaters situation, and she thought my solution would work well. 'I wonder if they'll get Seiji Ozawa to conduct?' she asked.

'He can't!' I said, alarmed. 'We have to get someone of our own, who can learn the pieces and get used to the timing. It would be a disaster to have a stranger, however distinguished.'

Rita looked thoughtful. 'Have you got someone?' she asked.

'Not yet. We had briefly considered an old client of Bill Judd's – Harry John Brown – but he's not exactly top of John's hit list right now. He was too old, anyway. It was the wrong image.'

'I might have someone for you,' Rita said. 'His name is Charles Barker, and he's the Director of the American Chamber Orchestra. He's also a fine violinist in his own right.' She promised to get in touch with Charles and see if he would be interested. I thought he sounded promising.

I was to leave that afternoon, so I went to say goodbye to John. He was still in his room, and seemed somewhat subdued. 'Did you work everything out with the Japs?' he asked. 'What a frightful ordeal that was!'

'How are you?' I asked. 'I was worried about you yesterday. You looked terrible.'

John sighed heavily. 'I suppose I'd better tell you, or you'll just keep pestering me. I went for an AIDS test yesterday. I've had several, all of them negative. I expect this one will be too, but I need to be sure. You see, a friend of mine has AIDS, and I thought it wise to keep a check on myself.'

'Oh, John – I am sorry. Do I know him?'

'It's Brian,' he said sadly. 'You do know him. He told me you were friends, and I don't think he would mind my telling you.' I was

161

stunned. Dear, sweet Brian, who was the gentlest and kindest of people. It seemed so unfair. 'Is it full-blown?' I asked.

'Not yet,' John said.

He stared into space for a moment. 'You know, sometimes I wonder what the point of struggling is. We live such a short time and we don't seem to have an opportunity to be happy. We're too busy trying to succeed. Did I ever tell you that I would like to have been a carpenter? I've always enjoyed working with my hands. I could have lived in the Colorado Mountains, or in Cornwall, and I could have had a small house with a garden. And I would have lived very simply, just making beautiful things . . .'

I found myself blinking back tears. 'You make beautiful things now,' I said quietly. 'Your life is all about creating beauty for people to enjoy.'

'Yes, I suppose so,' he whispered. 'But sometimes it seems to be very difficult.'

29

We received a signed contract for our engagement in the Royal Albert Hall, and this was quickly followed by the contract for Dubai. With these engagements secure, and the Japanese/Hawaiian tour already arranged, things were feeling slightly more solid. It was just as well, because the news from Canada was not good.

Rita invited me to dinner at her flat, and I met Charles Barker and his wife. He was much younger than I expected, but had an air of distinction that lent him weight. He was prepared to commit himself wholeheartedly to the Curry Company, and I felt John would enjoy his mixture of authority and boyish charm. 'We will need an assistant conductor,' he told me. 'You need that because he will go ahead to rehearse the next orchestra while I am conducting the first one. It's essential. The thing is, that conductor could also be our solo pianist. That way we can get double value from him.'

David called frequently from the tour. Seattle had gone very well indeed. John had been happy because of the full houses and because he had Dorothy there. The reviews had been hugely complimentary and his confidence was considerably bolstered. Canada, however, was another matter. The houses were poor, and the promoters were reluctant to pay. Almost everywhere our costs exceeded our income. We couldn't cancel at this point, and we just kept hoping that things would turn around. 'I keep telling myself', David said, 'that we are getting valuable experience. But at what price?'

I was busy juggling figures, and was becoming adept at dealing with crises. I went to Joe Concilio for advice, but he was less concerned than I was. 'It's a new venture, with start-up costs,' he told me. 'You have to expect things to be tight at first. They'll get better next year.'

John called from a small town in Ontario. It was very late at night and I was already in bed. 'I hope I didn't wake you up,' he apologized. 'I wanted to tell you about something that happened tonight.' I could tell by the tone of his voice that he was not calling to complain. 'We had a very small audience,' he went on. 'Just about four hundred people. There were so few that Richard invited them all to move down into the front rows. There was a school party among them – children of ten and eleven. When I wasn't skating, I watched them, and I was so inspired by their faces! They were enraptured, watching every movement. After the show they came backstage and asked for autographs, and one little girl told me that the show was the most beautiful thing she had ever seen. She asked me how she could learn to skate, and she wanted to know how old I was when I started. I knew, just from that one child, that it doesn't matter how many people there are in the audience – it can be two or three – it's how much joy we bring into their lives that counts.' I had no need to tell John about Pavlova – he had figured it out for himself.

Two days later I had another late-night call. This time it was from David in Kalamazoo, Michigan, and he sounded desperate. 'Elva, I don't think I can cope. You're going to have to fly out here tomorrow and see what you can do with John.'

'John?' I asked. 'I spoke to him two nights ago, and he sounded fine. Best he's been for a long time.'

David snorted. 'He must have been smoking funny cigarettes, then. He isn't fine now, I can assure you.' He told me the problem had started on the bus down to Kalamazoo. When it had pulled up at the hotel in the morning, the skaters had all climbed on board and chosen seats next to each other. Nobody elected to sit beside John.

'They guessed he wouldn't want them to,' I said.

'I know,' David answered. 'But he's convinced it's because they don't like him. He sat right in the back of the bus and travelled all the way down with his coat over his head. I tried to talk to him, but he wouldn't even answer.'

'Oh, poor John,' I said.

'You haven't heard the whole story yet,' David continued. 'When we got to the hotel, John went straight to the desk and demanded his room key. We were early, so none of the rooms were ready, but John made such a terrible fuss that the manager gave him the honeymoon suite to shut him up. He disappeared, and just as we were registering he came running down the stairs and threw his suitcase across the lobby. He started to scream at the desk clerk: "How dare you put me in a room with purple sheets! And a mirror on the ceiling! Do you think I'm some kind of pervert?" He turned on Richard then and shrieked at him: "This is all your doing! I won't stay here a minute longer. If you can't find me some decent accommodation, then I'll go back home."'

Richard had moved the whole company to another hotel and this time John seemed to be mollified. He went to his room and nothing more was heard from him until he came down to the dining room for a late lunch. He sat down beside David, who was having a quiet cup of coffee, and said: 'I want you to weigh Lori once a week. She promised me she'd lose weight and I don't see any sign of it. If she gains anything, then I want her fired. I won't have fat people in my company.' David said nothing, for fear of incensing him again. 'And another thing,' John went on, 'if I find out Dorothy is being paid more for Tokyo than the company members, I shall quit. Remember that.'

I flew in just before the evening show, and found the arena relatively full. This would have been a welcome relief, except for the fact that we'd taken a small guaranteed fee and no split of the gate. The show was well received but the skaters were edgy. John's mood had affected them all, and they were feeling insecure. On a whim, I called a company meeting at the hotel after the show.

We provided red and white wine and hot finger foods, and as soon as everyone was settled I started to talk to them. I told them how important they all were to the company, and how much we appreciated their loyalty and hard work over the past nine months. I explained what our long-term plans were, and told them of our dream to put the company into the Met in New York. They asked questions about the Albert Hall and Dubai, and then we discussed Japan and Hawaii. I could see from the looks on their faces that they were excited at these prospects. I referred often to John, who was sitting at the back of the room, and at the end I asked them to give him a round of applause. While everyone was clapping, JoJo ran over and hugged him. It was strange, but the very thing that John had longed for had come to pass. The John Curry Skating Company had become a close-knit family. The problem was that John was in far too much pain to notice it.

I went to John's room after the meeting, and ordered two salads, rolls and butter, and two glasses of white wine. Neither of us had eaten anything earlier, and I thought he might enjoy it. 'I hope that's all for you,' he said irritably. 'I certainly don't want any.' When it came, however, he ate ravenously and drank the wine in great deep gulps. Then he went into his bathroom and I could hear him vomiting. After a while he came out again and slumped into an armchair. 'Please don't ask me what's wrong,' he said miserably. 'I can't tell you. You wouldn't understand.'

'Try me,' I urged. 'Maybe I can help.' Two big tears slid down his face. He dabbed at them crossly and blew his nose.

'No, I'm afraid you can't. No one can. I just want to go to sleep and never wake up again. I want to stop living. It hurts too much.' I knew something must have triggered this, but I had no way to know what it might have been. The talk of death alarmed me, and I thought it might be a good idea if I took John back to New York for the three days between Kalamazoo and Windsor, Ontario. If he stayed, there was no telling what he might do.

As soon as John was back in New York, his spirits lifted. 'I'm sorry to be such a nuisance,' he said as I dropped him off at the Streeters' building. 'I feel better now, and when I go back I will try very hard to be nice to everyone.'

Bill and I took John to lunch with Margaret Carson, the doyenne of New York publicists. She handled a very few select clients, including Leonard Bernstein, and would take only those she personally believed in. It was clear from the first few minutes that they would get on splendidly together, and she was deeply impressed by the breadth of his knowledge. She told John quite candidly that she planned to build his image as the master skater by associating him with other leading artists from all disciplines. 'And the venue is very important,' she continued. 'Paramount. When you go into the Metropolitan Opera House this will tell the world that your company is first-class, and when you skate to music by Leonard Bernstein, and he is watching the performance, then this gives you an aura. You become sexy and sought-after.'

John looked surprised. 'You talk about the Met as though it is a reality. What makes you think they will take us?'

Margaret chuckled to herself. 'For the simple reason that I shall tell them to take you,' she said. 'I think it's time that you met Jane Herman. She runs the summer season at the Met, and she will no doubt want to be very much involved with the company. Jane never does things by halves, and I think she will find you quite captivating.' I was often to remember those words in the months to come.

The Metropolitan Opera House stands in the middle of the Lincoln Center arts complex, its starkly modern design arching against the river skyline. In front of the complex is a large quadrangle with a fountain in the middle. This is flanked by the New York State Theater on one side, and Avery Fisher Concert Hall on the other. To the right of all this, and slightly behind, is a large reflecting pond, dominated by a massive Henry Moore sculpture. There is nothing particularly beautiful about the complex, but it has an air of authority and permanence which gives it an unquestioned stature.

Bill, John and I entered the main hall of the opera house, with its baronial stairways curving to either side of the central foyer. Soaring above our heads was the disturbing Chagall mural, which drew the eye from every angle. We went to the reception desk and asked for Jane Herman, and a polite woman came from the interior and led us into a lift and down what seemed like miles of corridors. Eventually we were standing in front of Jane's door.

Jane Herman was a woman of about fifty with a commanding presence and a striking resemblance to Lauren Bacall. She exuded an odd mixture of cynicism and sensuality, and she greeted us politely and invited us to sit down. Bill, who already knew her, introduced us and I told her about our desire to play the Met. John then launched into an eloquent explanation of his company's aspirations. He ended with an impassioned plea for an opportunity to become a part of the legitimate arts world. 'You hold us in the palm of your hand right now,' he told Jane. 'I hope you will help us to realize our dreams.'

John flew to Windsor, and I had a second meeting with Jane to talk in minute detail about the company and what I would envisage the costs to be. In the end, she told me she was willing to commit herself to us for a trial period of three years. Each year would depend on our reception the previous year. We would start with a one-week engagement in July of 1984, and she was prepared to pay us a guaranteed fee of $50,000. For this we would have to offer three different evenings of work and at least three world premières by internationally established choreographers. She would also want the engagement to feature Dorothy Hamill. This last clause qualified everything that had gone before. The Met wanted to present Dorothy Hamill, who was currently the hottest box-office star on the ice. They wanted the John Curry Skating Company as a bridge between the sports and arts worlds. It would provide a beautiful and convenient backdrop for what they saw as an athletic *tour de force*. I was bitterly disappointed, but if that was the only way we could launch ourselves into the classical world, then we would have to find a way to deal with it. We might even be able to turn it to our advantage.

I called Michael Rosenberg, because if Dorothy refused to do the Met dates we might have to let the allocated slot go. I decided to tackle him head-on. 'Michael,' I said, 'we have been offered an opportunity to play a week at the Metropolitan Opera House in July of next year. It will be the first time ice has been laid on their stage and the event will attract a lot of attention. You know the quality of John's company. You also know his high regard for Dorothy's artistic potential. He would like to include Dorothy in the engagement and make two beautiful new pieces for her that will show off her lyrical qualities.'

Michael chuckled. 'Elva, we've known each other too long for this! Let's cut through the bullshit and get to the bottom line. The Met want Dorothy Hamill because no one has ever heard of the John Curry Skating Company and they're scared they won't sell any tickets. I *do* understand the quality of John's work, or I wouldn't even be having this conversation with you. I'm also not unaware that it would be good for Dorothy's image to be associated with a prestigious event like this . . .' He paused, then said: 'What about money? I presume it will be a hurdle?'

'Michael,' I said, 'we are getting a flat fee of fifty thousand dollars for eight performances. Out of that we have to pay for the ice, the skaters, their accommodation and travel, the publicist, the costumes, the rehearsals and our own crew.'

'Well,' he said slowly. 'I'll talk to her, but I know she won't do it without a substantial fee. I'm going to urge her to accept and see if we can work out the details, but I want to warn you that Dorothy is a tough negotiator. People think it's me, but I'm really an old softie at heart. I know how much this means to you, and all I can say is that I will do my best.'

Before Michael could come back to me, Jane had phoned to say that she could arrange a follow-on engagement for two weeks at the Kennedy Center in August. This would also require the addition of Dorothy Hamill, but she felt she might be able to negotiate a guarantee of $75,000 a week on our behalf. Suddenly things looked a little brighter, and I said I would let her know by the end of the week.

I called Michael again and told him of the new development. 'Well,' he said, 'this might make all the difference. Dorothy is keen to do the Met, but as I predicted the money is a sticking point.'

'How much is she asking for?' I demanded.

'You don't want to know,' he replied. 'But if we can add two weeks at the Kennedy Center, maybe I can persuade her to do the whole period for a fee of twenty-five thousand dollars.'

It was much more than we could comfortably afford, but, if it meant our being able to finalize the contract, it would be worth it. 'Fine,' I told him. 'See what she says.'

The Canadian tour had ended with nothing but debts to show for it. Windsor had cancelled two out of four performances, and the remaining ones were only a moderate success. The promoters, however, refused to pay us our share of the box office, claiming that it had to be offset against the cancellations. David went to our bank and persuaded them to advance us a small amount against the Albert Hall engagement, and we sat down one evening with Joe Concilio and figured out who and what should be paid out of it. There was no question of David or me being able to take anything, but we insisted that John was given a little of what he was owed. The skaters were all paid in full, and money was set aside for the ice equipment we would need in Hawaii. 'Is it all worth it?' Joe asked, looking at us curiously. 'Why are you doing it?'

I shrugged. 'It's hard to explain, Joe. It's just stronger than we are. We're committed to it – we don't even question it any longer.'

'But why not take your time, and do these things more slowly?'

I sighed. 'Because John has only given us three or four years to get this off the ground for him. He wants to retire from performing after that, and just be Artistic Director of the company. If he is to do that, we have to launch the company while he is still in it. There isn't a skater anywhere in the world who can do what he does. That's why he is so anxious to train his troupe, so that they can take over from him when he stops.'

Michael called me to say that Dorothy would do the engagements for the $25,000 fee. 'I talked her into it on the basis that she would be getting two wonderful new programmes made for her, which she wouldn't have to pay for. And costumes as well.'

'I don't understand,' I said.

'Well, after the Met gigs are over, then she will be able to perform those programmes in other situations. Other shows.'

'No, Michael. She won't. Those will be the exclusive property of the John Curry Skating Company. She can't have the rights to them. No dance company would grant such a thing, so how can you expect us to?'

'It's a deal-breaker,' Michael said flatly. 'Let me know.'

I knew that if I discussed the situation with John he would be likely to veto the entire project and retire. I didn't want to risk that, especially in light of his recent emotional outbursts. I went to see Bill. 'My advice to you is to solve as much as you can before presenting it to John,' he told me. 'That is your duty to him. He has lost two companies before this one, and I suspect it was because no one was willing to go out on a limb for him. If you work very hard, and take a great deal of the responsibility on yourselves, you and David can succeed where others have failed. But you must do it knowing that one day he may turn on you too. If that happens, there will be nothing you can do about it.'

I telephoned Michael: 'I've thought about your proposal, and I am willing to offer the following. Dorothy can have the twenty-five thousand dollars. We will retain copyright in all the choreography, and we will own the costumes. However, she can apply to us in writing if she wants to use it outside of our company and our permission will not be unreasonably withheld. If we allow her to use the choreography, then she will automatically be able to use the accompanying costumes. I will start by telling you that she would be granted permission to use everything in Pro Skate this year, and I know that has to be a big consideration as far as time and cost goes.'

Michael was silent for a moment, then he said: 'All right. I think she will agree to that.'

'There's one more thing,' I told him. 'She will have to agree to spend the month of June in Vail with the company. And that's a deal-breaker.'

He laughed. 'You drive a hard bargain!' he said. 'I'll come back to you later today, but I think you can assume you have Dorothy for the summer.'

I told John that the Met had asked if Dorothy could join the company for the summer season. 'On our terms, or hers?' he asked.

'Ours,' I told him. I did not elaborate on the negotiations with Michael. I simply told him that she would be paid $8,000 per week, and that this would include publicizing the performances, any television coverage and four weeks' rehearsal in Vail. He seemed satisfied.

'I know she gets much more than that normally,' he said. 'But it's probably best if the company members aren't told. She'll be getting eight times more than they are for a fraction of the work, and it really *isn't* fair. If they find out they'll give her a hard time, and I don't want that.' He seemed pleased. 'I'm going to make a very beautiful piece for her to Puccini – *Madame Butterfly*.'

One evening, John and I were invited to a performance at the Met. Afterwards we took Jane to dinner, and she talked animatedly about her plans for John and the company. 'I think it should be televised in July,' she told us. 'You should have a really good recording of your work.'

I told her we were already negotiating with someone about doing a special from the Met: 'Clem d'Alessio – he tells me he used to do a lot out of the opera house.'

Jane raised her eyebrows. 'The less said about that the better!' she laughed. 'Shall we just say that you need a top professional, not a has-been. I think you should use Brian Large.'

I opened my mouth to protest, but John glared at me and I kept quiet. I knew Clem well, and I also knew that he did stellar work. His departure from the Met had been politically motivated, and had nothing at all to do with his level of professionalism. Jane and John continued to discuss the television potential and I had the uncomfortable feeling that we no longer held the reins of our own company. In the months to come, I was to realize that this instinct was correct. The process of erosion, which would ultimately split us all asunder, had already begun.

30

The 1983 Pro Skate Championships involved as many of the Curry skaters as possible, and several were to take part in the Singles events. The fact that they all distinguished themselves was a further tribute to John's abilities.

John had been working intermittently with a young New York girl called Katherine Healy. Katherine had never competed as an amateur, having no interest in the world of skating as such, but she had been performing John's choreography in charity galas since the age of ten. She was an accomplished ballet dancer also, and had recently starred in a movie with Dudley Moore and Mary Tyler Moore. At fourteen, she was the epitome of everything John believed in, and at Pro Skate she stunned the audience with a dazzling performance of *The Dying Swan*. This was skating on a different level – the carriage, the extensions, the lovely soft arms and the fluid transitions – and the audience adored it. The judges, however, were sharply divided. The skating judges awarded her mediocre marks, but the artistic judges gave her several perfect scores. Later, John was interviewed by the ABC anchorman, and asked for his reaction to this apparent discrepancy. He replied: 'Everyone is entitled to their own opinion; that's what makes skating so peculiar.'

From the company itself, two skaters stood out in the competition. The first was Patricia Dodd, who at thirty-nine was the oldest member of the troupe. She performed to her own choreography, set to music by Gluck. It was starkly simple in its beautiful delivery, and she seemed to float above the ice. Once again, the audience reacted with spontaneous appreciation, maintaining absolute silence during the performance and erupting only after she had stopped moving. The judges again were divided – the two traditional skating judges awarding unnecessarily low marks, the two younger skating judges giving slightly better marks, and the artistic judges giving two perfect scores. In the Men's event, Nathan Birch – the youngest skater in the company – performed to Neil Diamond's *Jonathan Livingston Seagull* and brought the house down. He was dressed in a flowing white costume and he seemed to make the arena disappear. Instead the audience saw a bird, swooping, diving and soaring in space until he finally came to rest on the ocean. The skating judges were confused – they had never heard of this young skater and yet he was as accomplished and eloquent as any world competitor. John Curry was turning the establishment on its ear, but they had no intention of acknowledging him. The artistic judges heralded Nathan for his creative distinction, however, and John seemed satisfied.

At the party afterwards, I told John that I was disappointed with the judging system. 'I thought it would make a difference, but it doesn't seem to be working out,' I said.

John disagreed with me. 'There is one very big difference between this and amateur competition: this is not corrupt. You are exposing skaters to the public who deserve to be seen, yet because they are not politically acceptable to the establishment they would never be allowed in the top ranks of amateur competition. It makes no real difference whether they come first or last in Pro Skate – the important thing is that the public is being exposed to consistently fine skating. You must never underestimate the importance of that.'

The company returned to Vail immediately after the competitions, to spend two more weeks preparing for Japan. John seemed to be in an extremely good state of mind, and David opted to remain in Vail throughout the period. Christmas Day was a happy affair, with

John cooking dinner for the whole company. He bought each member a small gift and a card, and was showered with packages in return. When David got back to his own flat on Christmas night, he found a large brown paper parcel propped up outside his door. Inside was a new suit and a card saying 'I thought it was time someone gave you something really nice. I do hope it fits. Love, John.'

Last-minute preparations for the Tokyo engagement were becoming a headache. I still had no confirmation that the presenters had accepted the concept of having the Japanese skaters appear during intermission. Michael Rosenberg had announced Dorothy's demands for four first-class tickets to Japan for herself, Dino, Michael and his wife: thousands of dollars we didn't have in the budget, plus the extra hotel accommodation. Jack made it clear that these costs would have to come out of the company's money, West Nally weren't willing to allocate any extra. I talked to Joe about it, but in the end the only thing to be done was to give up the $10,000 production fee that would have gone to David and me. It seemed we would never be able to recover any of our personal money.

Rita Anichini and I flew to Tokyo two days ahead of the company. We travelled in the almost-empty economy cabin of the JAL plane and for fourteen hours we exchanged stories of our lives and watched movies. By the time we arrived, we had established a friendship that was to last way beyond the life of the company.

Jack kept us so busy that we hardly noticed the bitter cold. We had meetings with the sponsors that lasted many hours, and inspected the Yoyogi Stadium. It was a massive space – much larger than the average arena – and I was concerned about the effect this would have on the skaters' orientation. Charles Barker had already arrived to rehearse the New Japan Philharmonic and he was ecstatic about the quality of their playing. We saw nothing of Tokyo itself, outside of the hotel, the stadium and the West Nally offices, but in passing I had the impression of a highly motivated population, moving steadily about their business and being very careful not to disturb one another. Everything was spotlessly clean and I was particularly impressed by the taxis: the drivers wore white gloves and there were immaculate white headrests on the seats. 'It certainly beats the shit we have to sit on in New York,' Rita said.

David and the company arrived on the morning of 28 December, full of excitement and anticipation. Janet had joined them in Denver and she and John had travelled together on the plane. The airline had offered to upgrade them, but John refused. 'I'm perfectly content to sit with everyone else,' he said. 'But thank you for offering.' Dorothy's party was due in the late afternoon.

A large bus was waiting to bring us all to the city. When we arrived at the hotel, we saw television cameras outside, and a battery of photographers. 'Will you all please stay seated for a moment?' Jack asked. 'And would Janet please come with me?' Janet was embarrassed as she made her way to the front of the bus, clutching an armful of flowers that had been given to her at the airport. As soon as she stepped outside, the flash bulbs began to pop, and people fired questions at her. 'Are you pleased to be back? How are your children? What does it feel like to be skating again?' She smiled at everyone, posed for pictures and answered questions. John, in the mean time, was growing increasingly irritated.

'Is this really necessary?' he demanded. 'Couldn't they have set up a press conference for her after everyone had settled in? It's incredibly rude of them.'

I got up and went to talk to Jack. 'You have to invite John to be interviewed,' I said. 'What do you think he feels like?'

Jack just smiled. 'He will be,' he said. 'He'll have lots of opportunities. But this is for the evening papers and the news broadcasts. We need it for the sponsors.'

Eventually it was over, and the company were allowed off the bus and into the magnificent foyer of the hotel. 'Wow!' said Richard. 'This is a step up from the places I'm used to staying in.' They had all been allocated beautiful double rooms, and baskets of fruit, flowers and champagne were waiting for each of them. Their spirits were high as they left to unpack, but John was obviously unhappy. I could see the beginnings of a full-blown tantrum and I wondered desperately how we could prevent it erupting.

David volunteered to go and meet Dorothy, leaving me to deal with John and the skaters. At three in the afternoon, I rang John's room and he answered the phone in a whisper. 'John, I'd like to come and talk to you,' I said. 'Are you awake?'

'I haven't been asleep,' he snapped. 'But come up if you must.'

I got into the elevator and as it rose slowly to the top floor of the hotel I wondered why I hadn't chosen to work in Woolworth's. It seemed an attractive alternative at this point.

John's room was opulent. Jack had taken very good care of him, and he had gifts piled on the table. John sat huddled in an armchair, wearing the new bathrobe provided by the hotel. He looked grey. 'What do you want?' he said flatly. 'You can order some coffee from room service. I think they speak English.'

'I want to know what's the matter,' I said. 'You were all right when you left Vail, so what went wrong?'

'I'm always all right in Vail,' he said quietly. 'It's leaving it that's a problem. I don't like it here.'

I pointed out that he had only just arrived, and that maybe he should give it a chance. 'After all, you are building this company for the skaters, as well as yourself, and it's this kind of thing that makes it possible. Besides – they're all so excited about it. Do you really want to spoil things for them?'

He sighed. 'No, of course not. I don't mean to be like this, but I just find it all so depressing. It's always the same: people only want the "star" (whoever that might be at any given moment in time), and they won't treat the others with the same respect. Why aren't they interviewing Patricia or Cathy or Mark? Why not Nathan?'

'John, they *will* interview them one day, when we've achieved what we've set out to achieve. When we've made the ensemble itself the "star". But Cathy and Patricia didn't win the Olympics, and whether we like it or not that's what makes a skater famous at the moment. You know that – it's the very reason you fought so hard to win a gold medal. Now you have to endure another long fight – to make people accept your company in its own right, without guest stars. If you're determined enough, that day will come.'

He stood up. 'You're right, of course. Perhaps I'm just tired. I think I'll just sleep until tomorrow morning. Will you make sure everyone's all right?'

Dorothy arrived safely, and they were all delighted with their suites. Michael was visibly impressed with the hotel, and busily made plans to tour the city. Dino greeted me warmly and asked after John. 'I'm looking forward to this,' he said. 'Dorothy's terribly nervous, but I know she's excited.'

I gathered the company in one of the lounges later in the evening, and went through the plans with them. They seemed relieved that John was not present. 'I'll spend time with him tomorrow,' said JoJo. 'He'll be all right.' After the meeting, David and I went to the hotel bar and sat in a corner drinking cappuccinos. 'I have the most horrible feeling', David said, 'that John is going to fall apart here.'

'No,' I said firmly. 'He won't. He's had his outburst now. It's over.'

David shook his head. 'I hope you're right. That's all I can say,' he said gloomily.

The next morning was bright and sunny, and I went down to the hotel coffee shop looking for John. Several of the skaters were there, eating large cooked breakfasts, and Timmy called to me to come and join them. He was sitting with Nathan and JoJo and he pulled out a chair for me. 'We're going on a coach tour of the city this morning,' he said. 'Jack has arranged it all.' Keith, Shelley and Mark were sitting at the next table and when David appeared he was invited to sit with them. We spent a very pleasant half-hour, and I was just preparing to sign the bills when the door of the restaurant burst open and John came in, dragging his overcoat behind him. His face was contorted with rage, and he stormed up to our table.

'I hope you're all enjoying yourselves,' he said icily. 'I've just been informed I can't be served because I'm three minutes late.'

I got up. 'Why don't you sit here, John? I'll talk to them. I'm sure they'll serve you.'

He whirled on me. 'Thank you, but I'd rather starve. And I have no wish to sit somewhere that I'm not wanted.' He hurled his coat on to the floor with such force that it took a chair down with it. 'I presume you won't be needing me today,' he yelled over his shoulder, and pushed his way past the startled *maître d'* and a group of curious onlookers.

David looked at me in dismay. 'I think you misread him last night,' he said.

'Obviously I did. I think you'd better go after him. Perhaps you can find out what's going on.'

David searched for John for an hour, but failed to find him. He had disappeared. We decided to say nothing, assuming he would be back when he had calmed down. I had no time to dwell on it, as it turned out, because Michael descended on me looking as though he was about to commit a murder. He was waving a book in the air. 'I suppose you've seen this?' he demanded. 'Since it's your own souvenir book, you must have.'

I looked at it, and saw it was the programme for the Tokyo engagements. 'Not yet,' I told him. 'We were picking it up this morning but we were distracted.'

'I would just like to know why Janet Lynn has a whole page to herself, when Dorothy is stuck on a page with a skater no one ever heard of!'

I looked in horror, realizing that the promoters had completely ignored our instructions. 'Michael, I'm sorry,' I apologized. 'I had no idea this had happened.'

'Well, luckily for you Dorothy hasn't seen it yet, but if she finds out, I'm warning you, the shit will hit the fan. She'll probably refuse to skate.'

I had a thumping headache and I was already late for a meeting. 'Michael, we both know this wasn't deliberate. Try to keep it quiet for now, because it's too late to change it. I'll make sure she gets a really splendid build-up when she performs.'

The rest of the day passed in a blur of activity and at five o'clock I went to my room to lie down for an hour. The sponsors had arranged a dinner for everyone in the evening and I needed some quiet time first. I set my alarm and fell into a deep sleep. When I awoke, the room was dark and I felt my mattress vibrating. I thought it must be an electronic massage mechanism that I had turned on accidentally. I felt the side of the bed for a switch, but could find nothing. The vibrations were getting stronger, so I knelt on the floor to see if I could find any way to turn it off. It was then that I realized, with sickening clarity, that I was in the middle of an earthquake.

The floor literally rolled and buckled beneath my knees. The walls themselves appeared to be moving inwards, and the furniture slid across the room and back again in wild disarray. I was cold with terror and clung to the bed, praying for it to stop. I thought for one terrible moment that I was going to be crushed to death in a pile of concrete with no time to say goodbye to my family. Then, after what seemed hours, it stopped. There were a couple of brief hiccups and everything was still again. The power had gone, so I could see nothing. I crawled on to the bed and lay there with my heart hammering furiously. I wondered what had happened to the others, if the rest of the building was still standing.

Shortly afterwards, the power came on again and I began to dress. There was a hammering on my door and David stood outside, his face the colour of wet putty. 'I got caught in the elevator when it happened,' he said. 'I'm still shaking. I had no idea what was going on – the lights went out and the elevator was swaying from side to side. The floor was tilting – I thought I was going to die.' Gradually we heard from all the skaters, most of whom had run outside when it started. They had stood in the wind, shivering and waiting for it to pass. Janet, on the other hand, had been in a television station, waiting to be interviewed about the show. When the earthquake hit, she screamed and started to sob. 'I'll never see my babies again!' she wailed. Later, she told us that the Japanese took no notice of the quake, but simply continued to go about their business as if nothing was happening.

I found John in his room. He was calm, and offered me a drink. 'I think I might,' I said. 'Let me have one of the miniature brandies.' John handed one to me and took one for himself. He sipped at it thoughtfully.

'You know, it gives you a completely different perspective on things when something like that happens. All the things one worries about on a daily basis become unimportant, and only survival matters. It made me realize how silly I was being, yet the awful thing is that it will all revert once it's died down. I suppose that's why wars bring out the best in people.'

The time came for the company to go down to the stadium for the orchestra rehearsal. They piled into a huge bus and JoJo remembered to invite John to sit with her. She hugged him as he sat down and offered him a piece of fudge. 'This is so exciting!' she bubbled, her eyes shining. John was suddenly aware of the other skaters around him, and the air of anticipation that pervaded the bus. 'I'd almost forgotten what this must mean to you all,' he said to JoJo. 'You've all worked so hard for this. I mustn't let anything spoil it for you.'

At the Yoyogi, John was pleased by the trouble Jack seemed to have taken to make the dressing rooms comfortable and attractive. He had even included portable heaters to make sure that they were warm. They changed into their rehearsal clothes and went out to the ice. What they saw there made them gasp.

The vast space had been transformed. Across one end was built a magnificent plexiglass stage, lit with miniature bulbs embedded in the floor. It was multi-level, and on each surface sat musicians dressed in tuxedos. Charles Barker stood at the front of the structure, beaming happily, and overhead hung a huge array of lighting equipment. When the skaters were out on the ice, ready for the opening number, Charles raised his baton and the music filled the stadium, its magnificent tones rolling around the building. It soared and swept across everyone and transported them. John turned to me and said, 'This is what it's all about!' There were tears in his eyes, but this time they were tears of happiness. Part of his dream was now fulfilled.

The sponsors had spent a fortune preparing for the shows. In addition to all the follow-spots and other lighting equipment, they had brought in Japan's leading laser company to light Laura Dean's 'Burn'. I expected John to react badly to this creative assumption, but he was in an expansive mood. He watched as the technicians demonstrated the many possibilities offered by lasers, and laughed as the skaters raced around, jumping over the beams and being 'chased' by them.

'I would like to do a laser ballet one day,' he said, 'where I would choreograph to the lasers, instead of the other way around. The lasers would become animated characters, interacting with the skaters. It would be marvellous fun. I can hear some really lively music – maybe Scott Joplin.'

The stadium was packed for the show. Everyone was filled with nervous energy, pacing around behind the stage, trying to keep limber. The orchestra started to play the overture and I felt a chill of excitement.

31

The brother of the Emperor of Japan attended the opening show, and I was asked to go and sit with him in the front row of the stands. He was a slightly built man, very polite and with a sweet smile. He had once been a champion ice dancer, and he told me he had admired John Curry since he watched him win the Olympic Games. Also in the stands was the prima ballerina from the Tokyo Ballet, who had sent five dozen red roses to John that morning.

The show was a brilliant success, and the normally reserved Japanese audience were lavish in their praise. Dorothy skated with great flair and style and Michael was satisfied with the grandeur of her introduction. At one point I excused myself to see how things were going backstage, and John asked: 'Why are we having verbal introductions for every skater? I would much rather they didn't do that.' But Jack assured him it was Japanese custom and he accepted his explanation. When it was time for John and Janet to skate together, I returned to my seat.

As the lights dimmed, Janet and John appeared in the centre of the ice. There was a gasp and the building erupted in applause. They were skating to an extract from Tchaikovsky's *Nutcracker* suite, and for eight minutes they held the audience in thrall. They were so perfectly suited to each other, and their every movement was synchronized instinctively. The passion between them was palpable, and John lifted Janet with a mixture of strength and tenderness, in the manner of the great *danseurs nobles*. When they finished, they seemed unaware of the crowd, and remained for several minutes clasped together in a private embrace.

John was in his dressing room when the intermission entertainment was announced. Emi Watanabe was a popular star in Japan, and everyone stayed in their seats until she had finished skating. John was blissfully unaware of the addition to the programme, and it passed without incident. 'What he doesn't know won't hurt him,' said Rita. 'No harm done.'

I decided to relax and enjoy the second half of the programme. I sat beside the Emperor's brother again, and he told me how much he had enjoyed John's duet with Janet. 'I have seen nothing more beautiful, even at the ballet,' he said. Suddenly there was a commotion at the top of the stairs. Michael came running down and pulled at my arm. 'I need to see you urgently,' he hissed. I followed him backstage and he pointed to a television monitor. 'It's bad enough that this is being covered live,' he said, holding up his hand to stop me from interrupting. 'Let's put that on one side for the moment. What I want to know is, what are those numbers running in the corner of the screen?'

'What numbers?' I said blankly.

John and JoJo on a glacier in the Rockies *(Martha Swope)*

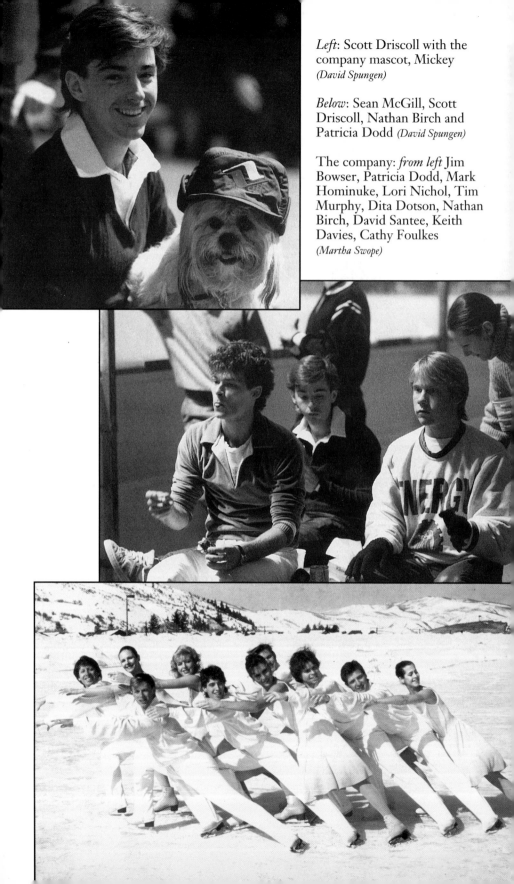

Left: Scott Driscoll with the company mascot, Mickey
(David Spungen)

Below: Sean McGill, Scott Driscoll, Nathan Birch and Patricia Dodd *(David Spungen)*

The company: *from left* Jim Bowser, Patricia Dodd, Mark Hominuke, Lori Nichol, Tim Murphy, Dita Dotson, Nathan Birch, David Santee, Keith Davies, Cathy Foulkes
(Martha Swope)

Kevin Kossi *(David Spungen)*

Rob McBrien *(David Spungen)*

John working with Cathy, Patricia, Dita and Scott *(David Spungen)*

Left: John outside the Metropolitan Opera House, New York, July 1984
(*Judy Hammond*)

Above: Curtain call at the Met
(*Judy Hammond*)

Below: John and JoJo perform a 'death spiral' in the *Skaters' Waltz* at the Met (*Judy Hammond*)

John skating to the
Moonlight Sonata in
Vancouver, 1983
(Christie Jenkins)

(Martha Swope)

John with the author
(Chung Young Kim)

Above: *En route* to Washington, August 1984
(David Spungen)

In discussion with Jane Herman *(Chung Young Kim)*

John in hospital with toxoplasmosis,
early 1994 *(Daily Mail/Solo)*

Rita and John at home in Binton
(Daily Mail/Solo)

Overleaf: The Albert Hall
(Peter Bolton)

'*Those* numbers,' Michael answered, 'the ones that go up and down every time there is any applause.'

By this time David had joined us and as soon as he saw the monitor he said, 'Oh my God! They're running an applause meter.'

'Thank you, David,' Michael said sarcastically. 'You don't seriously expect me to believe you didn't know this was happening, do you?'

'Know *what* was happening?' I asked.

Michael laughed. 'Oh please, Elva – you're intelligent. What is usually happening when there's an applause meter? It's a fucking competition, that's what it is. And I hope Jack Sakazaki has a good lawyer, because he's going to need one.' He paced furiously up and down, puffing on his small cigar. 'It's too late to stop Dorothy going on, or I would have,' he fumed.

Jack was talking to some of the television people in the corridor. I told him about Michael's outburst and asked him if it was true. 'Of course,' Jack said. 'It's the only way to sell it to television. It's no big deal – just based on the audience reactions.'

Dorothy was skating one of the pieces John had created for her at the Queen's rink in London. It was a character number, set to *Pennies from Heaven*. Her performance was charming, skated with total conviction, and she was obviously enjoying herself. When it ended, the ice was covered in red roses, thrown by the army of admirers who had come to see her. She bent impulsively to pick one up, skated over to the orchestra stage and handed it to Charles with a dazzling smile. The audience rose to their feet and gave her a thunderous ovation, and the orchestra joined in. The applause meter shot to the top of the monitor screen and stayed there. Dorothy had won the TV Asahi Competition.

Michael and I watched this together on the monitor, and he turned to me with a wide grin. 'You just got lucky,' he chuckled. 'If she'd lost you would have seen a very different side of Miss Hamill!' He stubbed out his cigar. 'Well, I'd better go and congratulate my little poopsie.' He turned in the doorway and added: 'We'll talk tomorrow about the additional fee – Dorothy wasn't hired to take part in a competition. *Sayonara!*'

The sponsors had arranged a dinner for us at our hotel, and had invited several Tokyo celebrities. JoJo arrived early, wearing a stunning silk suit, and Rita wafted around the room exuding gusts of exotic perfume. Dorothy came, with Dino, closely followed by

Michael and Nancy. Dorothy seemed to be completely at ease and enjoying the attention she commanded. Janet arrived, wearing an ice-blue chiffon dress which seemed to float as she walked, and one by one the company members came in, each with a mystique and an elegance of carriage that immediately placed them apart. Dino took me to one side. 'I don't know what John is doing with them, but I can't get over the difference! They all look so self-assured.'

We were served some very expensive champagne and talked animatedly with the sponsors. Suddenly I realized that John had not come. David rang his room and got a continual busy signal.

'Perhaps you should go up and get him,' I suggested. 'Jack will be royally pissed off if he doesn't come and meet the sponsors.'

David phoned John's room again from the lobby, but he still got a busy signal. He asked the telephone operator if the phone was possibly out of order. 'No sir,' she said, 'he's taken it off the hook.' David went up to his room and knocked on the door. There was no answer. He knocked louder and a muffled voice shouted: 'Go away.'

'John, it's David,' he called through the door. 'Why don't you let me in for a minute?'

'Go away and leave me alone,' came John's muffled voice again. David was alarmed. This didn't feel right. He went down to the manager's office and talked him into giving him a duplicate key, and raced back up to John's room. This time he could hear the distinct sound of sobbing. He put the key in the door and opened it slowly. 'John?' he called softly.

There was no answer and in the semi-darkness he could see John lying on his bed, curled into a foetal position. His eyes were wide open, staring wildly ahead of him. David crossed the room and sat on the edge of the bed. He touched John's shoulder gently. His body was shaking, but there were no tears on his face. In front of him, on his bedside table, there was a half-empty bottle of vodka, a bottle of pills and a framed drawing of Jesus wearing the crown of thorns. 'John, talk to me. Tell me what's going on.' There was no response. 'I'm not leaving here until I know what this is all about,' David said. He pulled one of the small armchairs up to the bed and sat in it. John focused on him slowly, recognized him and reached a hand towards him.

'Hold my hand, just for a minute. I'm afraid.' The tears came, running unheeded down his face, and he let out his breath in a long, shuddering gasp.

John began to talk to David; haltingly at first, then with the words tumbling out faster than he could pronounce them. He told him that he felt this deep depression every year at this time. 'You see, my father died at New Year, almost twenty years ago, and I can't seem to get over this terrible feeling that I'm lost. Alone. I get so scared, but I don't know why.' He stopped.

'Go on,' David whispered.

'Well, this year it seems to be worse. I feel I can't continue to fight. It's all much too painful and there's nothing left for me. No reason to go on living. If you hadn't come, I was going to take the pills. There were enough there . . .' David put his arms around John and held him as the sobs started again. When the spasms had finally subsided, he handed him a tissue and asked if he would like a bath and a cup of coffee. 'No,' John said quietly. 'I'm too tired. I need to sleep. Will you please stay with me?'

'Yes,' David said. 'I'll be right here in this chair. I won't go away. You're quite safe.' John pulled the duvet over his head and curled up beneath it. In a very short time, he was sleeping soundly.

When David failed to come back, I realized that something must be wrong. I went to the sponsors and told them that John had sent his apologies and asked if they would excuse him. 'He's ill,' I said, 'and he wanted to rest so he would be fit to skate tomorrow. I hope you understand.' They were very sympathetic, and John was hardly missed at the dinner.

By twelve-thirty I was back in my room, wondering what I should do. Then the phone rang. It was David, speaking so quietly that I could barely make out what he was saying. 'I'm staying here with John,' he whispered. 'I can't explain now, but he was in a bad way. I'm staying here, just to make sure he's OK. Don't worry – if I need you, I'll call.'

David fell asleep in the chair, and when he opened his eyes again John was standing in front of him holding out a cup of coffee. 'Here,' he smiled. 'It's just one of those instant things, but it's hot. You didn't hear me get up. I hope there's never a fire in your bedroom – you wouldn't hear the alarm!' John sat on the edge of his bed while David gratefully sipped his coffee. 'I shall never forget what you did for me last night,' he said. 'I'm not sure what would have happened if you hadn't come. But I feel better now, and I think I'll be all right. Why don't you go back to your room and see if you can get some sleep?'

David stood up and stretched. 'Sounds good to me,' he said. 'But just satisfy my curiosity on one score.'

'Ask anything,' John said quietly.

'Why the Jesus picture? I didn't have any idea you were religious.'

'I'm not,' he answered. 'But I do believe in something, and somehow that picture makes me feel safe. I'm not sure why.'

John came down to breakfast looking refreshed. Charles called out to him, 'We were just talking about how well the show went last night.' John sat down beside him. 'I thought so too. But you were the real star of the night. You made that orchestra sound fantastic!'

Later that day, David and I met with West Nally. Jack was in a peculiar mood, possibly because he sensed I was furious about the competition. I didn't wait for the usual formalities before I came to the point. 'How could you possibly put us in a situation where you ran a competition on our performance without even warning us it was going to happen? Did you take us for complete fools? Were you hoping we wouldn't notice so you didn't have to pay us any extra money?'

Jack became angry at this point. 'We don't have to pay extra money,' he yelled. 'This engagement has cost us so much already that we needed every cent we could make to cover it. You have to calm down and understand the economics of the situation, or we'll never survive as a viable company.' I stopped. I knew it must have been very expensive, and also that an orchestra like the New Japan Philharmonic would cost a fortune. I apologized.

'But you should have warned us,' I said. 'That wasn't a good idea.'

Jack had asked that John join us for lunch, and we met in the coffee bar of our hotel. We sat at a corner table by the window, and John thanked Jack for making our visit so comfortable. He asked a lot of questions about West Nally and the sort of things they normally handled. Over coffee, Jack said, 'Next year we need to do this a little differently. Your company was well received, but it lacks anything to attract children. I would like it next year if you could have a children's number, and also a comedy number. People expect it. It needs more variety. It's a bit too precious.'

'That's your opinion, is it?' John asked icily. 'Well, I suppose you're entitled to it, but you will have to forgive me if I don't share it.' I could feel his temper rising and I turned to Jack in disbelief. 'You must be joking, surely?' I demanded. 'You know John's company can't do the sort of things they do in the *Ice Capades*. I think you've probably just put it badly.'

Jack stared at me and finally seemed to understand what I was trying to tell him. 'John, you have to forgive me,' he said. 'I didn't mean to imply that you should have a variety show, just that you might need a little more variation in mood – after all, most of the ballet companies do humorous pieces as well as serious ones.'

John looked thoughtful. 'I've been thinking about doing something humorous for all the men in the company – a Western piece. And I would also like to do something based on Hans Christian Andersen. Is that what you had in mind?'

'Exactly,' Jack told him. 'We'll talk about it further nearer to the time.'

There was no performance that night, because New Year's Eve is a major holiday in Japan. Rita, Nathan, Timmy and JoJo ran into John and Janet in the lobby of the hotel just before eleven, and persuaded them to come with them to find a club. The concierge overheard them. 'No good tonight,' he warned. 'All booked up. You will never get in.' They decided to try anyway, and followed directions to a place Jack had recommended. At the door, John and Nathan approached the doorman, who waved his arms. 'Full up,' he told them. Just then, he saw Janet standing behind them and his face lit up. 'Janet Rynn!' he said, delighted. 'You come with me, please! Best table for your party.' Astonished, they followed him through the club to a very good table. Champagne was brought immediately, and all the waiters came over and bowed several times. Finally the manager arrived. 'Everything compliments of the house!' he said. 'We are honoured to have you as our guest.' It was a memorable evening for all of them, and John danced with Janet until well after three o'clock. He walked her back to her room afterwards and kissed her on the cheek. 'We have something very special, you and I,' he told her. 'If things had been different, I think we could have spent our lives together.'

32

As the plane descended into Honolulu Airport, we saw the Hawaiian Islands stretched out below us, lush green jewels set in the expanse of azure sea. The skaters were all buzzing with excitement, and craning their necks to get a glimpse of Diamond Head. John, however, was sitting alone in the rear of the plane with his eyes closed.

In the terminal, Jack was waiting to greet us. He was wearing a colourful Hawaiian shirt, and two young girls placed *lei*s round everyone's neck. Music wafted from the loudspeakers, and everything felt relaxed. Outside, the air was balmy and humid, and jackets were removed and stored in the overhead racks of the bus. 'This is fabulous!' said David Santee happily. John, who had barely been civil to Jack, again took the seat at the very back of the bus. The skaters were so used to John's moods by now that they took no notice of him. It was just John being eccentric, and if it didn't interfere with them they weren't concerned about it.

The bus sped past massive, contemporary hotel complexes, all glass and hanging plants: the Hilton, the Sheraton, the Marriott. About twenty minutes later, we came to a sprawling, low-slung group of buildings situated to the north of Honolulu. 'This is it!' Jack shouted cheerfully. 'Let me go and register.' Richard allocated rooms to everyone and cases were moved in from the bus. John emerged, looking tired, and asked for his key. 'I'll take you to your room,' said Richard.

'That won't be necessary, thank you. I'm quite capable of finding my own room.' And John reached for his case and disappeared down one of the passages.

It was not a luxury hotel, but it was bright and clean. Some of the skaters had rooms with little balconies, and this pleased them. Suddenly John came thundering down the corridor, clutching his suitcase. He bore down on Jack with such ferocity that Jack almost fell backwards. 'How *dare* you insult my company in this way!' he screamed. 'This hotel is abhorrent. We won't stay here a moment longer, and if you don't find us somewhere decent to stay before the next flight leaves for Denver, we shall not be keeping our engagement here. Is that understood?' He swept round and stormed out of the building, leaving a very startled hotel manager in his wake.

Jack was livid. 'This is your problem,' he said. 'This hotel is perfectly adequate for dance companies and orchestras, but it seems it's not good enough for His Lordship. I'll book him into the Hilton, but I want you to know that West Nally has no intention of paying for it. It will have to come out of your Hawaiian fee.' Everyone crowded back on to the bus and we set off back towards the beach area. John sat glowering in the back, and Jack was in the front, equally furious. Things seemed to be getting worse.

Jack managed to get rooms for everyone in the Hilton. Dorothy, Dino and the Rosenbergs were also staying there, although this time it was at their own expense. They were making a vacation out of the Hawaiian engagement and staying an extra week touring the islands. When John spotted them in the lobby, he came over to me. 'Isn't it a rather strange coincidence that they just happen to be staying here too?' he said. 'Did we put them in here?'

'No, we didn't,' I told him. 'They're paying for it themselves.'

John snorted. 'You don't have to lie to me,' he said. 'I know we're paying for them, and I also know Jack Sakazaki was trying to palm the real skaters off with a backwoods hotel.'

John was allocated an enormous room with a magnificent picture window overlooking the entire Pacific panorama. On the table were fruit, flowers, champagne and piles of the latest magazines. He put his suitcase down without bothering to unpack, crossed to the windows and looked out briefly at the view. Below him, on the hotel driveway, Nathan, Timmy, Mark and Keith were sauntering down towards the beach. He watched until they were out of sight, then he drew the curtains and climbed into bed. The loneliness was closing in again.

The flight carrying our ice generator had been delayed by several hours, costing us valuable preparation time. When it did arrive, it was not secured properly for the unloading process and was dropped on the tarmac. It sustained an ominous crack across the back, and Enrico Kossi was fearful that it would affect its performance. In the ninety-degree heat, it would take the generator running at full power to make ice. He promised to call us as soon as he knew the situation.

When the call came, the news was not good. The generator was running below capacity, and as a result Enrico had been forced to reduce the size of the ice surface. He felt that sixty by fifty feet was the maximum it could handle. I expressed concern about John's reactions, but Enrico waved this aside. 'John is a professional – he will understand. It's all we can do. He'll just have to change things around to fit.'

We had to delay the performance by one day because of the changes. The company couldn't appear without a rehearsal, and in order to rehearse they had to wait for the ice to freeze. The promoter seemed to accept the situation graciously, and the only problem was the cost of an extra night in the hotel. The skaters were delighted to spend more time at the beach. John, however, was incensed about the size of the ice surface. 'You promised me it would be full-sized,' he yelled.

'John, we have a cracked generator. It won't freeze a bigger area. We're just going to have to manage.'

'Then *you* do it!' he retorted. 'You go and restage it if you think it's so easy. I refuse to make a fool of myself on a postage stamp.'

I bit my tongue. 'The ice should be ready by three o'clock this afternoon,' I told him. 'The bus leaves for rehearsal at two-thirty, so I'll see you then.'

I went into the coffee shop and ordered a sandwich. Cathy and JoJo came to sit with me, and were full of the beauty of the island. 'It's hard to believe we're really here,' said Cathy. 'Some of us are planning to stay on here for a week after the show's finished and see the islands.' They talked enthusiastically about London and Dubai, and the Met season. They told me they felt as though they belonged to a very special group, and they were proud of the company. They avoided the subject of John, and I was grateful for that. I wasn't at all sure how we were going to cope with his latest outburst.

At two-thirty, John was nowhere to be found. He had simply disappeared. David was furious. 'I've just about had it with John,' he sighed. 'Every time I think we're back on track, this happens. He doesn't seem to give a hot damn about anyone else but himself.'

'You don't mean that,' I said quietly. 'You know how much he's hurting. He doesn't want to be like this.'

'Right now *I'm* hurting,' David said bitterly. 'And so should you be. Instead of us taking a week's holiday here, like everyone else, we have to go back to New York and try to find the extra money from somewhere. God knows how we'll get it.'

'Maybe Jack will do it, if the show goes well,' I said hopefully.

The company went off to the Blaisdell Arena with David. John had not appeared. The skaters were going to do their best to restage their numbers themselves, and Dorothy (who was used to skating on small ice) had offered to help them. I searched everywhere for John, hunting all over the beaches and hotels. No one remembered seeing him and finally, exhausted, I decided to stop. I took the lift to the revolving restaurant at the top of the hotel, to see if I could get some early dinner there. I was starving and I wanted time to sit by myself and think.

As I walked out of the lift, I saw that the restaurant was closed. It was still revolving, but the waiters' stations were all deserted. I turned to go back to the lobby, but as I did so I suddenly caught sight of John, seated bolt-upright at one of the window tables, slowly moving past the Honolulu skyline. It was like a scene from a Fellini movie.

I crossed to the table and sat down opposite him. He didn't appear to notice me. He was staring fixedly into space. I reached out cautiously and covered his hands, which were clasped together in front of him. 'John?' I said softly. 'Are you all right?' He seemed to become aware of me then, and his eyes filled with tears.

'Please,' he said. 'Please take me away from here. I can't do this any more. I don't want to have a company. I can't cope with it.' He looked at me beseechingly. 'You don't understand. None of you does. I'm so lonely. Everyone has someone else, but I don't. You have your family, and David. The skaters have each other.' He choked back sobs. 'I'm all alone,' he said sadly.

I felt tears pricking at my own eyes, and I wished I knew the right thing to say to him. 'You aren't alone, John,' I told him. '*We*'re your family. We love you. I wish you could believe that.'

He looked forlorn. 'But everyone expects me to be so capable, so strong. It's so hard sometimes to have everyone relying on me. I always have to be responsible, even when I feel like walking away from it.'

I looked at him for a moment. 'John, don't you think we feel the same way sometimes? That's part of being who we are. There are moments when David and I would like to throw up our hands and run away, but we can't do that. We made a pact, the three of us – remember? That we would stick together, no matter what.'

He was quiet for what seemed like a long time. Then he said:

'You know that's what I really want. I don't know why I get into these terrible moods. I do try not to, but sometimes it's as though someone else were inside me, making me say things.' He brightened a little then and added: 'Let's try to put this behind us. I'll make sure the performance goes well tomorrow.'

While we were sitting there, the restaurant opened again and I said to John, 'We are going to have a truly marvellous dinner for once – with some very expensive wine. I think we've earned it!'

After dinner, I left John watching a movie in his room, and went in search of David. He was prowling around the lobby. 'I've been worried sick,' he told me. I started to tell him what had happened, but he stopped me. 'No,' he said. 'Not now. You and I are going down to the beach, and we're going to sit in one of those expensive outdoor cafés and have two piña coladas and watch Diamond Head until the light goes. We never see anything but hotels and airports, and I need to do this for my own sanity.'

We sat there, watching the sky glow red and orange and gold. 'I think I shall always remember this,' I said. 'A moment of real peace in the middle of such constant chaos. Why do we do it?'

David sighed. 'Because we love it,' he said.

I flew back to New York the next morning, to keep a pre-arranged appointment with the Met. David stayed with Enrico and Kevin at the Blaisdell until he was sure the ice had settled. Then he went to find John. He was in bed. The curtains were drawn, and he opened the door to David reluctantly. 'I have to warn you, I am feeling terrible,' he said. 'I don't feel I can go to the rehearsal.'

David made him some coffee and pulled back the curtains. He could see then that John had been crying. His eyes were red and swollen. 'Elva told me you were feeling better last night,' David said in surprise. 'What happened?'

'It just keeps coming back. I feel better for a while, and then everything seems to close in again. I don't think I can skate today. Can't the company perform without me?'

'No, John, they can't,' David said quietly. 'You know that. They aren't ready to be weaned yet, but that day will come eventually. Then you'll be able to rest.'

The skaters had done an excellent job of rearranging the choreography, and John managed to alter his own solos quite easily. When the actual show took place, the audience was thrilled by the proximity of the ice surface. As their blades cut deep into the corners, the skaters kicked up a spray of ice which showered the front rows. 'You know,' John said, as he watched David Santee performing his 'Russian Sailor's Dance' from *The Red Poppy*, 'this size of ice has its own advantages. It makes everything look terribly exciting.'

Most of the skaters stayed on in Hawaii, but John flew back to New York immediately after the performance. He came to see David and me in our office the following morning. 'I want to talk,' he said. 'I'm not upset and I'm not depressed, but I have something important I need to discuss with you.'

He told us that part of his problem was with the constant necessity to marry his own artistic values to the dictates of the commercial world. 'I understand that everyone has their own agenda,' he said, 'but I need to work only with people who understand and support mine. Some time ago, Elva brought up the subject of not-for-profit status. I believe that is the only hope for this company to succeed, because it will enable us to shed all the materialistic promoters who are only around to see if they can make a buck out of us. If we go forward, it has to be just the three of us. No Steve Leber, no Michael Cohl, and certainly not those Japanese people. I won't work with Jack Sakazaki again.' I looked at David and smiled.

'Well,' he said, 'it's just us then. We'll start filing for not-for-profit status today, and we'll find a way to get out from under West Nally.'

'Just one thing,' I interjected. 'If we continue, John, it has to be on the understanding that you stay with the company until it can stand alone. Will you do that? Because it can't exist without you. Not yet.'

'If you can arrange charitable status for us,' he answered, 'I will give it three or four more years before I stop skating. Then I want to stop and concentrate on directing it. That, and running a school.' Then he added: 'But I need a commitment from you, too. The company needs you both just as much as it needs me.'

'This company has become our lives,' I told him. 'You know we'll stay with it.'

When he had gone, David and I wondered how we would handle Jack. West Nally, as well as Lewis Rappaport and Bob Harley, had legal ownership in *Symphony on Ice*, and we wouldn't be able simply to walk away from them. 'I can deal with Lewis,' David said. 'I'll find some way to make it right with him. And you know Bob will understand.'

'What about West Nally?' I asked.

'Screw West Nally,' he said. 'I'll bet they already made their money back in Japan.'

John had made it clear that in order to do the Albert Hall engagement, he would need nine further weeks of rehearsal to prepare. We had no idea how we were going to pay for them, but figured we could probably get enough in advances to cover the costs. John also told us he desperately needed someone to help him prepare the company, an assistant artistic director who was capable of taking over if John happened to be away. He recommended a young American called Rob McBrien, who was currently teaching at the Sky Rink in New York. 'He would be ideal,' John told us. 'He understands exactly what I am trying to accomplish and he is a wonderful teacher. I have already spoken with him, and if you agree he can start immediately.'

That weekend, everyone flew back to Vail and I went to meet with Laura Dean's lawyer, Jerome Landau, who specialized in not-for-profit companies. He promised to set the wheels in motion for us. Margaret Carson was delighted with our decision. 'Gives you a much better aura,' she said. 'I can do a lot with that. First ice company to be non-profit, first to play the Met . . . It's all solid stuff. We can announce it at the press conference.'

'When will that be?' I asked.

'Early February. I thought about the seventh. John will need to come back and bring two of his best skaters. I thought we could freeze the Reflecting Pond in Lincoln Center and have a short performance there. Then we would go into the Met itself for warm drinks and a question-and-answer period with the media.'

The rehearsals went very well, and David phoned to tell me that everyone seemed in high spirits. On 6 February, John, Patricia and Mark flew in to New York for the press conference. As they landed, it started to snow heavily, and the forecast was for intermittent snow showers alternating with high winds. 'Wonderful!' John said sarcastically. 'Jack Sakazaki must have arranged it with God.'

Over at Lincoln Center, Enrico was battling with the elements. He was not having an easy time of it. When I went to see how he was getting on, it was eight o'clock in the evening and he was standing in the empty pool with a brush and shovel. The snow had stopped, but the high wind was blowing shoals of leaves into the hole. 'Why didn't you just freeze the water that was in there?' I asked.

'If I do that, it expands bigger than the pool,' he explained. 'Then the sides go crack, and the big statue, he explodes.' It was bitterly cold, and Enrico was fortifying himself with swigs from a large brandy bottle. The conference was set for noon the next day, and I was concerned that the ice would not be ready in time. 'Don't worry!' beamed Enrico. 'It will be ready.'

By seven in the morning, the ice was still a soggy mass. Enrico had fallen into a stupor in his car and Kevin, his seventeen-year-old son, had taken over. ('Dad's exhausted,' he explained.) He worked furiously, pumping Freon through the miles of spaghetti-shaped piping coiled in the bottom of the pond. He directed a continuous fine spray of water on to the pipes until he had built up half an inch of ice. By eleven-thirty it was still soft, but it was just about skatable.

Margaret Carson had assembled the *crème de la crème* of the media world for the conference. Tony Bliss, the Managing Director of the Met, rushed about nervously wondering what Jane had let him in for. John, Patricia and Mark skated elegantly considering the treacherous surface that lay beneath their blades. They glided round the great Henry Moore edifice and by the time they had finished every journalist there was intrigued by the potential of the summer engagement. The next day the papers were full of it, including a front-page spread in the *Times*.

33

On 14 February John and JoJo sent out cards to everyone who had been helpful to the company wishing them a happy Valentine's Day. On the front was a photograph of a happy, smiling company dressed in their red and white *William Tell* outfits. Jean-Pierre Bonnefous went to Vail to make two pieces for the company, a *pas de deux* for

Mark and Cathy and a long version of Ravel's *La Valse*, for eleven skaters.

There were several works-in-progress performances in Vail, which were enthusiastically received, and some of the local luminaries expressed an interest in helping the company to establish their charitable status.

JoJo and John went skiing together and developed a comfortable rapport which translated on to the ice. They could often be seen coming home from the slopes, hand in hand. David, torn between worrying about the possibility of them sustaining injuries and the ever-present threat of John's destructive depressions, opted to condone the ski trips. In the end he felt it was better to take the risk than to have John wither away in miserable isolation. He kept me in the dark about it, however. 'You would have been like the proverbial mother hen!' he explained.

In mid-February, I flew down to Vail to see how the company was progressing. They staged a full run-through of the Albert Hall programme for me, and I found the level of the work to be vastly improved. The ensemble itself had matured and the twenty-minute piece John had choreographed for them, set to Glazunov's *The Seasons*, showed them off to perfection. The skaters were dressed in simple, flowing white costumes, and the work explained the full potential of skating, from the most simplistic to the most complex movements. It was, appropriately, called 'Glides'.

John seemed to be relaxed and happy. He was looking forward to being in front of a London audience again, and felt the company was evolving well. They were, however, prone to rumours. 'They're like any group,' he told me. 'If you don't keep telling them what's happening, they imagine the worst.' I decided to gather them together before I left and tell them about the not-for-profit decision, that we wanted to operate as a charitable organization. It was the only way for the company to have artistic autonomy. There was a round of applause at this announcement, and then John stepped forward unexpectedly. 'I realize I may have given you some bad moments recently, and I hope you will forgive me for that. But I just wanted you to know that my commitment to this company is absolute, and I will do my best to keep it all together.'

In New York, Mark and Sara Grayson, two young friends of Bill's, came forward to help us work out an appeal to charitable institutions who were known to support the arts. Mark took a great deal of trouble to prepare a fully detailed and indexed document which captured perfectly our aims and potential. They felt strongly that a core of young supporters could be nurtured, and also encouraged us to place a coupon in all our souvenir programmes, asking people who liked the work to send us their name and address so that we could keep them informed of the company's plans. This would enable us to establish a mailing list of Friends of the John Curry Skating Company.

The new air of well-being which suffused the company was to be shattered again. David got up one morning to drive to rehearsals and found a note pushed under his door. It said: 'Dear David: I quit. I am sorry to let you down like this, but I simply can't go on. Please forgive me, and thank you for all you have done. Love, John.' Horrified, David drove to John's apartment. John was standing in the living room, surrounded by suitcases. He was waiting for a taxi to take him to Denver.

'John? What happened?' David said wearily. It seemed that nothing could last. 'We need to talk. There is so much at stake.'

'I'm leaving,' John said flatly. 'I can't do this, David. It's too much for me – I don't think the work merits the fuss that's being made, and everyone in England is going to be baying for blood. Look what the critics did to Robin last year. Don't think it will be any different for me.'

David lost his temper. He took hold of John and propelled him to the sofa. 'Sit down!' he commanded. 'Listen to me for a minute, and then you can go on your way if you still choose to.' He glared at John fiercely. 'I am tired of hearing about your problems and your concerns about yourself. I don't hear you being concerned about the skaters. Yes, you made Jack give them a better hotel, but you didn't stop to think what that might do to them in the long run, whether the cost would affect their future! Because it well could. And you didn't stop to think about how it would affect Elva and me – she's up in New York still trying to find that money. You wanted nine weeks' rehearsal for the Albert Hall, but when push comes to shove you tell me you're throwing it all back in our faces because you're afraid of what the critics might say. Well, let me tell you, I think it stinks. And I am deeply disappointed in you. I don't think you deserve to have a company, and you certainly don't merit our own commitment to you. We have given up all our other involvements to follow what we believed was your dream. Now, when we are too far down the track to turn back, we find out it was a fantasy all along.' David walked to the door. His eyes were blazing. 'If you want to leave, you go right ahead and do it. Quite frankly I think it would be for the best. I don't think you're worth all the sacrifices.'

He slammed out of the door, got into the car and drove home. When he had stopped shaking, he phoned me at the office. 'Elva, I think I've just destroyed the company,' he told me. 'I blew up at John and I think he will be terminally offended. But what I told him was the truth – I couldn't let him continue to affect our lives in this way. It would be better if it just shut down.' He told me he would call me as soon as he knew anything, and I waited until eight o'clock, trying to concentrate on other things. Finally the phone rang. 'John came round,' David said happily. 'He apologized and we've hugged and made up. I think things might be better now.'

In early March, the celebrated ballet photographer Martha Swope flew down to Vail to photograph the company for Margaret Carson. She wanted to do some on-ice pictures, as well as some informal portraits of John and some unusual outdoor shots on one of the mountain lakes. The evening of her arrival there was a works-in-progress performance, and David drove her to the arena to watch. Afterwards, she was to shoot the company on the ice while the lights were still hung. The performance was late starting, and David went back to see what was going on. 'John's not here,' said Richard. At that moment, John arrived, looking flustered and unkempt. He hurriedly pulled on his costume and his skates and tried to warm up. He looked ill, but chose not to speak to anyone. David didn't disturb him, but went back to his seat. The show was very well received and Martha was deeply impressed. 'Phenomenal,' she said. 'They are really magical.'

David went backstage to make sure the skaters were ready for the shoot. He found them in a knot outside the dressing room, and Mark said, 'John's in there. He's in a terrible state.' David went inside and saw John huddled in a corner, sobbing uncontrollably. Lori and JoJo were trying to comfort him, rubbing his shoulders and telling him how much everyone loved him. 'What's going on?' David demanded. 'You know Martha is waiting to take the photographs.'

Keith came forward and asked if he could talk to David privately. 'It's me,' he told him. 'I'm the reason John's so upset. He's been pestering me for a long time now.'

'About what?' David asked.

Keith looked embarrassed. 'He's in love with me,' he said. 'He wants me to go to bed with him.' David did a double-take. 'Oh, come on, guy! Get real!' Keith shook his head. 'It's true. It's been going on ever since I came into the company. Every time I reject him, he has a fit of depression. Remember Kalamazoo? Tokyo and Honolulu? Two weeks ago? He's threatened to kill himself several times. He's also threatened to fire me. I won't resign, David. I haven't done anything wrong.'

While David was trying to digest this revelation, John had been persuaded to go back out for the photo shoot. He was somewhat subdued, but helpful and co-operative. Martha seemed satisfied, and asked if she could see everyone the following morning for the open-air shoot. 'Can you wear the white outfits?' she asked. 'I like that look. And John – you wear black. Not costume, just everyday choreographer clothes. I want a contrast.' She seemed unaware of the backstage trauma.

At midnight there was a knock on David's door. It was John, bearing a bottle of vodka. 'Peace offering,' he said. When he had taken off his coat, he told David he wanted to clear the air. 'I know Keith has told you about our problems,' he said. 'I thought I should come and talk to you about it.'

'Why didn't you tell me before?' David asked. 'Why all the red herrings?'

John sighed. 'They weren't red herrings. That was all true. But I suppose because of Keith I wasn't able to cope with it. I felt too wretched.'

He started from the beginning, and told him how he had been attracted to Keith back in the early days of Pro Skate. He had brought him into the company thinking it would be nice for him to have a romantic interest around, but things hadn't worked out. 'I thought he liked me,' John said quietly. 'But he only went to bed with me because I was the Artistic Director of the company. I suppose he was afraid to say no. Then he got scared that it was getting too serious and he backed off completely. He wouldn't even have dinner with me. I used to beg him, but he always made an excuse. I made a fool of myself – I used to push letters under his door, telling him how much I loved him. It's all horribly embarrassing.'

David sat in silence for a while, trying to take it all in. Then he said: 'Did you threaten to fire him if he wouldn't sleep with you?'

John's face flushed. 'Yes, I did,' he whispered. 'You see, I can't bear to be around him under the circumstances, and you won't let me leave. The only other solution is for him to go.'

David shook his head. 'Surely not, John. We can't fire him. We don't have any grounds. We have to find a way to make it possible for him to stay until June, when his contract is up.'

'There's something else,' John said. 'He's got his lover here from Canada. That's what happened tonight. He brought him to the arena. I just couldn't stand it, seeing them together.'

'What if I could persuade him to keep the guy away altogether?'

'That would help,' John said. 'It would make it easier.'

'Then let's give it a try. Let's see if we can't find a way to get through the next few months. Concentrate on our work, all of us.'

'I want to,' John told him. 'I *am* going to try.'

David went to see Keith early the next morning. He told him he had spoken with John and that John had promised to leave him alone, providing he could promise one thing in return. 'What's that?' asked Keith.

'That you will not have your lover around the company.'

Keith looked annoyed. 'But it's nobody's business. He can't tell me how to run my personal life.'

'It's only for a few weeks, Keith. It's the only way this can resolve itself.'

David found Richard at the arena. 'I want to bring you up to date on some conversations I've been having with John and Keith,' he said.

'Let me stop you, David,' Richard said. 'I know all about it.'

'You do?'

'Sure – we've all known about it. In fact, a couple of weeks back the skaters all offered to pay Keith part of their salary if he would agree to sleep with John.'

David stared at Richard with his mouth open. 'That's horrible!' he said.

Richard shook his head. 'Not from where they were sitting. Their company was falling apart. They had to do something.'

Keith kept to his part of the bargain, and sent his friend back to Canada. John seemed to settle down well, and spent time in Denver with some friends of his. He flew back to New York one weekend and I met him for lunch in the Russian Tea Room on West 57th Street. 'It's so crass to come here,' he said. 'But it's fun every once in a while. Everyone comes to see who they can see, and they all end up seeing only each other!'

Afterwards we walked slowly down 57th Street, looking in shop windows. 'I wanted to tell you about a little problem I've been having with someone in the company,' he began, but I interrupted him.

'There's no need, unless you want to. I already knew about it. Keith, you mean?'

He looked surprised. 'Did David tell you?'

I shook my head. 'No – I had an intuition from the first day you met him. I knew it was going to happen. It's a shame, because he's terribly wrong for you.'

'I know,' John sighed. 'But I can't help it.'

'John,' I began. He looked at me. 'What about the AIDS tests? I've been so worried.'

He smiled. 'All clear. I've stopped having them now. You don't have to worry – I'm not a saint, but I will be very careful from now on.' For some reason, the words sent a cold shiver down my back. I sensed that he wasn't being entirely honest with me.

34

The Royal Albert Hall was built in 1886. It is a unique building, like a cross between a cathedral and an opera house, and the red velvet boxes rise in tiers around the perimeter of the arena. The focus of the rotunda is a magnificent pipe organ, towering above the orchestra stage, and the audience can see the roof soaring up to an apex above them. It was originally equipped with ice-making equipment (a brand-new concept in 1886), but this was never used and was eventually covered. No ice had ever been laid in the hall until John Curry appeared there in April 1984. His company was finally fulfilling Queen Victoria's vision.

Enrico and Kevin encountered problems from the day they arrived. The resident crew resented them, and they were seen as oddities by some and as interlopers by others. A theatrical stage manager, Phil Smith, was drafted in to oversee things, and this caused a certain amount of mutual offence. The Technical Director, Pete Bolton, tried hard to keep things amicable but occasionally tempers boiled over. It was the hall itself, however, that forced everyone to put their differences on one side and pull together.

It seemed the power supply was insufficient to run the generator. Unless a solution could be found, there would be no ice. In addition, there was no loading bay, so the generator had to be parked outside in the street, and miles of wiring had to be run through corridors, up and down steps and over humps. By the time this was all sorted out, we were only forty-eight hours away from opening.

The company arrived, and were settled into apartments. John stayed, as he often did when in London, at the London Embassy Hotel in the Bayswater Road. It was bitterly cold, but the skaters were thrilled to be in England for the first time.

Charles had arrived and had two scheduled rehearsals with the Royal Philharmonic Orchestra. This was to be followed by a full orchestra and dress rehearsal in the hall. We had brought in Jennifer Tipton, the Broadway designer who was noted for her balletic lighting, to light the show. Victor was not happy about the amount of equipment she had ordered, and was nervous because she was not familiar with the hall's difficult configuration. It was too late to change this, but we realized we might have made a serious mistake.

Enrico and Kevin were having a very hard time. The ice equipment was American and some of the small parts they needed were not available. Enrico took refuge in a bottle of Scotch, but Kevin set about inventing ways around it. He managed to overcome most of the problems and, with thirty-six hours still to go, they were ready to start laying the piping. David went in to help, and worked through the night with Kevin and Phil. Occasionally Enrico would surface and lend a hand, only to disappear again. 'Right now we have no way to know if we'll make it or not,' Kevin said.

'We have to,' David said in desperation.

'If it's not set, they can't skate on it,' Kevin said practically. 'Let's not waste time speculating. Let's just get on and lay the ice.'

It became apparent that, even if the ice did set in time for the opening, there would be no time to rehearse with the orchestra and no time for a lighting rehearsal. Jennifer would have to light the show from memory. Pete Bolton was kept busy from morning to night, trying his best to help Kevin and Phil but spending most of his time with Jennifer. The huge square lighting rig had been slung before the ice pipes were laid, which was fortunate in the circumstances.

The skaters began to get nervous as the opening drew nearer. John himself, however, remained remarkably calm. He asked me to arrange for ice time in Richmond, because the skaters needed to rehearse somewhere and it would keep their minds off the show. This we did, and Charles sat watching, trying to gauge the tempo required.

The show had been sold out for weeks. Not a ticket was to be had. The press coverage was extensive, and John's fears about the kind of welcome he could expect turned out to be unfounded. London seemed to be embracing the John Curry Skating Company.

Bill Judd had been very sick all winter, but he was determined to see his favourite project in the Royal Albert Hall. He arrived the day before opening, looking pale and shaky, but nothing was going to dampen his excitement. 'I've been to openings all over the world,' he said, 'but this one is the one I've waited for.'

It was time to get ready for the show. The ice was now out of our hands, and the exhausted crew worked non-stop spraying fine jets of water across the pipes, not daring to stop even for a sandwich. I gave everyone in the company a red rose and a card from David and me. They were bubbling over with excitement and getting more and more nervous as they waited for news of the ice. Jennifer had done her best with the lights and would run them personally throughout the show. The audience filed in and filled the hall to capacity. Even the top of the rotunda was filled with hundreds of people standing around the perimeter, gazing down at the ice far below. What they saw was several men in dungarees, working furiously and ignoring the activity going on all around them. The ice was forming, but it was still very thin; the piping was clearly visible beneath it.

The official opening time arrived, and the skaters gathered in a little knot just behind the stage. They were dressed in their white 'Glides' costumes, ready for the opening number. Victor was frantic. 'We should cancel the show,' he said. 'It cannot happen.'

John, however, was completely unperturbed. 'It will happen,' he said firmly. 'All these people have come to see us skate, and they will not go away disappointed.' He took the skaters into a small room and told them: 'This is going to be a test of your maturity and your ability to cope under difficult circumstances. I must warn you that it will be dangerous out there tonight, because the ice is wafer-thin. But you will skate the show as though nothing was wrong. You must give this audience everything you've got – don't hold anything back. It will take a lot of courage, but you can do it. I know you can. Just remember: you're making history tonight.'

Then he went out on to the orchestra stage and walked to the front. The impatient buzzing of the audience stopped and John said, 'I want to thank you all for your kind patience tonight. I would normally never keep an audience waiting, but you can see for yourselves that our performing space is not being very co-operative. We would beg your indulgence for another half-hour, at which time we will be happy to perform for you. In the mean time, we have a very fine orchestra who I am sure will be happy to keep you entertained.' As he left the stage, the audience rose to their feet and applauded him. Then the lights dimmed, and the Royal Philharmonic began to play.

'Oh my God!' Victor said, wringing his hands. 'I don't think the Royal Philharmonic has ever been asked to be the opening act before!'

I raced into the stalls to make sure Bill was all right. He was sitting with a rapt expression on his face, dressed very smartly in his tuxedo and white silk scarf. 'Oh, my dear!' he said, his eyes shining with tears. 'John is definitely one of the great ones, in my book. What aplomb! How well he handled the situation! A champion in every sense.'

Backstage, David was looking very tired. 'It's terrible ice – it's rutted – but John says they can skate on it. Kevin is going to spray it once more, and then they'll start.' Just then a very fat policeman appeared, red in the face and out of breath.

'Whose generator is that, out in the road?' he demanded.

I was alarmed. 'Ours,' I told him. 'Why – is there a problem?'

'Problem is, madam, that it can't stay there. You'll have to move it.'

'Oh no!' I wailed. 'We can't – please, you can't make us do that. If you do, the Royal Albert Hall will be flooded with water. It's that generator that's keeping it frozen. I think we have permission.'

'Well, you don't,' he said irritably. 'It's typical of these rock bands not to bother to get permission. Just do exactly as they like!'

'Look,' I said. 'We can sort it all out tomorrow, but we must leave it there tonight. Why not come in and see the show? It's not rock, it's an ice show.'

His face lit up. 'Torvill and Dean, is it? My missus loves them. I can't come in now, because I'm on duty, but if I could have a couple of tickets for another day?'

'Done!' I told him, and he puffed happily down the stairs again. It wasn't until he'd disappeared that I realized I didn't have his name, and I hadn't even told him that it wasn't Torvill and Dean.

Finally Charles lifted his baton, and everything went dark. Then six follow-spots converged on a group of white-clad skaters, moving slowly across the ice in an elegant pose, like a floating statue. The audience erupted in spontaneous applause, and the orchestra began to play the Glazunov music. The hall was swathed in magic as each skater succeeded the other, elegant, dashing, poetic, lyrical, daring – they swooped in and out of the exquisite cameos like electric moths. In the middle of the piece, Nathan moved slowly across the arena, without apparent traction, his elegant lines effortlessly held, his head thrown back in undisguised joy. John, standing beside me, said, 'There it is – the future of this company. Look at them all. How splendid they are!' He clasped my hand so tightly that I almost gasped, and I could feel him trembling. I knew at that moment that he was where he belonged.

'Glides' lasted for twenty minutes and the skaters seemed to be handling the ice without difficulty. Even though there were intermittent wet patches that were treacherously slippery, they sailed across them securely. Then, as Nathan skated out for his second solo, he soared into a perfect axel jump. As he landed, his blade cut through the ice and a sudden stream of blue Freon spurted upwards. His foot slipped from underneath him and he fell heavily. It was one of those moments when the audience is not sure what will happen, but he rose again in one fluid movement and continued with his performance as though nothing had gone wrong. There was an audible sigh of relief and one or two people shouted 'Bravo!'

'Glides' established the ensemble as a powerful new artistic force, their carriage upright and open, everything co-ordinated in a continuous flowing line, their movements unforced and elegant. It was clear that at last John had established a company of rare beauty and consistent quality, and that he had extended the vocabulary of ice far beyond its existing range.

It was John himself, however, who emerged as the undisputed star of the evening. He performed 'Tango Tango' (by Peter Martins, Artistic Director of the New York City Ballet) first as a stylish solo and then as a witty duet with JoJo. His own solo, to music from the *Nutcracker*, underscored his passionate view of skating as art. He drew gasps of admiration from the audience as he soared across the ice in transcendent rapture, moving seamlessly in beautiful, open lines. But it was in the finale, Laura Dean's 'Burn' set to music by Jean-Michel Jarre, that he took the potential of skating into another realm. Laura's use of spinning, circling motions was enormously effective on ice, and Jennifer Tipton had lit the piece with eerie, candescent green lights. John skated with a power and authority that perfectly fused virtuosity and dramatic expression, and he commanded the ice with a hypnotic performance that left the audience dazzled by its range.

The response to 'Burn' was thunderous, and the applause continued unabated until Charles Barker raised his baton to indicate an encore. I was sitting by Bill, who had been totally captivated by what he saw. I leant over to him and whispered: 'This one is for you, Bill. This was your brainwave.' As the first notes of the *William Tell* overture began, he dabbed at his eyes. 'Oh, you can't imagine what pleasure this has given me,' he said. 'I have never had such an evening. Never.' The piece ended, John joined the company and the audience cheered and stamped their feet. There was an extra loud cheer, however, when John invited Kevin and Enrico to take a bow, still dressed in their Freon-spattered overalls. Everyone, even the audience themselves, felt as though they had contributed to this very special evening.

As soon as the encore finished, I ran backstage to find John. He was standing outside his dressing room, sweat running off his face, his eyes searching the corridor. When he saw me he hugged me so tightly I thought my ribs would crack. 'I'm so proud of you, John,' I told him. 'Proud of you all. You made everything worthwhile tonight and you need never again ask if people are willing to accept ice as an art form.' He smiled.

'They did seem to rather like it, didn't they?'

At the party afterwards, everyone was excited. Victor and Lillian were enormously enthusiastic, and Victor spoke of taking us to Scandinavia in November. 'It was a triumph!' he said. 'Quite remarkable.' John's British agent, Jean Diamond, was there and expressed her pleasure in John's new direction. 'It's a splendid company,' she said. 'He seems really happy.' Bill Kenwright, the producer of *Electric Ice*, had come and John greeted him warmly. 'I like Bill,' he told me. 'I'd like to do a show with him one day.' Finally, everyone had gone home, and David, Bill Judd and I went off to find a restaurant that was still open. We wanted to eat something hot, have a bottle of wine and talk about the show.

The next morning, the reviews were extraordinary. Without exception they hailed the new company as a superb group of artists. 'John Curry has finally succeeded in developing a team of colleagues who share his responsiveness to music, and his way of moving like a dancer who skates rather than a skater who dances,' wrote John Percival in *The Times*. Craig Dodd wrote in the *Guardian*:

> This is no anonymous, sequined chorus. This is a galaxy of superb skaters combining the hot Curry mixture of exciting technique and superb style; strong use of head and arms, good clean balletic lines and those moments of stillness and grace which are the Curry hallmark.

Of John himself, Clement Crisp said:

> He glides with a kind of rapt splendour ... the movement seeming to pour through the lines and beautiful open curves of his torso ... a rare and superlative artist in whom technique and expression are marvellously one.

It was clear that the appearance was a triumph in every sense, and John's deep misgivings about his British reception had been completely unfounded.

I called the London Embassy and asked to be put through to

John's room. 'John!' I said. 'What did you think of the reviews? You must be thrilled!'

'I don't want to read them,' he told me. 'They couldn't possibly be good. We had no ice. It was such a shame because everyone made such a gallant effort.'

'John, read the reviews for yourself,' I pleaded. 'They couldn't be better if I'd written them!'

'No thanks,' he said in a small, tired voice. 'I just want to sleep.'

I wasn't about to leave John in this state, not this morning of all mornings. I took a cab across London to see him. When I got to his room, he let me in reluctantly and I made him sit down. 'Here,' I said. 'Read these, and then tell me that England doesn't understand who you are – and, even more important from your point of view, that they don't understand what your company is all about.'

Finally he started to read, and by the time he had finished his face was flushed with pleasure. 'Are these real?' he asked. 'You didn't have them forged?'

By the second night, the ice was gleaming like a mirror and there were no further problems about the generator. The reviews had sent people scurrying for tickets to the already sold-out performances, and celebrities bombarded us with requests for our small supply of complimentary tickets. Princess Margaret came, slipping unnoticed into the back of the producer's box. She was so deeply impressed by the performance that she asked to be taken backstage to meet everyone. The skaters were thrilled to be meeting a real princess, and she spoke to each of them in turn. To John she said, 'You have one of the greatest dance companies in the world. Keep up the good work.' Later in the week, Alan Bates came at John's invitation and afterwards went backstage to congratulate him. He told John it was one of the best shows he had ever seen.

By Friday night, Shelley was very sick. She had developed a high fever and a searing headache. I arranged for a doctor to come and see her, and he told her she should not skate that night. She had severe bronchitis. 'I must,' she said. 'They're relying on me.' The doctor gave her a heavy dose of antibiotics and painkillers and told her at least to stay in bed until it was time to go to the Albert Hall. Shelley did manage to get through the performance. She was off, though, and missed a couple of difficult lifts. 'Don't worry,' I told her. 'It's not your fault. It's enough that you're even here.'

On closing night there was another party, and Keith turned up with his Canadian friend. I couldn't believe my eyes. 'How can you do this, tonight of all nights?' I demanded. 'I thought we talked about this?'

Keith shook his head. 'We did, but it just seemed too much to ask. Everyone else can bring their partners, so why not me? I don't think it's fair. He's stayed away all week, surely that's enough.' It was difficult to dispute what Keith was saying, and since they were already here and the show was over, I felt that not much harm could come of it.

The party went well, everyone went home happy and David and I took the technical crew out for a drink afterwards. When I got back to the flat, the phone was ringing. It was John. 'I want you to fire Keith and Shelley,' he said. 'I will not take them to Dubai, so it's only fair that you tell them tonight.' I was devastated. I had no grounds on which to give them notice and I felt they had done an outstanding job for the company. On top of that, they had become a seamless part of the ensemble and would be very difficult to replace. 'John, please think about what you're doing . . .' He cut me off abruptly: 'Elva, this is not up for discussion. Your personal feelings about them are not the issue. My own survival is. I'm afraid if you refuse to fire them then I will have to resign.'

I couldn't sleep for worrying about the situation. I agonized about what would be the right thing to do. Morally it was reprehensible to fire two people when they had done a very good job, even in the face of serious illness. Emotionally, it was terribly distressing because I liked them both so much. On the other hand, if John were to resign, there would be no company and all the skaters would lose their jobs. It seemed to be an impossible situation.

35

The company was scheduled to leave for Dubai a week after the Albert Hall engagement. Most of the skaters took the opportunity to go on holiday, and when I phoned Keith and Shelley the next morning to arrange a meeting, I found they had already left for Scotland. No one knew where they were staying, and we had no way to reach them until our rendezvous at the airport. I felt terrible. I knew we were doing something unprincipled, yet I kept hoping there would be some way to salvage the situation. David was equally upset, and we must have looked a sorry pair as we scanned the terminal for them. Finally, we saw them climbing out of a taxi and we went to meet them. They were relaxed and smiling, and the sight of them broke my heart.

They knew immediately something was wrong. 'It's John, isn't it?' Keith asked.

'Yes,' David told him. 'I'm afraid he has asked us to let you go.'

Shelley was dumbfounded. 'On what grounds?' she demanded.

'None,' I answered truthfully. 'Except, if you stay on, then he will resign and the company will collapse. Keith – the thing is, we can't go on like this, can we? It will only get worse.'

He looked tired. 'I suppose that's it, then. I don't seem to have a choice, do I?'

'I wish there was some other way,' David told him. 'You have to know how awful we feel. We hate having to do this.'

'Yes,' Shelley said bitterly. 'But you're doing it, aren't you?'

Keith stood up and gathered his things. 'I suppose you will pay our way back to Canada?' he asked.

I told him we had exchanged their Dubai tickets for a Toronto flight, to leave later in the morning.

'And what about salaries?' he asked. 'We will both expect to be paid up until our contracts expire.'

'Yes, of course we have to do that,' I answered. But I had absolutely no idea where this would come from, since we would have to replace them for the Met engagement. It seemed that every time we thought things were improving they just got worse again.

We watched as they walked towards the tunnel leading to the

other terminal. Shelley stopped and turned around. 'You will say goodbye to our friends, won't you?' she called. And then they were gone.

'I feel like a piece of shit,' David said angrily. 'We should never have let that happen.'

'I know,' I said. 'I feel horrible. What kind of people have we become?'

We had expected the company to react badly to the news of Keith and Shelley's departure, but they were surprisingly calm about it. John was in a radiantly good mood, sitting with Cathy on the plane, and talking animatedly to everyone. He seemed to be enormously relieved.

It was a very long journey, and we flew across barren territory and vast stretches of water. Eventually the pilot announced our descent into Dubai, and we entered a different world. We were subjected to very severe customs searches, and warned that any use of drugs or alcohol would carry dire penalties. We were met in the terminal building by our promoter, Simon Wall, and someone who seemed to be the Minister of Culture. He invited us all to have our picture taken with him, and then we were taken by coach to a five-star hotel.

Once everyone was settled in, John and I met again with the government minister, who proceeded to tell us that we would have to divide the company into two units for the shows. Each unit would perform in a separate building. 'I beg your pardon?' said John. He wasn't sure what was being said. 'In Dubai, we cannot permit physical contact between men and women in public,' he announced. 'And they do not perform together.'

John was struggling to suppress a smile. 'I'm afraid, if we have to do that, then we won't have a show at all,' he said. 'There wouldn't be enough people.'

Simon, listening to all this, had a bright idea. 'How about staging a rehearsal, so the minister can see for himself if the show is at all offensive?' he suggested.

John laughed. 'All right,' he agreed. 'We're willing to do that, if it will help.'

David had flown back to New York to sort out the various administrative details still to be arranged for the next rehearsal period. He called me that night to see how we were getting on, and I told him the story of the segregation policy. 'We're auditioning for the moral watchdogs tomorrow,' I laughed. He told me that Lewis Rappaport's son, Billy, had loaned the company $2,500 to help bridge the gap until the arrival of the Met money. 'What a great guy,' he said. 'He and Lewis have both come through at crucial moments in the company's history.'

The hotel was gorgeous, and the skaters were delighted with it. They revelled in the strange atmosphere of the United Arab Emirates and went shopping for gold in the souk. 'It's amazingly cheap,' announced JoJo. John noticed Mark Hominuke passing the coffee bar, and chuckled to himself. 'They're so predictable,' he said. 'Look at Mark – he's covered in gold jewellery.' There was a magnificent indoor pool, and a whole avenue of shops inside the hotel. The performance rink (if we could pass the audition) was inside the vast lobby, surrounded by steep tiers of seats. 'You mustn't mind the Arabs,' Simon told John. 'They are used to walking about and eating during performances. They aren't being rude. It's just the custom.'

'I'm glad you warned me,' John told him. 'I might have taken it personally.'

The audition went very well, and apart from cautioning John and JoJo about a particularly torrid scene in 'Tango Tango' they gave permission for them to perform together. There were seven shows in all. On the opening night, the appreciative audience was largely European. The second night, several government ministers came and there were a large number of people in the audience. We prepared the skaters for the fact that they would be noisy and inattentive, but it was an unnecessary exercise. The Arabs were quiet, polite and fascinated by the new experience. They had not seen an ice show before and they loved every moment of it. We were a hit in the desert.

On the Sunday we had a day off and Simon arranged for a coach to take us all to the Gulf of Oman for lunch. John wanted to stay in the hotel and rest, and later asked JoJo to have dinner with him; he seemed genuinely happy.

The last night we were there we were warned to go to bed early because we would have to get up at four a.m. in order to catch our flight to London. John and I ate dinner together, and afterwards he asked: 'Do you have difficulty in falling asleep early? I'm afraid I do – I'm rather an insomniac.' I didn't, but I offered to stay up with him. He was obviously pleased. 'I have some excellent red wine in my room that Simon provided. You might like some because I know you haven't had any since you came here.' We sat in his room, which was furnished with white sofas and chairs and a huge glass-topped table piled with fruit of every kind. He opened the wine ('It's apparently something people collect. I think I'll try some') and after two glasses he was thoroughly relaxed. He began to talk to me about his struggle with the amateur world, his disappointments with his early companies, his dislike of the skating establishment and his long-term hopes for the company and the school which was to follow. ('If we handle it properly, it will change everything for the better.') At midnight, he was still wide awake and he decided to open another bottle of Simon's vintage wine.

He spoke about his family, his mother, his experiences at school and his difficulty in communicating with his father. ('He made it plain he didn't really like me very much. It affected me a little, I'm afraid.') He sat in silence for a while, and when he spoke again he sounded as though he was fighting back tears. He told me about his father's drinking problem and his tendency to abuse his mother when he was drunk. Then he began to tell me about how his father had beaten him. ('He was always sorry afterwards, but how much of that can you be exposed to as a child and not be affected by it?') He poured a fourth glass of wine and apologized for subjecting me to his life story. ('I rarely speak about these things, but I feel you might be able to understand.') Then he told me, in a very quiet voice, that his father had committed suicide. It had been on 30 December 1965, and I recalled that this was always the period of John's darkest depressions. He faced the same thing every year, he said, when he was forced once again to come to grips with the manner in which his father had come to leave them. ('I still wonder sometimes why he would have been so lonely when he had all of us.') There was one more glass of wine in the bottle and I insisted that he have it.

It was three o'clock, and John asked if I was tired. 'I have been talking about myself for hours,' he apologized. 'It must be so boring for you.' I told him that I was far from bored, and that if he would like to keep going I wanted very much to listen. He started again, telling me of his lifelong struggle to discover his sexual identity. He spoke of his loneliness and his feelings of isolation and his longing for a permanent partner in life.

'Do you only love men?' I asked him.

'No, not at all,' he answered. 'I've loved three women, in the sense that I could have spent my life with them. Janet Lynn, who was married already; Sam, who was madcap and wonderful, but who in the end was too much for me to handle; and someone now, who I love enough to think I could marry her. If I tell you who it is, I am terrified you might say something.' I promised I wouldn't and he told me it was JoJo. How marvellous, I thought. What a perfect match they would make. 'Do you approve?' he asked. I laughed. 'I can't think of anything that would make me happier,' I told him.

At four, we boarded the bus and headed for the airport. I was terribly tired, but I understood a great deal more about John, and I felt an empathy for him that was to stand me in good stead in the days to come. He requested a seat beside JoJo on the plane, and I felt that he had started a new chapter in his life, one that would bring him the peace and happiness he so longed for.

36

We arranged to meet West Nally at their Manhattan offices in early May, to seek their formal approval for the establishment of the not-for-profit entity to be known as the John Curry Skating Company. Jack flew in for the meeting and we were also joined by our four shareholders. These were the people who had provided crucial help and support during the formative period of the company: Lewis Rappaport, who had put up the $10,000 needed to complete the initial funding phase; Bill Judd, who had provided invaluable counsel as well as booking the Canadian tour and the Met season without payment; Bob Harley, who had given freely of his legal services; and Bill Weylock, a friend of mine who had offered us office space when we could no longer run the company out of Steve Leber's premises. They had all been given a percentage of our equity in *Symphony on Ice* as a way of thanking them for their generosity.

The meeting was amicable. The success of the London season had bolstered our credibility, and it was now obvious to everybody that the John Curry Skating Company belonged in the non-profit sector. To run it as a commercial venture would inevitably compromise those very qualities that gave the company its unique status in the rarefied world of the arts. In little more than a year, the fledgling group had been propelled by sheer momentum from tentative experimentation in a small mountain arena to the door of the Metropolitan Opera House. Now David and I needed to find help before the financial weight of the venture collapsed on top of us.

West Nally were willing to support the switch to a non-profit company providing they could retain the rights to merchandising and sponsorship and could turn part of their original investment into a long-term loan. 'We can recoup it from your share of sponsorship and merchandising income,' Jack told us. What we didn't know (and Rita was to explain this to us later) was that Jack was alone in his enthusiasm for the company. The West Nally offices in London and New York ignored the potential for sponsorship and merchandising, electing to concentrate their efforts on their rock-and-roll clients and their lucrative association with major boxing tournaments. The John Curry Skating Company was too small a fish for them to fry.

Our four shareholders voted unanimously to turn their shares into long-term loans, and accepted an invitation to sit on the board of the non-profit company when the time came for it to be formed. We were now free to go forward as a charitable organization.

I had several meetings with Jane Herman in June. She was extremely well connected in the arts world and with the movers and shakers of New York society. She offered to find some heavyweight board members who could be helpful to us in the fund-raising area, and also to see if any local corporations might be willing to donate money. In the mean time, however, we needed to make some fundamental changes to the overall structure of the company.

Foremost among these changes was the question of a new booking agency. Jane had strong connections with the powerful Columbia Artists Management agency (known as CAMI) and worked closely with both Peter Gelb, head of their television division, and David Foster, one of their senior agents. I met them both, but heard nothing that was particularly encouraging; I felt that Bill Judd was much better able to handle our peculiar and very specific requirements.

'Bill is a has-been,' Jane said dismissively. 'He's not right for John's company.'

'He's one of the main reasons there *is* a company right now,' I told her. 'It's easy for people to look now and see the potential, but Bill recognized it when it was still in the dreaming stages.'

'Nobody cares,' Jane said. 'You're in a different world now, where power talks. You won't survive without it.'

John and I went to see Shelley Gold at International Creative Management (ICM), the other major booking agency in America. They represented many fine classical artists and had great respect for Bill. Shelley was warm and hospitable, and proved very well versed on the subject of ice. 'I think we can work on this together,' he said. 'Bill and I can work as a team.' I felt this to be an excellent suggestion and went to the Met to tell Jane. She was furious. 'You can't be serious!' she said. 'Shelley Gold is *persona non grata* at the Met. If you go with ICM, it will *seriously* affect your future with us. I strongly suggest that you think again.'

I went out to spend a long weekend at Bill's summer home on Long Island. While I was there, Jane invited John to dinner with Margaret Carson and David Foster. He came to see me as soon as I returned, and he was clearly upset. 'I've been taken to meet David Foster – he seems to be a booking agent, and he wanted to represent our company. I'm afraid I told Jane that I wanted nothing to do with him. You and Bill have done a very good job so far, and I can't see why we would need him.'

It appeared Jane was not used to having her recommendations turned down. I went to see her, and told her I would appreciate it if she would not in future try to recruit John's support behind my back. 'I want nothing more than to have you in our corner,' I told her. 'I like you. But we've worked too long and too hard to hand our company over to someone we don't feel is right for us. You must have excellent reasons for supporting David Foster, but unfortunately we are not particularly impressed. We're going to stay with Bill Judd for the time being.'

Jane looked at me quizzically for a moment, then she held out her hand. 'I apologize. I underestimated you.' She pulled out the bottom drawer of her filing cabinet to reveal a collection of bottles and glasses. 'Vodka or Scotch?' she asked. 'You do take yours straight?'

*   *   *

In the middle of May, John decided to have knee surgery. He had been suffering considerable pain over the last eighteen months and the prospect of appearing in the Met with an unreliable knee was worrying him. 'There will be such pressure to be at one's best,' he told me. 'If I have orthoscopic [keyhole] surgery now, I have time to recover before we go back into rehearsal. If it's successful, I could be good for another four or five years.' I was greatly encouraged to hear him speaking of the future so positively, and went with him to the Doctors' Hospital on the Upper East Side.

While he was recuperating at the Streeters' apartment, we talked at length about our plans. He seemed to have new energy and had been making copious notes. 'I want you to arrange for us to go back to Vail at the beginning of June,' he said. 'That will give us eight weeks of rehearsal and we'll need every bit of it. Tell David we need more ice time than before. If necessary, we'll take night ice. And I want Rob to set up auditions for the end of the month. We need to get some new skaters – the Met stage is a hundred feet by eighty, and we're too few for that size at the moment. And we need a new pair . . .' I listened to his enthusiasm as it tumbled on. He seemed to have emerged from his depression, and I wanted above everything to prevent its recurrence. I couldn't bring myself to tell him that we had no idea how to pay for all the things he required. David and I would just have to find a way to cover them.

We sat down the next day and went through our possible sources of income. The obvious one was fund-raising, but that would take time. There were to be two events in Vail, organized by a community group called the Vail Associates, and one or two events connected to the Met season. The BBC still owed us £6,000 for the televising of the Royal Albert Hall shows, and we had a small amount still to come from Dubai. The major potential was from the sale of our own equity in Pro Skate and *Electric Ice*. We had already negotiated an advance on this back in January, when Steve gave us $8,000 to cover the company's air fares to Vail and one week of rehearsals. Now we needed to settle on the balance as quickly as possible. 'It should give us enough to carry us over for a few weeks,' David said.

Jane managed to tie up two weeks at the Kennedy Center directly after the Met, which meant that we could keep the company working. Victor called from England to say he could get two weeks in Scandinavia in November, culminating in the brand-new Bergen Opera

House in Norway, and Bill Judd managed to get us a week in Boston's Wang Center at the beginning of September. Things were looking up.

We met with Kevin Kossi to discuss the formidable task of icing over the great expanse of the Met stage. John wanted the ice to cover the wings as well, so that the skaters could enter and exit at speed. 'My father's equipment won't do that job,' Kevin told us. 'You should think about buying an ice machine for the company. In the end it would pay for itself, and you wouldn't have to worry about renting it.'

'Who would run it?'

'Me,' Kevin said. 'My father isn't really up to it any longer, and I know exactly what needs to be done.' John thought it a very good idea; he trusted Kevin.

The question of how to pay for such a major piece of equipment was another matter. David went to the Chemical Bank, which held the company account, but was turned down instantly. 'Sixty-five thousand dollars is out of the question,' said our account executive, Nan Miller.

'But what if we put the machine itself up as security?'

'Please, Mr Spungen. There isn't exactly a brisk trade in used ice machines, is there?'

And that was that. We each tried our personal banks but got firm refusals from both of them. 'There's only one thing left to do,' David said with a sigh. 'We have to tell John. Remember he told us we were to ask him if it was ever a question of something important to the company.'

John's response was immediate: he would do whatever was necessary. He talked it over with Joe Concilio and decided to purchase the equipment through his own company, Frozen Assets. This would apparently give him a much-needed tax break. The order was placed with barely enough time to take delivery before the Met opening. It seemed we were destined to live on a cliff-edge.

Rob had set up an audition for new skaters at the Sky Rink on 27 May. It was to take place at eleven p.m., when the regular sessions had finished. John and I rode down to 33rd Street together, excited to see who would come; so much depended on having the right mix in the ensemble.

216

There were about twenty skaters on the ice, most of them men. Rob asked them to skate around for a while in a general warm-up session, then John called them out one by one, questioned them about why they wanted to join the company and asked them to skate on their own. He made them do spirals, spins, spread-eagles and footwork. Then they had to jump, first to the left and then to the right. Dexterity was for John an essential quality of an ensemble member. It was at this point that most skaters were eliminated, but John was gracious to each of them, encouraging them to keep trying and thanking them for taking the trouble to come. Finally he leant over and said, 'I want four of them. Can we afford it?'

The truth was that we couldn't afford anyone, but we knew we had to increase the size of the troupe. 'We'll find a way,' I told him. He chose Adam Lieb ('because he has an earthy quality we're lacking right now and because he's so strong'), J. Scott Driscoll ('because he's so wonderfully animated – he skates with such joy!'), Joan Vienneau ('because she's the only woman here who could do the job, and we're desperately short of women') and Sean McGill ('he reminds me of Jack Courtney, and I think he has the makings of a principal'). We told them the pay was $300 a week for rehearsals and $800 a week for performance, and there was no guarantee of how many weeks they would work. Everybody got the same level of accommodation and transport, and billing was alphabetical. They all accepted the offer.

Two days before the company was due to leave for Vail, David called me late at night. 'There *is* a god!' he said. 'I just got home and there was a Diners Club card in the mail. Can you believe it? I can put all the flights on it, and there might even be a bit left over for the rental cars.' The same day, Joe called to say the ice equipment had been discounted by $20,000. Things looked distinctly brighter.

When the company arrived in Vail, there was no ice available. There had been a problem with the power cables, and this had necessitated major repairs. John was beside himself: he felt that the delay would put an end to any possibility of a successful Met season. Rob, however, managed to turn the situation to advantage, and persuaded John that the time could be used to carry out valuable off-ice training. He set out a plan for the week which included pair lifts, working with weights, aerobics and dance, and the regime seemed to put everyone in very good spirits.

I had heard recently that Billy Fauver and Lee-Anne Miller were planning to turn professional. They were an attractive and talented pair, and ranked among the first five in the world. 'I love their work,' John said, 'but I'm sure they'll already be involved with one of the big shows. Anyway, they'd never work for the kind of money we're paying.' I thought it was worth trying, however, and I met with Billy to discuss it. He was charming and he told me that they would very much enjoy the opportunity to work with John. They were willing to accept the money offered, and had no problem with alphabetical billing. 'Where else can we do this kind of work?' he asked. 'In such a company?' By the time the ice was in the Dobson Arena, they were installed in Vail with the rest of the ensemble. Our company was now complete.

The advance ticket sales for the Met were going so well that it seemed we were assured of a large audience. Jane invited me for a drink (from her filing cabinet) one afternoon, and told me that the time had now come for us to acquire a professional general manager. 'We can't afford it,' I told her. 'David, John and I aren't even drawing a salary right now.'

She shook her head. 'You really can't afford *not* to have an experienced manager. You need someone who's used to dealing with the unions and so on. In the end, it would save you a lot of money.'

'I'll think about it,' I promised, but she was insistent.

'I have to warn you that the Met won't feel comfortable unless you have an experienced pro on board.'

The following week she invited me over again, this time to meet Darryl Dodson, her recommendation for general manager. She had told me on the phone that he had impeccable qualifications and was perfect for our purposes. When I met him I was somewhat taken aback. He had Persil-white hair and a high facial colour which could have been caused by drinking. When he shook hands, his palms were perspiring and I could feel him trembling. I was not immediately impressed.

I called David in Vail that night and we agonized over the question of Darryl Dodson. Left to our own devices we would not have hired a general manager at all, let alone this one. But Jane had indicated that he was the Met's personal choice and that we were expected to hire him. 'We already turned down her booking agent,' I said. 'Maybe we have to go along with this chap. I think, politically, we'll be in a difficult situation if we don't.'

David sighed. 'I guess you're right. But a thousand a week! Jesus – that really hurts.' The next day I told Jane we would start him in mid-June.

One morning, Darryl was late coming into the office. We were still working out of Bill Weylock's premises, which happened to be a block away from the Met, and Bill told me he was concerned about Darryl. 'Something isn't right,' he said. 'Forgive me if I'm poking my nose in, but it seems to me you've been forced to hire a guy who obviously couldn't manage his way out of bed in the morning. You do all the work, and he gets the salary. It doesn't make sense.' Darryl came in then, full of apologies and looking shaky. He shuffled some bills and wrote a few cheques and then went out again. 'I'll be back later,' he said. 'Things to do.'

'I think he's on drugs,' Bill told me. 'All the signs are there. And look at his writing – it looks as though a spider fell in the ink.' I called Jane to tell her of our misgivings. She was dismissive: 'He's terribly respected. I'm sure you're imagining things,' she said.

Darryl soon raised the subject of an assistant general manager. I was appalled. 'Absolutely not,' I told him. 'You know the state of our finances – how can you even suggest it?' But he persisted. He knew someone with very good credentials who might take on the Met season for nothing. 'Why would he do that?' I asked.

'He's a friend of mine,' he replied. 'He'd do it to help me, and maybe later when we have income we could hire him.' I thought this was fair enough, and Darryl set up a meeting in the Mayflower Hotel.

Nate Barnett was six feet tall, black, and had a nervous tic. He was arrogant, overbearing and condescending and I did not take to him. After thirty minutes of excruciating conversation I excused myself and left. The next morning I told Darryl that, if he wasn't going to cost anything, I couldn't really ban him from helping.

On 14 June Lar Lubovitch, a noted American choreographer, went to Vail to create a ballet for the ensemble. It was to be called 'Court of Ice', and it was set to music by Bach. It was a difficult and demanding piece but when it began to take shape it was obvious it was a stunning departure from the normal skating idiom. Lar left

John to rehearse it for two weeks, after which he would come back and polish it.

In July, one of the most respected of all the New York choreographers flew in to make a solo piece for John. Eliot Feld was not certain he wanted to do it, but Jane had talked him into it. He chose to work with an eleven-minute unaccompanied piano prelude by Ravel, and he rejected any of the known skating moves. He called the work 'Moonskate'.

From the beginning there was tension between Eliot and John. On the second day, Eliot fell on the ice and cracked a bone in his arm, but he strapped it up and continued to work. He seemed to resent John for some reason and made no effort to befriend him. David was worried about it – it was the first time he had encountered any problems with visiting choreographers. 'Think about it,' I told him. 'Eliot has a distinguished company of dancers, and has been a hugely lauded artist for many years, yet his own company is not considered suitable to play the Met. There he is, making choreography for an ice skater whose company is making its American debut there. It's no wonder he feels some resentment.'

I now engaged Howard Phelan, a professional fund raiser from Connecticut. He was offering to help us organize a fund-raising event based around the Met, and would work for a small percentage of the profits. 'You need to get the corporations in,' he told me. 'We should give them complimentary tickets and a reception after. It will pay off handsomely in the long run.' We also needed a lawyer with some clout to help us organize the legal side of things. Since we had no money, this was difficult, but Lewis Rappaport introduced us to a prominent Manhattan attorney called Shelley Cammacker and he agreed to come on board. Things seemed to be relatively well in hand; then I got a late-night call from David. He sounded frantic. 'The Marriott Hotel has just threatened to jail me,' he said.

37

When David had calmed down, he told me the story. Apparently, for the last week of the December rehearsals the company had been housed in the Marriott Mark Resort Hotel in Vail. This had been done with West Nally's approval, and the hotel had extended credit until late January on the understanding that West Nally would take care of the bill. Unfortunately, West Nally had reneged on the promise and now, six months later, the hotel was after the only person they could reach. David.

'It's a ten-thousand-dollar tab,' David said miserably. 'How am I going to come up with that kind of money?'

I advised him to call Jack. 'After all, he's not a monster. Surely he'll understand the position it's put you in.' Without any real hope, David placed the call and got an unexpectedly sympathetic response. Jack told David he would make sure West Nally took care of the matter, and within twenty-four hours the money had been wired to Vail. We breathed a sigh of relief.

On Thursday morning, David called again. I knew from the tone of his voice that something had gone horribly wrong. 'It's in the papers,' he told me. 'The *Vail Trail*. All the gory details – except they left out the fact that it was a West Nally obligation in the first place. They made it sound as though it was a personal bad debt. My credibility has been shot to ribbons.'

'Does John know about it?' I asked. 'I think it's very important you go and explain it to him in person.'

David was dreading what he assumed would be a major confrontation with John, but he was surprised by the reaction he got. 'You seemed to have handled a difficult situation very well,' he said. 'Don't forget what they say: today's newspapers are just tomorrow's trash. I wouldn't worry about it.'

David's concerns about his credibility were well founded. The incident jeopardized the company's standing with the town council, which had been on the verge of extending substantial support. An emergency meeting was held, and David went to address them. 'Look on it as damage limitation,' he told me. 'I'd like to know they had the facts, at least.' He was granted a hearing, and everyone listened to him attentively. When he called me later, he said, 'I think the jury's still out, but it can't have hurt us.'

The company's financial status became the subject of widespread gossip in the small mountain community, and credit facilities were rapidly withdrawn. David went to the company's Vail bank to ask for a temporary loan, citing the advances imminently due from the Kennedy Center and Boston, and the recent international sale of the BBC tape, which would net us over $40,000. He asked the bank for $15,000, but was turned down. 'Of course,' the Manager said, 'if you can find someone of repute to co-sign it, then we could reconsider.'

David thought of George Webster, the President of the Vail Associates, who had been so supportive of the company in the past. He had often indicated he would be willing to make a donation, and David thought this might be the time to approach him.

He telephoned just after midnight to tell me about the meeting. 'It was horrible,' he said. I had rarely heard him sound so grim. 'First of all, he made it plain that he wasn't going to make a donation till the end of the year. This year's foundation money has already been allocated. Then I asked him if he would be willing to co-sign a note at the bank for us, and he seemed shocked. He asked me why he should do this, and started to grill me. I've honestly never been so humiliated in my life. He made me turn my soul inside-out. I was on my knees, begging him to do it. I must have looked like an unprofessional nerd, but he agreed in the end. I can tell you, though, it didn't feel good.'

Howard Phelan got a $10,000 donation from a lady in Connecticut called Kit Wright. He also invited sixty-five potential donors to the Met, and asked us to throw a party for them afterwards ('somewhere rather nice. You'll have to impress these people'). On top of this, Mark and Sara Grayson were bringing thirty young friends, who were all very well connected, to the same performance. It was costing us a fortune in complimentary tickets.

By the second week of July the money from the television sale had come through, and Lewis Rappaport had made a short-term loan of $15,000. It became obvious, though, that if we were to make it to the Met we would need to come up with some fairly hefty bridge financing. The costs were escalating rapidly, many through circumstances beyond our control.

Jane Herman had recommended we use the Broadway costume designer Willa Kim. Willa's work was stunning, but very expensive, and the set of costumes created by her went far beyond our existing costume budget. Margaret Carson was doing a phenomenal job, but we were having to pay her office $5,000 a month for her services. We had extra insurance costs, because of the ice (no one would believe it wasn't going to ruin the stage), and huge down-payments for the various unions involved. On top of this were all the extra costs for choreographers and costume people to go to Vail, and the added expense of Dorothy Hamill's training in Vail. The worst shock, though, came from Darryl's quarter.

For two weeks now I had noticed the balance in the company bank account falling well below the expected level. I confronted Darryl about this, and he told me that he had been obliged to withhold payroll taxes and unemployment insurance, plus large amounts earmarked for the Inland Revenue Service. These payments had not appeared on Darryl's cash-flow budget, so I was rather annoyed about the discrepancy. However, he explained that he felt it imperative to do this immediately, as we had no way to predict future income and we could not risk violating federal and state law. Since this seemed to make sense, I didn't question him further.

Jane recommended a production supervisor to us. His name was John Paull the Third ('Sounds like we've hired the Pope,' David said). John Paull in turn hired a veritable army of people – electricians, carpenter, stage manager, assistant stage manager, assistant ice engineer, wardrobe assistants and a sound engineer. We had also found an assistant musical director for Charles. Steve Masi was a brilliant pianist, and besides helping Charles he was to play the Ravel piano solo for 'Moonskate'.

Nan Miller at the Chemical Bank agreed to advance short-term loans to the company on condition that the notes were personally guaranteed by three people: myself, David (who had to fly up from Vail for the signing) and Bill Weylock, who was acting as the company treasurer. Of the three of us, Bill stood to lose the most, since he owned a thriving research business. Every asset of David's and mine had already been put into the pot; we had very little left at this point. However, we had come too far to turn back now. We all signed the papers, and the finance to cover the weeks leading into the Met was made available to us. The only provision Nan Miller insisted on was that Darryl Dodson become the sole cheque-writing authority for the account: he no longer needed our permission to issue payments. This was an error of judgement that was to jeopardize the future of the John Curry Skating Company.

Dorothy settled in well in Vail and seemed to thrive on the demanding schedule. The skaters were nervous but excited, and on the whole John seemed satisfied with their progress. There was one exception, however: Lori Nichol.

'She's just plain fat,' he told me.

'John, she isn't fat at all,' I said. 'How can you say that? She's such a beautiful girl, and a lovely skater.'

'I wasn't complaining about her skating,' he said, 'but I can't have a great blonde blimp out on the Met stage. She claims to be dieting, but it certainly hasn't done any good if she is. I think she binges. I've asked the others to try to help her. Keep an eye on her.' Poor Lori had to suffer the indignity of being weighed twice a day every day. 'I feel like an elephant,' she said sadly.

Lar returned, with Jane Herman, who had come down to check things out for herself. What she saw impressed her. She told John that it looked like we might have a sold-out season, and asked if he could fly back to New York for a couple of days to do some publicity.

I saw no evidence, on my visit, of the closeness that had sprung up between John and JoJo in Dubai. I had dinner with John before I went back and he told me that was all over. 'It was a dream,' he said. 'It would never have worked.' Later, Rob told me that John was now in a relationship with Sean McGill, and that he thought it might last. 'He seems happier now than for a long time,' he said. 'Can't you tell the difference?'

I made time to talk to all the skaters personally before I left Vail. I felt it was important to make them feel there was someone they could go to if they had problems, and I wanted to understand how they viewed the company and how they fitted in to the overall plans. It was an interesting process. They all needed the opportunity to discuss their feelings, their insecurities and their dreams. Everyone felt that John was a brilliant artistic director: ruthless and demanding, but able to draw magical performances out of them. But everyone also felt that he could be very mean sometimes, making cutting remarks and cruel observations.

'We do try to understand him,' said Dita, 'but sometimes he is just so nasty. It's hard not to cry.' I explained to them the problems he had, the pressures of the company. 'That doesn't give him an excuse to be shitty to us,' said David Santee. 'We're all giving up stuff too, you know.' It was JoJo who had the last word. 'I guess he knows in the end that we all love him,' she said in her soft voice. 'No matter what he does.'

38

The final two weeks of rehearsal were extremely positive. Everyone seemed to be in good spirits, and even John was unusually optimistic: 'If we're not ready now, we never will be,' he said. He had devised programmes for three separate evenings, and had made certain that everyone in the company had solo time on the stage. The whole season was very well balanced.

On the last Saturday, there was a works-in-progress performance at the arena, and Pat Dobson was extremely encouraged by the results. The company shone, and the word-of-mouth in the community was that, no matter what kind of teething troubles they had experienced earlier in the summer, the company had now triumphed. 'You can stop worrying about the Marriott business,' Pat told David. 'It's blood under the bridge at this point. This company is a major asset to the Vail community and I think you'll find them anxious to keep you here.'

The Met season sold out, and Jane arranged for an extra performance at the end of the run. 'We'll split the box office, fifty per cent to the Met and fifty per cent to your company,' she said. We shook hands and it went on sale. Within a week, this too had sold out. I called David.

'We've got an extra fifty thousand dollars sitting there for us,' I told him. 'When we add that to our split of profits from the rest of the performances, we should come out of this with over a hundred thousand dollars.'

'From your mouth to God's ears,' David laughed. 'I daren't even think about it. Does this mean we might actually be able to draw some salary soon?'

The company arrived in New York four days before the opening. Darryl had booked them into his favourite hotel, the Mayflower, which he informed us he had an excellent deal on. The skaters were delighted, because it was a beautiful old-world hotel, only a block away from the Met. It had a coffee shop overlooking Central Park, and the traditional New York horse-drawn carriages gathered there waiting for passengers.

John was staying with the Streeters, which gave him some much-needed breathing space. He was strong and calm, and as confident as I had ever seen him. Everything about this engagement seemed right to him: the name choreographers and designers, the prestigious venue, the magnificent stage, the matured and cohesive ensemble, and the marriage of great music, lighting and costume to ice. It was the culmination of everything he had hoped for, and he was determined to make it work.

The Sunday before the performance, John was on the front page of every newspaper in the city. He was presented as the master of his genre, someone who had fought against impossible odds to bring his young troupe to the Met, someone who would not compromise under any circumstances. In the photographs he appeared relaxed, smiling and handsome, and he spoke in glowing terms of the fulfilment of his dreams. Margaret Carson had monitored the interviews carefully, and the overall impression was of a sensitive creative force at the helm of a superlative company of artists.

We had always known that the ice machinery would arrive at the eleventh hour, but we now knew that it would be delayed until two days before opening. There was nothing to be done except to make the best of it. We would have no time to test it – it would have to go straight in on Sunday night, to be ready for Tuesday's opening. It was going to be a very close call.

On Monday morning we ran into our first union problems. This was new territory to us, and we were not prepared for the level of power they exerted. The main problem was that Kevin was not a member of the stage-hands' union, but he clearly saw himself as being in sole charge of the ice-making operation. At nine, David arrived and rolled up his sleeves to help. 'Just like the Albert Hall!' he joked to Kevin. 'It'll take all of us pulling together if we plan on opening tomorrow.'

As he stepped forward on to the stage, one of the men caught his arm. 'Where d'you think you're going?' he asked. 'If you don't fuck off and leave us alone, we'll call a stoppage.'

David went to find Jane. 'This is dumb,' he fumed. 'They won't let anyone help; they won't take orders from Kevin; but they've got no idea how to do it themselves.'

'Doesn't matter,' she said. 'He's on their stage, and he only has a temporary card. You have to understand, he's an eighteen-year-old kid and he's bossing these old union hands around. They don't like it.'

David was exasperated. 'What I understand', he said, 'is that if they don't pull their fingers out, we won't be opening tomorrow night.'

By four in the afternoon it became clear that we were facing a crisis. Jane called a meeting in her office. 'When will this ice be ready?' she demanded.

'At this rate, never!' David said.

'The truth is,' I told her, 'they have delayed things so much that the best we can hope for is good ice by opening time. We wouldn't have a rehearsal, and the skaters wouldn't be familiar with the stage.'

John suddenly slapped his hand down on the table. 'We have to postpone until Wednesday night. This is too important for us to make a mess of it. It seems we aren't able to hurry these union people, so we will just have to accept it. I won't let the skaters perform cold. They must have a rehearsal first.' No one was arguing with this point of view, and we assumed the cancelled opening would become a joint responsibility of the Met and the company. 'I think people will understand,' John said. 'It's nothing to be ashamed of, is it?'

The cancellation was handled well by the box office, and virtually no one asked for their money back. We managed to schedule an extra matinée on Sunday to accommodate the demand for tickets, and those few people who couldn't make that performance were squeezed into the last night. John was concerned about the physical demands the extra performance would place on the skaters, but everyone voted to go forward. It seemed we had averted the immediate crisis.

On Sunday night, John and I sat in the stalls of the opera house, watching Kevin as he struggled to complete the huge ice sheet. 'He's unbelievable,' John said. 'He takes no notice of all the fuss going on around him – he just gets on with what must have seemed an almost impossible task.' He chuckled. 'You know, when I asked him if he could run ice right out into the wings, I didn't really expect him to do it! I think we must be the first ice presentation to have anything other than a square tank.' He was in a mellow mood. He had taken the skaters to Connecticut to rehearse that morning, and he was comfortable that everyone was ready. 'I just want to tell you,' he said quietly, 'before everything gets too hectic, that this appearance in the Met means more to me than anything that has gone before. I know how hard you and David have worked to pull it off, and I hope you know how grateful I am. I'll try not to let you down.'

I smiled. 'Remember,' I said, 'we're in this together, the three of us.'

By Tuesday morning the ice was shining like glass. The technical rehearsal went well, although Jennifer Tipton wondered why she had let herself in for lighting such an odd-shaped space. 'It's impossible,' she said – but she managed to bathe everything in a mystical, magical glow. 'I think it's the best thing she's ever done,' said Jane.

The orchestra rehearsal in the early afternoon was spectacular. It was the first time I had seen the pieces performed in costume, with full lighting, and I sat in the stalls watching in delight as the splendour of the company unfolded. Tony Bliss, Manager of the Met, who came in to watch for a while, was astonished. 'I had no idea,' he said frankly. 'This is an extraordinary experience.'

Jane, pacing about between the rows of seats, felt that the company had matured since her visit to Vail. 'They're so in synch with one another,' she said, 'like they've been together for years.' Later, she watched John and JoJo rehearse 'Tango Tango'. 'There's something going on between those two,' she said. 'It comes across the footlights.' I said nothing, but I knew exactly what she meant. There was a definite chemistry. The sad thing was that it only seemed to manifest itself on stage.

When John rehearsed 'Moonskate', I heard the doors open at the back of the auditorium. I looked round and saw Eliot Feld standing just inside. He watched for a few minutes, then turned and left. 'Why didn't Eliot stay?' I asked.

'He won't,' said Jane. 'I've pleaded with him, but he's not to be persuaded. He isn't coming tonight either.' I thought this was terribly sad, because 'Moonskate' was very much a combined achievement. John's unique talent was set alight by Eliot's undoubted genius.

For the rest of the afternoon we raced around tying up loose ends, finding last-minute seats for guests and answering an avalanche of phone calls. At the Met office, Darryl dealt with hundreds of complimentary tickets, writing on the envelopes in his spidery hand. I went backstage to check out the dressing rooms and David Santee called out to me. 'I was just looking for you,' he said. 'Who's the black guy who hangs around back here? He's a real pain in the butt.' I knew immediately he must be talking about Nate.

'I'll deal with it,' I told him. 'He's a friend of Darryl's.'

'Figures,' David muttered.

I found John sitting quietly inside his room. 'Are you going back to the Streeters'?' I asked.

He shook his head. 'No. I brought everything I need. I just want to sit here by myself for a while and prepare.'

I hugged him. 'I'm so proud of you,' I told him.

He smiled. 'I haven't performed yet! I might fall all over the ice.'

'It has nothing to do with any of that,' I said. 'I'm proud of you for what you've done to get to this point. You *and* the others.'

As I approached Lincoln Center at six-thirty, crowds of people were already milling around in the quadrangle. It was a balmy summer evening and the outdoor café was full. Near the entrance to the Met itself, I could hear people trying to scalp tickets and I was offered a pair of 'excellent seats in the stalls' for $400. 'No thank you,' I smiled. 'I already have mine.' It was a strange feeling to know that our little band of skaters had become such a hot ticket in the sophisticated New York theatre world.

The dressing rooms were already abuzz with excitement. Gayle was bustling about, hanging the costumes on racks in performance sequence. She took John's into his room and hung them in the small cupboard. 'Break a leg!' she told him. Charles was pacing nervously up and down, muttering to himself. Bouquets of flowers were arriving for the performers, and good-luck telegrams were pinned to the company noticeboard. I had bought small first-night gifts for everyone, and I distributed them with a red rose and a hug. 'From David and me,' I told them, and we received a small avalanche of beautiful cards in return. Dita had written: 'Remember when I skate tonight, my smile is specially for you!' I knew that Dita had found it difficult to adapt to John's rigid regime, and over the past months David and I had spent a great deal of time talking her through it. Now, though, she was happily integrated and enjoying a wonderful new relationship with Jim Bowser. John had sent us both flowers and thank-you notes which said: 'I want you to know how much I appreciate your dedication and hard work. Tonight is your night as well as ours. Love, John.' We were deeply touched.

Finally, it was half an hour to showtime and there was nothing more to be done backstage. I made my way to the foyer, and found David talking to Jane. 'Good crowd,' she said: 'lots of critics.' People were streaming in, pushing their way towards the staircases and the stalls entrances. Kevin's mother, Ruth, arrived and we found her a seat in the production box. Bill Judd came, slightly out of breath, and sat beside Ruth. Lewis and Billy Rappaport were there, with Bill Weylock, Bob Harley and several skaters' mothers. The bell sounded and the lights flashed the five-minute warning. The orchestra, hidden in the pit, began to play the overture, Charles standing in front of them resplendent in his white tie and tails. David and I stood at the back of the box. 'Here we go!' he whispered to me. 'There'll never be a more important night than this one.'

39

The auditorium lights went out, the great crystal chandeliers rose slowly upwards, and the musicians were quiet. The magnificent golden curtains twitched, parted and opened to reveal a shimmering sheet of mirror ice. There was an audible gasp from the audience. The follow-spots converged on the back of the darkened stage, and illuminated a moving tableau of skaters dressed in flowing white costumes, gliding silently forward like a living Rodin statue. Applause burst from every part of the house, and 'Glides' had begun. The John Curry Skating Company was finally in the Met.

'Glides' was rapturously received with a ten-minute ovation. David Santee's 'Russian Sailor's Dance' was thrillingly placed near the edge of the stage, silver blades spraying ice across the orchestra pit, and Dita's new solo, to music by Alexander Scriabin, showed her range and presence to perfection. John and JoJo skated the sultry 'Tango Tango', with Peter Martins watching appreciatively in the wings, and Billy and Lee-Anne earned shouts of approval for their dizzying pair number, 'Tarantella'. It was 'Moonskate', however, that brought the greatest response of all.

I sat in the front of the box, wanting to share this moment with Bill Judd. When the lights picked out the lonely, white-clad figure and the haunting piano music began, a hush fell across the house as though every person there had stopped breathing. We were in the presence of a consummate artist who moved through space with effortless grace, who tore at our hearts with the depth of the pain he portrayed, who floated, devoid of gravity, in search of spiritual peace. He held us transfixed for eleven minutes without a jump or a spin, and at the end he stood, head bowed, hands clasped, in a moment of stillness more powerful and more eloquent than any movement. The audience leapt to their feet, cheering, stamping and screaming 'Bravo!' John moved slowly to the front of the stage, bewildered by the level of response, surrounded by bouquets of flowers, trying to take it all in.

In the production box, Bill turned to me and I could see his face was wet with tears. 'Ah, my dear,' he said, his lip trembling, 'he belongs with the great ones, and he has found his signature piece. He performs with such feeling, it is difficult not to weep.'

I nodded. 'He suffers every time he skates it, because, for John, "Moonskate" is autobiographical.'

At intermission, everyone buzzed with excitement. I saw Peter Martins on the stairs and congratulated him on 'Tango Tango'. 'They do it so beautifully,' he said. 'They made my work into something more than it was.' This was gracious of him, but also typical of great dance choreographers working with ice for the first time; they tended to stand in awe of the skater's art.

John skated 'After All' with a throwaway nonchalance that

bewitched everyone, and Jean-Pierre Bonnefous sat in the front of the stalls to see his exquisite adagio, 'Meditation', skated superlatively by Cathy Foulkes and Mark Hominuke. They infused the work with a mixture of tenderness and passion which mesmerized the audience, and their lines were beautiful and open and clear.

The ensemble shone throughout the evening, emerging as a mature and well-rounded troupe. When they came out to skate the finale, dressed in their red and white *William Tell* outfits, the normally reserved Met patrons clapped their hands in time to the music and laughed at the bit of nonsense taking place on stage.

The performance was over, and one by one the skaters came forward to take their bow, each one receiving a thunderous round of applause. When the ensemble was complete, they came forward to take a group bow and the house erupted, whistling, stamping and cheering loudly. Then they parted and John came from the back of the stage to stand in the middle of his troupe. His eyes were shining with pride as people rushed down the aisles to get near the front. They stood in knots, calling 'Bravo!' over and over again. Flowers rained down on to the ice, and John called Charles Barker up on stage to join them. Then he called for those choreographers who were present to take a bow also. Lastly he motioned to Kevin, who came out dressed in his blue jeans and received a new round of applause. It was a warm feeling, a family atmosphere. I thought John must be very, very happy at that moment.

'Don't worry about me,' Bill told me. 'Go and tell John how proud you are.' I ran downstairs and through the stage door directly beside the proscenium arch. The area was empty, except for John, still standing among his cascades of flowers, sweat pouring from his forehead and tears coursing down his face. I could see from there that he was trembling, and I went over to hug him. He clung to me for five minutes, his heart pounding furiously, his breath rasping. Finally he calmed down.

'We did it, didn't we?' he asked.

I smiled. 'I would say you not only did it, you have changed the future of skating.'

He hugged me again. 'And no matter what happens after this, no one can ever take this away from us, can they?' I laughed.

'No, John – they can't. It's an indelible moment, not only for us, but I suspect for the people in the Met tonight.'

The dressing-room area was swarming with people, all talking and hugging, shouting across heads to other people, analysing and marvelling. I visited all the skaters in turn, to let them know how very moved I had been by their performances, how special they were and how valued. David was close behind me, enveloping people in bearhugs, teary-eyed with pride. We shook hands with Charles, who had done a magnificent job throughout the evening, and there were more hugs for Steve Masi, whose haunting version of the Ravel piano prelude had contributed so much to the success of 'Moonskate'. We found Gayle ('Can't stop for all that sloppy stuff, I've got costumes to put away') and Jane, who extended a hand to each of us and said, 'Well done. We must do two weeks next year.' Then John called everyone together for a few moments and told them how much it meant to him to have such a loyal and brilliant team.

'Every bow I took out there tonight was on behalf of all of you,' he said. 'I could not have done this alone.'

There was a party afterwards, in a large, ornate room somewhere in the vast expanses of the Met. Champagne flowed and toasts were made in abundance. Everyone was in celebratory mood. I cornered Dorothy and Dino, who had disappeared to their hotel to change after the show. Dorothy was glowing. 'I thought I would die of nerves,' she said. 'But once I was out there, I had a ball!'

'You were fantastic,' I told her. 'The best I've ever seen you.' I also thought she was the happiest I'd ever seen her.

As I was leaving, Dino walked outside with me. 'This whole experience has come at a very pivotal point in Dorothy's life,' he said. 'She's been a bit down lately, to say the least, and working with John and the group has made such a difference to her. She's loving every minute of it.'

Before I left, John took me aside and asked if David and I could have breakfast with him the following morning. 'I want you to read the reviews first and then tell me about them,' he said. 'I couldn't bear to do it by myself.'

The reviews turned out to be extraordinary. They were, if anything, even more extravagant than the British ones. This avalanche of praise was all the more remarkable because – unlike Britain, where he was an established celebrity – in New York John was relatively unknown. The critics lauded not only John himself, but the entire galaxy of skaters in his company. The *Daily News* said: '. . . this company leaves the audience with a sense of awe and a very special glow'. John was 'breathtaking, superb'. The most eminent of the New York dance critics, Clive Barnes, wrote:

> John Curry and his company of superb artists swept into the Met on Wednesday night and took it by storm. They have left us all in little doubt that a new art form is here . . . This gifted young troupe can hold their own with any of the world's great dance companies, and I doubt that skating (or for that matter, the Met) will ever be the same again.

He called John 'The morning star, the undisputed leader of his genre . . . his "Moonskate" was (and I rarely apply this word to any artist) pure genius and stands among the finest work I have ever seen.'

The prestigious *New York Times* was equally expansive: 'A night of pure magic . . . this dazzling troupe of skaters have proved beyond doubt that skating is, indeed, an art form of the highest order.' They singled out most of them for individual praise, including Mark ('in the best tradition of the *danseur noble*') and Cathy ('sublime artistry, unbelievable extensions and exquisite lines'), while Patricia was described as 'an otherworldly presence, a creature of heartbreaking sensitivity' and Nathan was picked out for his 'beautiful, uncluttered lines and noble carriage'. It was once again John, however, who won the highest praise.

> He has burst onto the New York arts world like a comet and exploded on the stage of the Met . . . he is divinely talented and has a rare and special beauty . . . John Curry's rendering of 'Moonskate,' so masterfully handled, showed Eliot Feld's delicate choreography off to perfection. This must be the best thing Eliot Feld has done in any medium.

When I had finished reading them to John, in a small Greek coffee shop near Columbus Circle ('Please, not the Mayflower! I need to be private for this'), he sat looking stunned. 'It's difficult to absorb,' he said. 'It's all so overwhelming. So many years of struggle – always at odds with the establishment – and now this! Am I dreaming?' I laughed.

'No, you're very wide awake. All you need to know is that you've found acceptance from people you respect. All you ever needed was the right team of skaters and the time to prepare. Once you had that, you could do everything else.'

He smiled. 'It wasn't easy for you either, was it?' he said. 'But I hope things will be different now.' He looked at me anxiously. 'People *will* want to support us, won't they?' he asked.

'I hope so, John. All I can say is that, if they don't, I shall be very surprised.'

The week was an overwhelming success and the response from the public was phenomenal. We were heartened by the number of people who bothered to fill in the coupons to become Friends of the John Curry Skating Company. 'Maybe we'll have an influx of donations after this week,' said David. 'Howard's thing tomorrow night should help.'

On Thursday night, Howard Phelan's potential donors enjoyed the performance enormously and were lavish in their praise at the party afterwards. They were somewhat disappointed not to meet John in person, but I had already explained to Howard that we couldn't expect him to attend anything until the closing-night party. The demanding schedule, coupled with the extra rehearsals he was conducting every morning, took all the strength he had. If anyone looked particularly promising, we could always arrange a special lunch.

Mark and Sara's group were also very impressed by what they saw. 'It's stunning,' Mark said, 'absolutely fabulous. The company has to be a cinch for corporate sponsorship.' I thought he must be right. Where would a commercial enterprise find a purer, more wholesome image? John had cautioned me against any involvement with cigarettes ('I know some of the skaters smoke, but they shouldn't. Cigarette companies are no better than murderers – I don't want their money'), and he also refused to contemplate anything to do with South Africa or any company that dealt with fur: 'I abhor the wearing of fur. It's the ultimate act of barbarism, to strip a defenceless animal of its skin in order to wear it. I was presented with a fur coat at the Olympics and I gave it back. I told them to return it to its rightful owner.'

On Friday evening we premièred 'Presto Barbero', set to Leonard Bernstein's theme from *On the Waterfront*. At five that afternoon, Margaret Carson's office rang to say that Leonard himself was planning to attend the performance. This news threw everyone into a panic, as there was not a single seat left in the entire house. The production box was full, but I looked down the list to see if there was someone who might agree to come another evening. 'I can't ask Bill Judd, because *On the Waterfront* was his idea. It means too much to him. And my mother has flown in all the way from Ohio – she would never forgive me.' Finally we decided to ask David's parents, who were gracious about it and delighted to give up their seats to the man who had written *West Side Story*.

The curtain went up before Leonard arrived. He came, huffing and puffing, with only ten minutes to spare before 'Presto Barbero'. Margaret steered him to the front of the box, and he became so excited at the sight of the ice that he almost fell into the stalls. He sat down noisily, emitting squeaks of delight every time a skater came out. He was clearly enthralled by 'Meditation', and let out loud, ecstatic sighs and muttered exclamations of pleasure. Down in the stalls, several people looked up to see who was causing this disturbance, but none of us felt able to tell him to stop.

The stage went dark, and flashes of red and blue could be seen moving slowly forward. The drumbeat from the *Waterfront* music began to throb, and as it quickened the lights came up to show three of the men dressed in stunning, primitive costumes. They raced around the ice, jumping repeatedly, often perilously close to the edge of the stage. They were joined by three girls, also dressed in Willa Kim's clever, inventive costumes, and the piece gathered momentum. Lenny was beside himself. He began to hum the music, and beat on the side of the box in time to the drums. 'Hah!' he shouted in delighted approval as he watched the choreography unfolding. My eighty-five-year-old mother could finally stand it no longer. She leant forward and poked him firmly in the arm. 'Shut up!' she hissed. I was horrified and rushed down to stop her.

'Mother!' I whispered. 'You mustn't – that's Leonard Bernstein.'

'I don't care who he is,' she retorted. 'He's got no business spoiling this lovely music.'

The piece ended to a rapturous ovation, and Charles Barker invited the audience and orchestra to stand and acknowledge Leonard, who was already weeping copiously. Backstage he spoke to all the skaters, and told John he had rarely been so excited by a perform-ance. He would, he said, like to write something original for the company. John should give him a ring and they would have drinks.

On Monday morning we met with Jane to go over the finances of the engagement. Darryl came with us and I thought he looked particularly glum. I found this odd, since the season had completely sold out and had received such a triumphant response. I soon discovered, however, what was wrong. Apparently we were not to receive any further monies from the Met and, even worse, we were informed we now owed *them* money. I exploded. 'This is outrageous! How can this be so? The box office has taken over eight hundred thousand dollars – minimum! Without programme sales. And we have received to date only fifty thousand. What happened to the split of the balance? Or the promise to share the final performance equally, right down the middle?'

Jane was calm. 'Sorry, but there's nothing left over. The missed opening night is not our responsibility, it's yours. And the costs were horrendous. Extra box-office staff, stage-hands, press releases . . .'

David stopped her there. 'What extra stage-hands? I can buy the other two items, but we had no need of stage-hands on Monday or Tuesday.'

Jane shook her head. 'As long as Kevin was there on the stage, they had to be around. It all has to be paid for.'

We argued back and forth for two hours, but it seemed that somehow the Met costs had escalated to the level of $810,000. The total take was just over $860,000, so we had already had our $50,000 share. There was no more forthcoming. I turned to Darryl, who hadn't spoken a word. 'What about insurance? Surely we're covered for such an event?'

'No,' he said. 'We aren't. Unfortunately I thought it was too expensive. We couldn't afford it.'

I wanted to scream, but I managed to hold it back. I turned to Jane. 'Let me get this straight,' I said slowly. 'We have performed a sold-out season, to great public and critical acclaim, and we have actually set a box-office record. We lost an opening night, largely because your union guys were being such unadulterated arseholes, and yet for some reason the Met – this multi-million-dollar monolith – doesn't feel it has to take any responsibility whatsoever. Am I right so far?'

237

'Perfectly,' Jane said icily.

'*And*,' I went on, 'it seems your hand-picked candidate for General Manager, hired at your insistence, hasn't even bothered to insure us. Isn't it strange that David and I, the two naïve *ingénus* who weren't considered capable of managing this engagement, had always bought insurance before?' At this point, David said:

'What about tonight's performance? You told me yourself that it was a separate thing. That if we could do it you would split it down the middle with us.'

'No. I told you I would recommend it to our board of directors. Unfortunately, they wouldn't approve it.'

I was dumbstruck. It was almost inconceivable but it seemed we had managed to sustain a loss on the Met engagement.

40

Monday night was to be our last performance, but the earlier meeting had left a very bad taste in our mouths. We made a deliberate decision not to discuss it with John ('What on earth could he do about it? And it will only upset him at a time when he needs to be positive'), and accepted the fact that we would have to deal with it in the best way we could. It had taught us that the non-profit world of the arts was just as capable of cut-throat dealings as any rock organization.

Early in the afternoon, Timmy Murphy called to ask if we could meet him for a coffee; he wanted to talk to us urgently. 'I won't keep you long,' he said, when we found him sitting in the Mayflower coffee bar. 'I've written all this in a letter, but I thought it was important to tell you in person.' We sat down and ordered coffees. 'I'll take mine with whisky in it,' I said. 'I have a feeling I'm going to need it.'

Timmy Murphy was a slightly built boy with a perfectly proportioned skater's body. He was intelligent, artistic and intensely musical and he was in many ways a pivotal member of the group. He looked at us both now, and said, 'I'm afraid I have to hand in my resignation.' I felt as though someone had just let all the air out of my lungs. No skater had resigned since the group began public performance, and the imminent loss seemed unbearable.

'What's wrong?' I asked. 'Aren't you happy?'

Timmy was silent for a moment. 'Happy? It depends what you mean by that. I've been part of this family since the beginning, and it means a great deal to me. Not just the other skaters, but you two and Rob and Charles and Kevin ... but I'm afraid I just cannot continue to work under John. I cannot condone the things he has done, and I don't want to be a part of that any longer.' He looked up. 'I hope you can understand that it's nothing to do with you. You have always done your best for us and I appreciate that more than you know.' Then he handed us the letter and left. In it, he informed us that his resignation was effective immediately after the evening performance.

For several minutes David and I sat in shocked silence. I found myself fighting back tears. Timmy was like one of our children – all the skaters were – and to have him leave us under these circumstances seemed infinitely sad. I couldn't even begin to countenance it. We knew, of course, the reason for his stance. He had been a close friend of Keith and Shelley and felt John's behaviour in their regard had been reprehensible. It had never occurred to us, however, that he would actually resign.

We walked over to the Met to check on Darryl, and were greeted by Mark Hominuke: 'The people from the American Federation of Television and Radio Artists are here – they say we all have to join their union,' he told us. It seemed we had to have a full company meeting with the AFTRA representatives before tonight's show, or they would close us down. 'What next?' David groaned. 'What else could possibly go wrong?'

I found Darryl and asked him what on earth this was all about. 'We're not on television,' I said. 'And we're certainly not on radio. What are they talking about?'

Darryl shook his head. 'They cover all kinds of performers,' he told us: 'anyone who doesn't come under some other union. Since the skaters don't belong to anything, they're susceptible.'

The meeting was held in one of the large dressing rooms. John was already a member of Equity, so he didn't attend. By the time we got there, some of the skaters were leaning towards membership. I asked the union rep to outline for me, one by one, the potential benefits for the skaters if they should vote to join. 'Financial,' she said. 'They would be assured a minimum income of two hundred and eighty-five dollars per week.'

'For performing?' I asked.

'Yes.'

'But our skaters get three hundred a week just for rehearsals, and they get eight hundred for performing. What else?'

'Well – the workload is important.'

'How many shows a week can they do?'

'No more than twelve,' was the answer.

'But ours do a maximum of eight, often less. What else?'

'Benefits – you would have to pay unemployment and a contribution to a welfare and retirement fund.'

'We do that voluntarily. And they also get their accommodation for free.'

'How many to a room?' she asked.

I looked surprised. 'One, of course.' And that was that. The skaters decided to form their own union, and Mark and Dita were elected to become their representatives. Another crisis was over.

The last performance was perhaps the best of all. It had the feeling of a party about it, and the audience was in an expansive mood from the moment the curtain went up. They cheered, stamped, whistled and shouted, and when it was over they stormed the stage. It was more like a rock concert than the Met.

Afterwards we went to a party thrown by Patricia's partner, Stanley Taub, a plastic surgeon who owned a huge loft space in Greenwich Village. From the outside the building resembled a derelict warehouse, but on the inside it was a sprawling, contemporary apartment, with glass skylights, deep sofas, soaring pillars and a massive black grand piano. There were bronze sculptures everywhere, including an impressive bust of Patricia sculpted by Stanley. It was a warm and relaxed party and the company members were in a festive mood. John seemed bemused but happy, sitting quietly at the side of the room watching everyone enjoying themselves. Someone was taking photographs and he asked them to take one of him with David and me. He was the first to leave: 'Do you think anyone will notice? I'm so very tired.'

I saw Timmy standing alone beside one of the big glass windows and I went to stand beside him. 'Timmy,' I said, 'I want you to do something for me – something that will mean a great deal to everyone in the company.'

'I won't change my mind, Elva,' he said.

'I'm not asking you to change your mind. But I *am* going to ask you to wait until we've played the Wang Center in Boston. It's very important to us.'

He thought for a moment, then he said, 'All right, I'll stay until then. But it has to be understood that the day Boston ends I am no longer a member of this company.' He smiled and added: 'In a way it's for the best, because my Mum lives in Boston and she was really looking forward to seeing me perform.'

'One thing, Timmy,' I said: 'John must *not* find out about your intentions, because if he does he will make things very difficult for everyone in the mean time. You can tell him when you've skated your last show.'

There was a week between the Met and Washington, and we decided to keep the skaters in New York and rent rehearsal ice in Connecticut rather than send them all back to Vail. 'We'll just leave them in the Mayflower,' Darryl said. 'It'll work out much cheaper in the end.'

'How much cheaper?' asked David.

'Oh – I haven't worked it out exactly, but it's considerable.' The skaters were delighted.

The ice equipment had been slightly damaged in shipment, but because of the timing we had been unable to have it repaired before the Met. Now, Darryl told us, it would have to be overhauled before leaving for Washington. John Paull had made the arrangements. 'How much is it going to cost us?' I said. Darryl wasn't sure, but said he would let us know. 'But isn't it under warranty?' David asked. 'If something is damaged before we even take delivery, surely the manufacturer is liable for repairs?'

'I expect you're right. I'll find out about it,' Darryl promised.

I spoke to John about the stance the Met had taken over the box-office receipts. 'I must have misunderstood Jane's intentions,' I told him. 'I had no idea she had to seek board approval before she could make a deal with us.'

John shook his head. 'She told me herself that she would split the Monday-night box office with us if the skaters agreed to do it. That's why I told them we'd give them a hundred-dollar bonus. She said nothing about approval. Why not talk to her again? I'm sure it's all a mistake.'

I went to see Jane. She was in a mellow mood and told me the season had been an unqualified success. 'Except for the lost opening night,' I said.

She laughed. 'Oh yes, let's not forget that.'

I took a deep breath. 'Jane – according to you, the postponement cost just under a hundred thousand dollars. We received fifty thousand, and you have documented the Met's own costs for the week as just over four hundred and fifty thousand. By my reckoning, that comes to approximately six hundred thousand dollars in outgoings, leaving a two-hundred-and-sixty-thousand-dollar profit margin on the income of eight hundred and sixty thousand. What possible reason can the board have for refusing to share that?'

'It's business,' Jane shrugged. 'They're tough.'

'But they're a non-profit organization. They're not General Motors,' I said. 'No one stands to gain personally from such a coup.' I paused a moment to gauge her reaction. 'Or do they?'

She leant forward. 'Let's just say the best thing you can do for the John Curry Skating Company is to swallow this situation, and make a bloody good deal for yourselves for next season. On paper.'

We arrived in Washington on a steaming August morning. The city was built in a geographical bowl around the banks of the Potomac River, and the heat rose in a visible cloud as though we were driving into a giant sauna. 'It must be nearly a hundred degrees,' David groaned. 'Poor Kevin, trying to make ice in this!'

Darryl had arranged accommodation at a luxury hotel only a ten-minute walk from the Kennedy Center and a few hundred yards away from the infamous Watergate Hotel. Everyone had a small suite, furnished in contemporary style, with a small, fully equipped kitchen. 'They can all make their own meals, if they want,' Darryl said.

Over at the opera house, Kevin was struggling. He had set up a huge dehumidifier just inside the loading bay. 'It's murder,' he said.

'What do you think?' I asked him. 'Will we make the opening?'

'Of course!' he grinned. 'The ice is already beginning to freeze. It'll be ready for technical rehearsal in the morning.' His eyes were like black hollows and it was obvious he'd had no sleep. He had brought an assistant with him, but there was no way he would rest until the ice had formed.

David stayed to help Kevin, and I went in search of John. He was having a late breakfast in the hotel coffee shop, and looked relaxed. 'Darryl's done a very good job for us,' he said. 'I'm beginning to warm to him.' I wondered what he would say if he knew about his failure to take out insurance, but I was pleased he liked the hotel. 'How are the ticket sales?' he asked.

'Respectable,' I told him. 'The first night is sold out – Roger Stevens has filled it up with senators.' Roger Stevens was the legendary President of the Kennedy Center, best-known for having bought and sold the Empire State Building at a vast profit. 'He wants to invite you and Dorothy, David and me to dinner,' I said.

John looked slightly cross. 'What about Dino?'

'Oh, I'm sure he'll go too.'

'Then tell him I'll be happy to go if I can bring Cathy and Patricia with me.'

Howard Phelan was arranging a fund-raising party at the Watergate, to be linked to one of the performances. 'I'll need to have tickets for everyone – they're the cream of Washington society,' he told us.

'What about the Met party? Did we raise anything?' I asked.

'Too early to tell,' said Howard.

The complimentary tickets set us back another $5,000, but it seemed the wrong thing to economize on. If Howard was right, we could expect to get several hundred thousand from his efforts – 'They're all crazy about the company. Never seen anything like it!'

David and I stayed at the opera house until two in the morning. By the time we left there was an inch of good ice covering the eighty-foot stage and spreading into the wings. 'There'll be an inch and a half by morning,' Kevin said happily. 'I'm going to take a quick nap.' He had set his bed up in one of the dressing rooms, just in case anything went wrong with the machines, and everything was attached to an alarm system. He slept with a beeper in his hand so as to be instantly available at the first sign of a problem. 'Kevin takes this very seriously,' David said; 'we're so lucky to have him.'

At five-thirty my phone rang. It was Kevin, and he sounded hysterical. 'You'd better come quickly,' he said. 'Someone's just punched a hole in the middle of the ice.'

I woke David and we raced over to see what had happened. There, right at centre-stage, was an enormous hole. Kevin was sitting with his head in his hands. 'It was two men. They came rushing in with a sledgehammer and it was all over before I could even see who they were.'

'Why would anyone do such a thing?' I asked.

'The fucking unions,' David growled. 'It's the same old stuff. They don't like it because Kevin's not a member. He's doing a job the unions would have fourteen people doing.'

'What can we do?' I asked Kevin. 'Can it be repaired?'

He shook his head. 'No chance. I will have to strip it all down and start over.'

David and I looked at one another in horror: another lost opening night. There was no way we could avoid a postponement. 'This time,' I said, 'the Kennedy Center will surely pay. This isn't our fault.'

I left a message for John to call me as soon as he woke, though I had no idea how he would take this latest catastrophe. I rang Darryl and asked him to come down to my room. He sounded extremely groggy, but I told him he had to wake up, we needed his help. He came half an hour later, looking ghastly and uncharacteristically unkempt. When he heard the news he turned even paler. 'Darryl,' I said, 'you did get insurance this time, didn't you?'

He looked wretched. 'I couldn't – it came as a package.'

'What did?'

'The Met and the Kennedy Center.'

I tried to stay calm. 'But you had no insurance for the Met.'

He nodded. 'That's right. So we don't have any here either. It doesn't start until Boston.' I thought there was little point in saying anything right now, but I was determined that Darryl would go. I didn't care what Jane had to say about it. He had cost us enough already.

John appeared at seven, looking worried. I asked Darryl to leave us alone: 'Go down to the Kennedy Center and see if you can help David.' I explained the situation to John and he groaned.

'It's going to look like we aren't capable of making an opening,' he said. 'Can't we possibly do it?'

'No,' I told him. 'Kevin had to take the ice right down to the piping, or it would have been rutted.'

'Of course,' he said. 'He was right.' We ordered breakfast, and I called Jane in New York. 'When can you open?' she asked.

'If nothing else goes wrong, tomorrow night.'

'Set up a press call for one,' she said. 'I'm coming down.'

In the morning, the skaters went to Maryland to rehearse. Kevin was working non-stop, spraying layer after layer of fine mist, and trying to ignore the remarks from the union reps who were standing around watching him. 'Can't we do anything about them?' I asked Jane. 'Kevin says the two guys who made the hole are there.'

'Where's his proof?' she asked. 'And even if he had proof, it's more than his life's worth to go up against them. That's a no-win situation. You don't throw gauntlets down in front of the unions.'

'Shit!' I said. 'They're sitting there laughing at us.'

When the time came for the press call, John was nowhere to be found. 'We need a skater to speak to them,' Jane said. 'Sympathy vote. And Kevin too.' Roger Stevens was in the opera house, talking to JoJo and Dorothy; I asked if they would be willing to make the postponement announcement to the press, and they both agreed.

'But don't say anything about the hole,' Roger warned. 'Just say it's due to the excessive humidity.'

'But why?' JoJo asked. 'That'll look bad on Kevin, as though he wasn't able to cope.'

'Darling, just do it this way,' said Roger. 'I promise we won't make Kevin look bad. In fact, we want him to tell them about how difficult it all is. He can show them all the equipment – they'll be fascinated.'

The conference went extremely well, and by the end of it Dorothy and JoJo had the journalists laughing. Kevin took them on a tour of the equipment, and the photographers took pictures of it all. The evening papers carried the story on the front page, and by six o'clock the box-office phones were ringing off the hook. 'Great publicity stunt!' teased Alan Wasser, the General Manager of the Kennedy

Center. 'Ticket sales are booming!' The disaster had been turned to good advantage, but the postponement set the John Curry Skating Company back another $30,000.

41

The unions hadn't finished with us yet. That afternoon, Kevin moved one of the electrical cables and the shop steward was called. The members all sat around backstage, while the steward paced up and down with his hands clasped behind his back. We argued back and forth for over an hour, and at precisely four o'clock he called a halt to proceedings. 'If he makes sure never to do it again, then we'll forget it this time,' he said abruptly, and strode away. We found out later that he was going to see one of his stable of racehorses running at Arlington.

Jane was increasingly strident as the day wore on. John was concerned about her: 'I've never seen her like this,' he said.

'I think she's drunk,' David said bluntly. 'She had four whiskies at the press conference.'

'Surely not?' said John, surprised.

We asked her to have dinner with us, and she continued to drink all through the meal. She held it amazingly well, but her tongue became sharper by the minute. John left early, and I went down to the opera house to see how the ice was coming along. It was almost ready. Suddenly I heard a commotion erupt. When I got back to the stage, Jane was screaming hysterically at Kevin, telling him he was a 'fucking disaster, not fit to be out of short trousers'. Kevin was livid, and I stepped in to steer her away before he lost his temper. She whirled on me. 'You! You're no better yourself. You and that partner of yours – you're fucking amateurs! If you knew what you were doing, none of this would have happened. You're unprofessional losers!'

I was mortified. The production crew were watching with their mouths open, expecting a good catfight, but I didn't answer. I just walked away and left her there. I could hear her screaming at Darryl in the distance. 'You're just useless!' she was yelling. 'How come you didn't get insurance?'

By the following morning, Jane was contrite. 'Sorry I had such a go at you,' she said. 'It was the pressure. It got to me, I think.'

'I was more concerned about Kevin,' I told her. 'He's done such a good job, I hated you to speak to him like that.'

She laughed. 'He'll live!' she said.

Opening night was a glittering affair, filled with dinner jackets, evening gowns, senators, movie stars and sports celebrities of all kinds. The company was extremely calm, and John was again in very good spirits. When I was backstage before the show, JoJo and Dorothy handed me an enormous box. 'We went shopping,' they told me. 'We wanted you to have something nice.' When I opened it, there was a beautiful grey woollen trouser suit inside, and a wine-coloured silk shirt. Inside the card they had written: 'You always take care of us, so we wanted to tell you how much we appreciate it.' 'Wear it tonight, for luck,' said Dorothy. I did, and it fitted me perfectly.

Dino and I stood at the back sipping warm champagne out of plastic glasses, and he told me how much he had learnt from being around the company. 'I went through such hell-raising years with my rock band, then on the celebrity tennis circuit, then on the motor tracks. I was looking for ways to make myself happy, ways to please myself. I wasn't a real person at all – I was Dean Paul Martin, son of the famous entertainer, trying to live up to his image, trying to make him notice me. I only realized recently, since I've been married to Dorothy, and particularly since we started hanging out with this company, that you can only be happy by pleasing *other* people.'

The show went up late, since so many people were still finding their seats. 'It's like that here,' one of the ushers said. 'People always come late.' It was quite unlike the starkly elegant Metropolitan Opera House. The exterior of the building looked like it had been erected with the sole purpose of withstanding the atomic bomb, and the inside of the building resembled nothing so much as a French bordello. However, once the lights had dimmed, and the curtain was swept back, the ice sheet worked its usual magic on the audience. From the moment the first knot of skaters appeared, they were captivated.

Every skater drew prolonged applause, and John's exquisite 'Moonskate' was received with wonder. The first half ended on an exuberant high with the throbbing 'Presto Barbero', and the audience filed into the foyers, chattering excitedly about the performances.

The second half opened with Jean-Pierre Bonnefous' 'Valse', which had its most rapturous reception to date, and David Santee was loudly applauded for his 'Russian Sailor's Dance'. It was to be the night that Patricia Dodd stole the show, however, with her hypnotically beautiful solo, 'Blessed Spirit', set to Gluck's haunting melody. She skated so sublimely, as though transported to another level of consciousness, that the audience was overcome. As her final spin slowed to a stop, they erupted in wild cheering, and all over the house people were screaming 'Bravo!' Pat was unused to this response, and had already hurried backstage to make the quick change necessary for her next number. The audience continued to shout for her, and she stood, half in and half out of her costume, not sure of what to do. 'Patricia!' John yelled. 'Get back out there and take a bow!'

She pulled on the dress, Gayle zipping it up as she went, and moved forward to centre-ice. When she appeared, everyone got to their feet and cheered her again, and she stood with tears streaming down her face, completely taken by surprise. 'That's exactly what this company is all about, isn't it?' Dino said. 'Giving opportunities to such wonderful skaters who were lost in the amateur shuffle?'

'Yes,' I said. 'It is.'

'Do you realize that Dorothy has won the Olympics and the Worlds, yet she could never skate like that?' I started to protest, but he stopped me. 'I'm not putting Dorothy down. Far from it. She is a star, and rightly so. But Patricia is an artist, and she deserved to be honoured tonight. Dorothy would be the first to say so.'

At the party afterwards, John came over to me before he left. 'Don't tell me – I'm to bring the reviews to breakfast!' I said. He laughed.

'Let's make it late. I'm very tired.' He had no cause to worry, however. The major Washington critic, Alan Kreigsman, was lavish in his praise, calling the company 'artistically rewarding and aesthetically daring, elegant and superior in every way'. He called John a 'master builder' and showered him with superlatives. It was clear that Washington had fallen in love with the John Curry Skating Company.

The adulation didn't stop with the press. Roger Stevens had taken an enormous liking to the troupe and invited everyone to a glittering party at the Ritz Carlton. It was crammed with Washington's élite and celebrities from the diplomatic world. JoJo and Dorothy made the rounds, enchanting everyone they met, but John stood in the middle of the crowd, looking lost. 'I have no idea who all these people are,' he said. 'Or why we're here.'

'Just do your best,' I whispered. 'It's just Roger, showing you off.'

John turned to the imposing man standing next to him and held out his hand. 'I'm John Curry,' he said. The man took his hand. 'I'm General David Jones,' he said, 'Chairman of the Joint Chiefs of Staff. What do you do?'

By the third performance, the tickets for the two weeks had completely sold out. Roger Stevens cornered us backstage and asked us if we would consider cancelling Boston in order to add a third week. John immediately turned it down: 'I won't let the Wang Center down. And lots of people have already bought their tickets.' Roger persisted, and when Dino and Dorothy, John, Cathy, JoJo and myself went to dinner at his house he brought the subject up again.

'You know, the Kennedy Center can do a lot for this company,' he said. 'We might even consider taking you under our wing. Officially. I have a particular sponsor in mind, who might be talked into putting up two hundred and fifty thousand dollars for the project.' This sounded too good to be true, but he offered to meet me the following day to go into more detail. 'Now,' he said. 'What about this extra week?' John looked disappointed.

'So that's what this is all about?' he said. 'And I thought you were really interested in our welfare!'

I met with Roger the next day, but his interest in the company was vague, and nothing specific was ever offered. It seemed John's gut reaction had probably been accurate.

The fund-raising party at the Watergate Hotel was a huge success. The problem was that it didn't produce any prospective donors. For some reason, John took a dislike to him. 'I don't want that man having anything to do with the company,' he said. 'Are we paying him?'

'No,' I said. 'He works on commission.'

'Well, just thank him for his efforts and tell him we don't need him any more.' I didn't argue with John, because the truth was that we had already become disillusioned with Howard's fund-raising skills. To date, he had cost us thousands of dollars in free tickets and hospitality.

When we came to settle our hotel bill, it was eighteen thousand dollars, more than the budgeted estimate. I was horrified. I took Darryl to one side. 'What the hell is going on?' I asked him. 'How can you do this to us?' He told me he had been promised a deal which hadn't materialized. I was too upset to bother arguing with him. I rang Jane and told her of the latest incident. 'I don't understand why everyone is forcing us to accept whatever Darryl chooses to do. You have us in a vice – on the one hand he is allowed to run us into more and more debt; on the other, we are the only ones responsible for paying it.'

'I don't run your company,' said Jane matter-of-factly. 'You must do what you think is best. Perhaps Darryl's not as efficient as he used to be. If that's the case, then you must let him go.'

This was easier said than done, since the Chemical Bank had manoeuvred us into a position where Darryl controlled the purse strings of our company. David went to see if he could get them to revert this decision. He was turned down flat. He appealed to Joe for help. 'I really can't do anything. You'll have to wait until Nan Miller comes back from her vacation at the end of September.' We were trapped. We would just have to survive the coming weeks the best way we could.

We went straight to Boston from Washington. Kevin had left in the early hours of the morning, travelling in the truck with the ice machine. When we arrived, it was to find we were booked into a very nice hotel, just a few blocks from the Wang Center. I knew it must be expensive, but I was too tired to worry about it at this point. There was nothing I could do about it anyway; I would just enjoy it.

When Timmy told John he was resigning, the optimism that had characterized his demeanour during the last few weeks crumbled away. He sank into a black depression and shut himself away in his room. When I tried to reach him it was to be told he had asked not to be disturbed. He refused to come out for the company practice at a nearby rink. Rob took over and organized the session, but he was worried about John. 'He's been so different recently that I thought the old demon had gone away,' he said. 'But it looks as though it's back with a vengeance. He's been chewing everyone out today.' Company morale was so low that I decided to go to practice with them. It seemed to help. We held a company meeting in the dressing room at the rink, and they told me several things that were bothering them. Top of the list, of course, was Timmy, but he begged them not to make a fuss. 'I want to move on,' he told them. 'It's time. I want to compose music and write scores.' Their other worries revolved around Darryl ('He gives us the creeps – he always seems to be drunk') and John.

Their problems with John were complicated. It was a kind of love/ hate relationship for them, and they desperately wanted him to like them. They also wanted him to be all right in himself. 'We worry about him so much,' said JoJo. 'He gets so down, it's scary.' 'He seems to be cross with me all the time,' Dita said sadly. 'I try so hard, but I never seem to be able to please him.'

The ice went in perfectly, with no problems, and I took a bottle of champagne down to the Wang Center and opened it. 'Don't spill that on my ice!' said Kevin. I gave him a glass and toasted him.

At ten p.m. I was reading some papers at the hotel when everything went black. I went to the window and pulled back the drapes, but the entire area was in darkness.

42

I pulled on a jacket and raced out of my room. The corridors of the hotel were dimly lit by emergency lights and the lift was out. I ran down the stairs and into the deserted street. I would normally have been nervous in the city, late at night, but I didn't stop to think about it. I hurried along, looking neither right nor left, and found the Wang Center almost by accident. An eerie orange glow was showing through the windows.

Inside the building, the emergency lamps were burning. There seemed to be no sign of activity and everything was silent, but when

I found the stage area Kevin was there, frantically covering the ice surface with clingfilm. 'Here,' he said, throwing me a roll. 'Can you help? The quicker we do this the better.' We worked together, sealing the long strips, until the entire surface was covered. Kevin let out a sigh of relief. 'It won't hold for long, but at least it'll retard the warming process.' I felt so sorry for him. He was exhausted. 'I can't believe it,' he said, sinking to the floor with a sigh. 'We get the ice in on time, and we have a power cut. It makes you wonder.'

I went down to the theatre office and found the manager sitting in the murky interior. 'What do you hear about the problem?' I asked. He shook his head. 'They say it was lightning, but I don't know. I think it might take a while. What about the ice?'

'We have to try to keep it in,' I told him. 'The only thing I can suggest is that we try to find a generator from somewhere. It'd need a big one.' He started to search through a tattered phone book.

'I could make a few calls, but it'd cost a bit.'

'That can't be a factor,' I told him. 'We have insurance so it doesn't really matter.'

He located one in Maine, several hundred miles away, and arranged for a private helicopter to airlift it in. It arrived at six a.m. and the commotion it caused attracted the media. The story was on all the morning television news programmes, and the interest was so intense that we arranged a press call for later. 'The ice is more famous than the company!' I told Kevin. 'Perhaps we should just get rid of the skaters!'

The huge generator was running by seven. Kevin had lost almost half an inch of ice, and the whole expanse was now softened. 'I have a choice,' he said. 'I can either work really quickly, refreeze what's here and build up from there, or I can strip it all down and start over. Starting over would mean a postponement, but if I do it the other way, the ice is going to be brittle. John won't like it.'

'Kevin, to be absolutely honest with you, I don't think John will give a bugger if the ice is brittle, just so long as it is frozen. The worst thing that could happen would be that we have yet another postponement.'

Later in the day, the power was back on and we were able to hold an orchestra rehearsal. Charles was perturbed by the musicians.

'They're supposed to be members of the Boston Symphony,' he said. 'But I don't think there's anyone under eighty. We had to give the trumpeter oxygen just now.'

'I'm sure you'll manage,' I said. 'There are a lot of things happening in Boston this week – I think Darryl had a problem finding any musicians.'

John came down for the rehearsal, but he was still in a very bad mood. He ran through 'Moonskate' and 'Tango Tango', then sat in the stalls by himself watching the others rehearse. Billy Fauver asked me if I could do something about him. 'He's making us all nervous. Maybe you could talk to him.'

I sat beside John, and for a while we didn't speak. Then I said: 'In some ways this will be the most difficult engagement of all.' He turned to look at me.

'Why?'

'Because it's not exciting, the way the Met and the Albert Hall, the Kennedy Center and Dubai were. It's not the first, not the last, not the most important – it's just Boston.'

'I think you might be right,' he said. 'I've been feeling a bit blue today.'

'Post-natal depression!' I teased him, but he couldn't bring himself to smile.

Boston was to be our first American date without Dorothy as a guest skater. It was reflected in the advance ticket sales and we were concerned about the company's ability to stand alone in a major US city. David, who had stayed in New York to work on the fund-raising, called to see how the box office was performing. 'Mediocre at the moment,' I told him. 'But we have to remember this is Labour Day weekend. It's the worst theatrical date in the calendar, other than Christmas. All the commotion over the ice helped a bit, though.'

That night the opening went very well indeed. The vast cavern of the Wang Center was ninety per cent filled, and the performances were spectacular. At the end of the show the audience stood and applauded as loudly and enthusiastically as any of our previous houses. The reviews ranged from complimentary to lavish, and the powerful *Boston Globe* said: 'Forget the Olympics! If it's real skating you want to see, go on over to the Wang Center and see the John Curry Skating Company.' Cathy Foulkes was singled out for special praise, not only because of her outstanding talent, but also because she was a home-town girl who had once trained with the Boston Ballet.

Jane called me to find out how things were going. 'David Foster is coming up to see you today,' she said. This wasn't good news.

'John's not really in the frame of mind to be able to deal with that right now,' I told her, but she was insistent.

'It's you he wants to talk to. I think you should listen to what he has to say.'

John had taken the skaters down to the Wang Center for a rehearsal when David arrived, so I was able to meet him in the hotel coffee shop. He began by apologizing for his previous meeting with John: 'We should have discussed it with you. It was a silly mistake.' Then he told me that CAMI believed strongly in the potential of the company and would like to manage us on a trial basis. 'Give me six months to show you what we have in mind. We can take the headache out of the difficult markets – CAMI has power and influence. We'll get you more money and better deals, and we can open up new performing possibilities for you.' I asked him for an example. 'The arenas. They're notoriously complex and very hard to break into.'

I shook my head. 'John doesn't want to play arenas. We've already done an arena tour, back in 1983. He made us promise we would never book the company into another arena.'

David sighed. 'That's a pity. You could have made some really good income that way.' We talked for half an hour, but nothing he said made any impression. It was all things we had already thought of. Finally, I leant towards him and said:

'David, I don't want to waste your time. I must be honest with you. There's only one reason we would consider signing with you, and that's if you can guarantee to solve our financial crisis – not just for the time being, but on a long-term basis.'

He stared at me thoughtfully. 'How much money do you need?'

'A quarter of a million dollars in the first instance.'

'And later?'

'That depends. If we have sufficient bookings next year, then we might become relatively self-sufficient. And maybe we could even get a sponsor by then.'

He drew his breath in sharply. 'A quarter of a million isn't actually that much, considering you've set up an entire company and developed three evenings of ballets for it. Let me think about it carefully and talk it over with my colleagues. Why don't we meet next week, when you get back from Boston?'

Meanwhile, the rights to the BBC special from the Royal Albert Hall had been bought by a Manhattan entrepreneur called Sander Jacobs. He showed a keen interest in the welfare of the company. His lawyer now called to say they would like to come to Boston to see the show, and would like to invite myself, John and JoJo to lunch.

Sander was a generous host. We had a pleasant and relaxing two hours, and over coffee he said: 'Now, let's talk about the company. What can I do to help?'

John smiled. 'You're one of the few people who seem to understand our needs. Perhaps you might consider coming on to our board?'

'I could do that. But on a more practical level? What if I were to endow a ballet? Is there something special you would like to do?'

John's face lit up. 'Oh, yes – Stravinsky's *Firebird*. I've always thought it would work beautifully for ice and now I have the skaters who could do it.'

Sander smiled. 'You figure out how much it would cost and come back to me. You will need an exact budget. I don't like to be vague.'

Dorothy and Dino were at the Saturday-evening performance. They sat in the front row of the dress circle and Dorothy rewarded every performance by whistling loudly through her teeth. 'My brother taught me to do that when I was five,' she said. 'What a great show this is! I've never had a chance to sit out front and watch it before.'

Monday was our last day, and I cornered Darryl in the hotel lobby. 'We need to talk,' I said. We sat in the coffee bar and ordered toast. He seemed nervous, and I noticed his eyes checking the entrance every few moments. 'Are you expecting someone?' I asked curiously.

'No, no,' he said quickly. 'Just a lot of things still to do.'

'Well, this is one of them,' I told him. 'I need to know *exactly* where we stand financially, because we have the potential of a large influx of cash from CAMI, and the last thing we need is to take it and then find it isn't enough.'

Darryl cleared his throat. 'I would need to work with Joe on that – it's a bit difficult because Bill's computer system isn't one I'm used to. It'll take me some time.'

'But surely,' I persisted, 'you can get the information from your own records? When you joined us, the books were up to date. Just work forward from that point and you'll have the answers you need.'

'Yes. Well, that's what I must do then.'

I stood up to leave. 'By the way,' I said, 'how long do you think the insurance claim for the generator will take? It's ended up costing just over five thousand dollars and I told the Wang Center you would settle it as soon as the insurance company paid up. They were OK with that.'

Darryl looked surprised. 'Insurance? Didn't I tell you? We can't claim for the generator because the power cut was caused by lightning. It comes under acts of God, and it's an exclusion.'

In Boston, John decided to fire Lori Nichol, angry at her apparent inability to lose weight. 'Lori, we just can't continue like this,' he told her. 'I don't believe you've tried at all, and I wash my hands of you.' Lori burst into tears and Nathan, who was a special friend of hers, pleaded with John to give her another chance.

'She's making herself ill,' he said. 'She throws everything up, and she's undernourished.'

'Then she should see a doctor,' John said. 'She may have hypoglycaemia.' As they boarded the bus, John stopped her and said: 'Lori – if you can overcome this problem, then let me know. You're one of the most beautiful skaters I know, and I don't want to lose you. See what you can accomplish over the next few months.'

The final show was full. The houses had been increasing all week and the Wang Center was keen to have us back the next year. 'No doubt next time you would do very well indeed.' This was exciting news – it meant the company could sustain itself without the addition of external guest stars.

It was Timmy's last night and we had planned a party for him back at the hotel. Everyone had clubbed together to buy him a state-of-the-art synthesizer, and we had champagne and cake. John had got wind of this celebration, but was not invited: the reasons for Timmy's departure made his presence impossible. As I was leaving the theatre, I glanced into the darkened auditorium and saw a solitary figure sitting motionless in one of the stall seats. I knew it was John, and something about his forlorn figure made me want to cry. I felt afraid for him for the first time in many weeks.

43

The next morning we flew to New York on the Boston Shuttle. David met us at the airport because he was to go to Vail to resettle the company in new accommodation. I was sorry to lose him: we desperately needed time out to discuss our situation.

When I got back to the office, there were two brown envelopes waiting for me. One contained our official notification of 501(c)(3) status, which meant we were now legally able to solicit funding and seek grants. The other was paperwork from the Equal Opportunities Commission, regarding Keith Davies.

I was appalled. I knew that Keith's firing had been grossly unfair, but had no idea that I could be prosecuted for it. I telephoned their officer, Joseph Wiznewski. 'What can I do about this?' I asked him. 'Is there any way to settle it?'

'Possibly,' he answered. 'It will all depend on the offer.'

So I went to see James Berry, John's personal lawyer. He listened while I told him the Keith Davies saga from beginning to end. 'We must try to settle it,' he said. 'What do you think he wants?'

'A pound of flesh at this point, I should think,' I said. 'He has nothing to lose, that's the problem. Should we tell John?'

James shook his head. 'No, I don't think so. We'd better keep this between us for now. If John finds out he'll insist on fighting it, and then it will go before the discrimination board. He won't want to settle it.'

I sighed heavily. 'It's all so complicated. But we don't have a leg to stand on, James. We can't possibly deny that Keith was fired because of John's emotional problems.' James suggested that I leave the matter with him for the time being and he would see what he could negotiate.

David Foster now came back to me with a definite offer. CAMI would underwrite a $250,000 loan from the Chemical Bank to the company. The bank would carry the loan on payment of a monthly interest rate of $3,300, until such time as we were in a position to repay the capital. CAMI would require us to sign a three-year contract with them for representation, and they would take over the booking of all future dates, as well as servicing the existing ones. I

257

discussed it with David and we felt we should accept. We also felt that the size of the loan would give CAMI an incentive to do a good job for us as our agents. I told John what we wanted to do. 'You must do what you think best,' he said. 'If we need the money, go ahead. I won't object, just so long as I don't have to deal with David Foster.'

I met with the agents at CAMI, David Foster, Catherine Gevers and Peter Gelb. We discussed the future of the company, and where we might be able to find suitable bookings. I told them that we had three weeks in Scandinavia in November, plus return visits to the Met and the Kennedy Center in 1985. Victor had not located a suitable London venue yet. Boston would most probably want us back, and we had interest from the Miami Center for the Performing Arts and the San Francisco Opera House. What we needed was a cohesive plan for 1985 which would keep the company working and provide enough income to enable us to begin paying off our loan.

Darryl announced that he had the possibility of a week in the Arie Crown Theater in Chicago. 'It's a good house,' he said. 'I think you would do well there. Shall I book it?'

'What are they offering?' I asked.

He looked blank. 'Offering? Nothing. We would have to promote ourselves.'

'How can we afford to do that?' I asked him.

'I don't think it would be too difficult,' he said. 'With the company's recent record, we could probably find local funding.'

David told me he thought Chicago would be a godsend, since the skaters were all anxious to perform again. Their recent unbroken stretch had made them hungry for more. He suggested I talk it over with CAMI.

I imagined CAMI would advise us not to self-promote, but to my surprise David Foster thought we should go ahead. 'CAMI can't be involved in the date, but all the evidence suggests that you would do well. You sold out in New York and Washington with a guest artist, and you did seventy-five per cent in Boston without one. You have great reviews to go in with, and you have the added advantage of David Santee being a local boy. It seems a fairly safe bet.'

Darryl's budgeting showed that we could break even in Chicago at less than fifty per cent. This was an acceptable risk by any standards, and we felt reasonably confident that we would do much better than that. The estimated cost of the date was just over $300,000, which included $50,000 for advertising. We now had to find a way to front this amount.

We signed the CAMI contract and the loan was finalized with the Chemical Bank. David and I discussed the essential disbursements and I gave Darryl a list of those things that needed to be paid immediately. This included $6,500 to Bill Kenwright's office in London to cover a cheque we had given him during the Royal Albert Hall season: unfortunately, it had arrived in our bank during the pre-Met crisis, and had been returned to London unpaid. We needed to take care of several short-term loans and a number of expense accounts, and it was also time to make a payment on David's American Express card.

James Berry had arrived at a tentative settlement with Keith Davies. The deal hinged on Keith getting a US work permit, which would cost approximately $1,500, and in addition we would have to pay out the balance of his skating contract, including compensation for his lost appearances at the Met and Kennedy Center. It seemed an eminently fair settlement. The question arose as to who should actually pay these sums. It was rightfully John's responsibility, but I knew that we couldn't effect such a payment without telling him about it. 'I guess the company will just have to swallow it,' I told James. 'I can't see any other way to handle it.'

It had become an emergency to free David from his duties in Vail. It was going to take both of us to handle the enormous task of launching the non-profit company, and to set in motion the many-faceted fund-raising campaign. Also, we needed to find investors for the Chicago season. I had recently hired someone to help me in the office, a former World Champion roller skater called April Allen, and I approached her now with the idea that she might go to Vail in place of David, and look after everything down there. Additionally, she could take class with the company each day with a view to joining the ensemble. She was dubious. She had two jobs in New York (including ours) which gave her an income of $600 a week. If she went to Vail, she would have to be paid a minimum of $400 or she couldn't afford to go. It was more than the skaters were earning, but it balanced out because she would have to work much longer hours and she wouldn't get the increased performance pay when the company was on tour. It was agreed, and she left straight away. David came back as soon as she arrived.

John was very enthusiastic about April: 'She has an amazing natural grace on the ice,' he told me. 'I'm going to work privately with her because I think she's worth it. She could well be in the company before long.' April told me that one or two of the skaters were giving her a hard time, but that on the whole she had been well received.

Jane Herman had become very friendly since the CAMI contract was signed, and offered us all kinds of advice. She thought we would do well in Chicago and put David in touch with a friend of hers with a view to finding some investors. He flew down two days later and within twenty-four hours he was back with a cheque for $70,000. 'It's a great start,' he said. According to Darryl, we would be safe if we could raise a further $100,000, since $170,000 would carry us until the box office kicked in.

A Canadian acquaintance of mine, David Doucet, told us about a man in Wisconsin who sometimes invested in shows, and called to see if he would be interested. The answer was a tentative yes, and he suggested that one of us go down to Wisconsin and meet the man. David went the next day, and spent several hours explaining the project. When he came back, he had the $100,000. We were all set.

I had lunch with Bill Judd, and we talked extensively about CAMI. Bill was concerned with the apparent lack of action, and suggested he come with me to a meeting to see if he could find out what the problems were. CAMI was a powerful office with excellent connections, yet they seemed to be getting nowhere. Bill worked from a very small office with part-time help, yet he and I between us had managed to put together a total of sixteen weeks of performance, most of it booked when the company was virtually unknown.

When we got to CAMI's offices on West 57th Street, we were told David Foster had been called away to an urgent meeting, and asked to wait while Catherine Gevers was located. Bill was not pleased by this apparent lack of courtesy, and felt it did not bode well. When Catherine arrived, fifteen minutes later, she seemed ill-prepared to talk about the company's prospects. She spoke at length about the next year's bookings for the Met and the Kennedy Center, and about the San Francisco Opera House. Bill eyed her irritably. 'Am I not right in assuming those dates to have been booked through my office?'

Catherine looked startled. 'Well, yes,' she said. 'But we're negotiating the contracts for them.'

'Quite so,' said Bill. 'But we've come here today to hear all about the new opportunities CAMI has developed for the company. You do have some new ones?'

Catherine's face flushed and she began to thumb through her file. 'I'm sure David has something on the horizon, but I have to admit I'm not sure what it is. You should talk to him about that.'

'That is precisely what we were hoping to do today,' Bill said archly. 'Before our good friend was urgently called away.' He snapped his folder shut. 'So I take it that you don't actually have anything pending at all?'

Catherine shook her head. 'Not specifically. It's really too soon.'

'And may one ask how much longer you will require before we can expect something to materialize?'

'Oh, it shouldn't be too long. We'll let you know as soon as we have something, of course.'

Afterwards we went for a glass of wine in the Italian café next door. 'I can't understand why we don't have any bookings,' Bill said. 'It's very worrying.'

Jane called me the next day. 'What on earth were you thinking of, taking Bill Judd up there to David's office?' she demanded.

'He's our booking adviser,' I replied. 'I wanted his opinion.'

'Well, it was in the worst possible taste. And apparently he was terribly aggressive to poor Catherine.'

'He wasn't at all aggressive. He was just asking questions that needed to be asked.'

Jane was obviously upset. 'Well, it hasn't done you any good,' she said. I thought this a very odd conversation, but I didn't ask her to elaborate.

I flew down to Vail to see John. I had sensed some tension in his voice recently and I wanted to see for myself what was happening. I realized very quickly that we had made a serious mistake in leaving him down there without David.

44

Suddenly, John seemed like a stranger to me. He even looked different. He seemed weary and lethargic, and he was unusually off-hand. I went to Rob's chalet and asked if we could talk. 'What's wrong with John?' I asked straight away. Rob looked uncomfortable. 'He's just a bit tired, that's all. He has a lot on his mind.' Down at the Dobson Arena I found April in the office. 'Now,' I said. 'I want to know what's going on.'

She was reluctant to talk about it at first. 'You won't say anything?' she asked anxiously. 'If John thought I was discussing him, he'd throw me out.'

I was appalled. 'April!' I said. 'You have to tell me if there's something wrong. That's why you're down here. I can't help if I don't know what's happening.'

She told me that John had been in a terrible mood for over a week. He'd screamed at several of the skaters, particularly JoJo, Mark and Patricia. Yesterday, Patricia had broken down and cried. He had asked April to ban them from rehearsals. 'I couldn't do that, could I? He put me in an impossible position, and when I didn't do it, he turned on me too.' I told her not to worry about it, and that I would try to sort it out. It was clear that David would have to come back if we were to get the company to Chicago in one piece.

That evening Rob invited John and me for dinner at his chalet. I arrived slightly early and he handed me a glass of red wine. 'We need to talk,' he said. 'I've asked John to come at nine, so we have an hour.'

'I really don't know what's happening to John. And, much as I love him, my concern is now for the effect he is having on the others. They are becoming demoralized. Not just the ones he's fixated on, but all of them. They're such a close-knit family now, and when John is unkind to one of their members, they all feel the pain.'

'But what's wrong?' I asked. 'He seemed in such good spirits all summer. What's happened to change things?'

Rob was silent for a moment. 'It's partly your fault,' he said. 'You used to be so light-hearted around John. David was always here for him to talk to when he felt concern about anything. Or when he just felt in a lousy mood. David would take him off for a walk and make him laugh. Now you both have so little time for anything except running the business of the company. I know it sounds strange, but John feels left out. He feels as though you and David have taken over and excluded him. He also feels he isn't being told what's happening.' I was shocked. Much of what Rob said was true, but I had always assumed that John understood.

'We feel we have to protect him,' I said. 'He's so vulnerable, and we felt he would never have been able to handle the summer season if he'd been worrying about the money all the time.'

'Well, you're right, of course,' Rob said. 'But you have to find a way to make him feel secure. I think David has to come back here again. Things were very different when he was around.'

At rehearsal I saw for myself what had been causing the concern amongst the skaters: 'You're not exactly Pavlova, Patricia! Stop behaving like a prima donna and just try to be a good member of the ensemble. You're forty years old, not six.' He singled out Mark, and told me he wanted him fired.

'Fired?' I said. 'Whatever for? Surely you aren't serious?'

'I've never been more serious in my life,' he answered. 'Mark Hominuke is an inferior skater and a pain in the backside to go with it. I want him out.'

'John,' I said carefully, 'please don't do this. We need to get through Chicago, which is only ten days away. Let's put this on hold for now, and after Chicago we'll sit down and discuss it.'

John drew a very deep breath and let it out again sharply. 'All right. We'll wait until after Chicago. But then I want him out. It doesn't need to be discussed.'

David made arrangements to go back to Vail immediately. 'I'll go down via Chicago, and I can check out what's happening there.' The initial ticket sales had been brisk ('I think they were all bought by David Santee's mother'), but now things had slowed to a worrying trickle. David wanted to meet with Margie Korshak, the local publicist, and see if anything could be done to boost sales.

Two days before we left for Chicago, Darryl told me that he had revised his budget. His requirements had increased by almost twenty per cent. 'How is this possible?' I asked him. 'You assured us your figures were accurate.'

263

'Some things are running over cost,' he said. 'Hotel, advertising, flights . . .'

I was horrified. 'What you are really telling me is that your original budget was all guesswork,' I fumed. 'Now you're actually doing the figures, you're finding out a different story. But you went to Chicago and made a deal with the hotel. What happened to that?'

He shook his head. 'I'm not sure. They reneged.' I felt the beginnings of panic. I had always worried about Darryl, but now we had a self-promotion riding on his assumed expertise. I called David Foster. 'Darryl was always a good man,' he said. 'But I must admit he doesn't seem himself these days.' This was not a comforting observation.

John knew nothing of all this, but down in Vail he was becoming increasingly difficult. David called me the night before departure and told me John was in a state of extreme melancholia. 'He's taken to his bed again and he's telling me he won't go tomorrow.' I tried to phone him, but the phone was off the hook. I called David back. 'You'll have to go over there,' I said. 'If he doesn't turn up in Chicago we'll have to cancel the whole engagement.'

David went over to John's chalet and found him in an appalling condition. He was unkempt (which was extremely unusual for John) and looked as though he had been crying for hours. David embarked on a mammoth heart-to-heart talk, which lasted until the early hours, and eventually managed to get John to drink a vodka and orange and have a shower. They called me at this point, and John sounded relatively cheerful. 'I've been a bit of a nuisance again,' he said happily, 'but David's given me a big vodka and I feel a bit better. Don't worry about anything.'

By the following morning, however, he was in a completely different mood. He was surly and aggressive and he again demanded that Mark be fired. David was too tired to bother arguing. He bundled John into his car and set off for Denver Airport with the radio playing. The skaters went down in the minibus, and when they got into the terminal John saw Mark in the coffee shop. He whirled on David: 'I thought you told me that he wasn't going to be here?'

David was getting increasingly irritated. 'I said no such thing,' he said. 'In fact, you had promised Elva and me that you would call a moratorium on Mark until after Chicago.'

John was already walking towards the exit doors. 'I told everyone

I wouldn't go if he was going, and I meant it,' he called over his shoulder. By this time the flight had been called and the skaters had disappeared towards the plane. David lost his temper.

'John,' he said through gritted teeth, 'you are getting on this plane if I have to drag you there. I don't know what your problem with Mark is, and for all I know you might be perfectly justified in your attitude, but whatever it is can wait until we have finished the Arie Crown shows. Now, shall we go?'

On the plane, David managed to talk the stewardess into upgrading John into first class. For once he didn't argue, but sat there in studied silence until the plane landed in O'Hare Airport. David waited until the skaters had disembarked, then he took John's bags and propelled him off the plane.

I had arrived in Chicago earlier that morning. I was desperately worried about the ticket sales, which had barely risen above thirty-four per cent of capacity. It seemed that Chicago simply wasn't interested in the John Curry Skating Company. Our only hope now was that the box office would pick up after the reviews, and that we would get good word-of-mouth. I heard the company arriving and went to meet them. They were excited, as they always were before the start of a new engagement. The hotel was a slightly seedy, old-fashioned facility and I watched anxiously to see how they would react. No one seemed bothered by it, and they all went off happily to their rooms. 'Where's John?' I asked Darryl.

'David's bringing him after us in a taxi,' he told me.

I sat in the lobby waiting for them to arrive, and Mark and Nathan came downstairs. 'How is it?' I asked.

'Fine,' Mark said cheerfully.

Ten minutes later, John came through the revolving doors, closely followed by David. He walked over to the desk and registered in silence, then he took his key and went upstairs. He refused David's offer to help with the bags. David sat down beside me with a weary sigh, and buried his head in his hands. 'You have no idea,' he groaned. 'This is worse than it's ever been, and I don't think it's over yet.' No sooner had the words left his mouth than John appeared again, running down the staircase, dragging his bags behind him. 'I will *not* be made to stay in this hellhole,' he yelled. 'This may be your idea of a luxury hotel, but it certainly isn't mine. It's a cesspit – in fact, the whole city is a cesspit, and I'm going back to New York.' The hotel manager watched this scene with his mouth open, and John stormed over to the revolving door and disappeared.

Darryl was so shocked that he ran out after him into the pouring rain. John was climbing into a taxi, and Darryl tried to stop him. 'Don't TOUCH me,' John screamed, and pushed him so hard that he fell backwards into the gutter. The door slammed and the taxi drove away into the gloom.

We knew John must be heading for the airport. 'We have to stop him,' David said. 'If he gets on a plane, it will all be over.' Darryl had just come back inside, brushing furiously at his muddy suit. 'Do you have a rental car?' David asked him.

'Yes. It's outside in the parking lot.'

'I need the keys in a hurry,' David said. 'We have to go and get him back.'

David and I drove towards O'Hare at eighty miles an hour, swerving in and out of the traffic. I was sure we would be killed. When we got there, we had no idea which terminal to search, so we drove round peering through the windows. Suddenly David slammed on the brakes. 'There he is!' he yelled. 'In the Delta lounge.' He parked outside and told me to wait with the car. 'It's illegal to stop here,' he said through the window. 'You'll just have to make something up if anyone tries to move you on.' I watched him as he went inside and tapped John on the shoulder. They talked for what seemed hours, and I managed to persuade the traffic warden to let me stay for a few minutes longer. 'You better not let me find you here when I get back, lady,' he warned. Eventually they came out, and John climbed quietly into the back of the car. I could hear him sobbing. David climbed into the front and drove quickly away. 'John's going to a different hotel,' he told me. 'He's going to put it on his credit card.'

We settled John into the Chicago Hilton, and he asked if we could come back and have supper with him. David was dubious: 'I don't really think we have time. I was planning on getting a McDonald's.'

'Please,' John persisted. 'I don't want to eat alone.' In the end I stayed there and David went back to the Arie Crown Theater to see how the ice was progressing. John and I had an early supper in the revolving restaurant ('These things always seem to crop up when there's a problem!') and talked about everything except the real reason he had run away. He had created a new piece especially for

266

Scandinavia (set to the *Holberg* suite by Grieg) and seemed pleased with it. I tried in circuitous ways to find out what was bothering him ('How's the knee? Has Sean settled down well?'), but his answers were polite and non-committal. He became animated only when he told me he was considering the purchase of a permanent home in Vail.

David Santee's mother arranged for the company to rehearse at her local rink, and the following morning we went over there in the bus, stopping to collect John on the way. When we pulled up outside the Hilton there was murmuring among the skaters, and I realized it was the first time he had ever separated himself from the rest of them in this way. It was to leave a permanent scar on the company.

The Skating Club of Chicago had cleared the ice for the company to rehearse, and had also prepared a buffet lunch for the skaters. It was a warm, pleasant rink and I sat upstairs with David in an observation room overlooking the ice surface. John left Rob to run the rehearsal and seemed to take no part in it. At twelve o'clock he came upstairs and pulled me over to the window. 'Look down there and tell me what you see,' he demanded.

I wasn't sure what was expected of me. 'The company,' I said. 'Why?'

'Because I want you to look at JoJo Starbuck and Mark Hominuke and tell me you think they are good skaters. *Look* at them! JoJo has no line at all. Mark is all over the place. They're hopeless and I want you to admit that you can see it for yourself.'

I watched quietly for a moment, then said: 'John, I can't understand what you mean. They are the same two skaters they have always been. They both have excellent lines and you've always said so yourself.'

'Then I have to tell you that you lack judgement,' he retorted. 'Either that or you have your own reasons for protecting them.' He slammed out of the door and reappeared down below.

When the session ended, Dita came to find me. 'You should go and see JoJo,' she said. 'She's a bit upset because John's just pulled "Tango Tango" from the show.'

The week opened to generally good reviews, but the company's morale was not high and it showed in the level of performance. John's heart was definitely set on making life miserable for everybody so long as Mark and JoJo remained in the company, and in the end

I was forced to confront him. 'You can't go on doing this,' I told him. 'It's undermining everything you've worked so hard to achieve.' He looked sad.

'I do understand that,' he told me. 'But I can't help it. It's not fun for me any more, and I just want to stop. I want to go back to Vail and stay there.'

'John,' I said, 'that day will come, and it isn't far away. But if you do this now, and destroy the whole company, you will never forgive yourself. I know you. You must keep going a little longer, and you must try to keep the morale high. We have four days left in Chicago, and then eighteen days in Scandinavia. Once that's finished, you'll be free until after the New Year.'

He hugged me briefly. 'I know you're right. I'll apologize to everyone at the company meeting tomorrow.'

'And what about Mark and JoJo?'

'I'll talk to them personally. And I'll put "Tango Tango" back into the programme for Scandinavia. I really am sorry. I wish I knew how to stop this happening.'

I knew he was sincere, but I also knew that it would happen again, and the strain was beginning to tell on us all. 'John,' I said carefully, 'have you ever considered getting some kind of professional help?'

He shook his head. 'What could they tell me that I don't already know? They'll just fill me up with tranquillizers and turn me into a zombie.' He sighed deeply. 'I have to try to fight it on my own.'

The audiences loved the shows at the Arie Crown. Once the curtain went up they were enchanted by the magic of the ensemble and the reactions were ecstatic. There were standing ovations after every performance and several people offered to form a local support group for the company. The great Canadian Olympic champion, Barbara Ann Scott, came twice and told John he must fight to keep the company together. 'The weeks of rehearsal are evident,' she told him. 'Nothing else exists in skating quite like this.' It was all very encouraging, but when the week ended, we had managed only thirty-eight per cent of capacity and we were $330,000 in debt.

When the full financial impact of the Chicago disaster became apparent, I had a showdown with David Foster. 'Why did you suggest we self-promote?' I asked him. 'How could you encourage us to leap into such a dangerous situation, knowing how volatile it could be?'

He shrugged. 'I only offered advice,' he said. 'I'm not always right. You had to make up your own minds in the end.' He had a point.

'But can't you help us to sort it out? You're our agent, David. If you believe in us – and presumably you do – then help us get back on our feet so we can go on to make money for everyone.' But he was already gathering his things.

'I'm sorry,' he said. 'Chicago is nothing to do with CAMI. You must handle it yourself.'

45

David was to return to Vail with the company while I went back to New York. At the airport, he told me he was not looking forward to the next three weeks: 'I feel as though I'm struggling through quicksand. I don't know what's happened to us all – is it because we're so tired? Or is it because, no matter how much people tell us they love and applaud what we're doing, there is never any offer of substantial help? It's all loans that have to be repaid. If only Columbia would book some new dates, or someone very wealthy would offer to become a benefactor . . . What a dream!'

Suddenly, over David's shoulder, I caught sight of Darryl crossing to the ticket counter. He was in deep conversation with someone and when he turned around I could see it was Nate Barnett, his 'assistant'. 'I don't believe it!' I said. 'Did you know Nate was here with Darryl?'

'Of course not. I would've said something. I must say he's done a good job of hiding him.'

I was furious with Darryl, but he couldn't understand my attitude. He admitted taking Nate, but told me it had only cost the company his bare expenses. 'What!' I said. 'You understood how we felt about Nate, and you promised he wouldn't come anywhere near the company again. We're not paying any expenses for him, Darryl. Not a cent.'

'But he helped me,' Darryl said. 'I needed that, and he was willing to do it for nothing.'

Something wasn't quite adding up. 'Who paid for his room?' I asked.

'No one,' Darryl answered. 'He shared mine.'

I stared at him, realizing for the first time that Nate Barnett was Darryl's lover. Now it all began to make sense to me.

When I came to ask Darryl for an accurate accounting of the Chicago engagement, and a list of who was still owed money, it seemed that hardly anyone had been paid. We were in dire straits and Margie Korshak had frozen what was in the box office. 'Can she do that?' I asked our lawyer. 'Yes, I'm afraid she can,' he said. 'You won't see any of that money now.' We spent a whole afternoon going over the figures, and in the end I found we still owed $33,000 to the Chicago musicians, as well as numerous smaller amounts to creditors all over that city. We also still had thousands of dollars outstanding in loans, as well as the major loan from the Chemical Bank. Darryl had paid nothing. I looked at him: 'I'm afraid we don't have any alternative but to let you go.' He wasn't surprised. He showed no emotion, but packed up his things and left the office within an hour. I never saw him again.

I was still desperately worried about John, too, and I decided to ask Brian Grant if there was anything he could tell me that might help me to deal with him. He sounded very sleepy on the phone, as though I had just woken him. 'Come over at eight,' he said. 'I'll make some dinner for us. I would really like to see you.'

When I saw Brian, I was shocked. His handsome face was gaunt and drawn, and his usually flawless skin was covered in unsightly blotches. I felt such an overwhelming sadness that all I could do was put my arms around him and hold him tightly. Eventually, when the tears had subsided, we sat by his fireplace and shared a bottle of red wine. 'Oh, Brian,' I said, 'I'm so sorry – I wish there was something I could do.'

He smiled at me. 'There is something. If you would come to see me when you have an hour or two to spare, I would really like that. People are afraid of me now, and some of my friends don't come any more. It can get rather lonely.'

'Are *you* afraid?' I asked.

'No, not really. Sometimes I worry about not being able to cope.

But there are wonderful organizations that will help when things get really bad. My one wish is that it will end quickly. I couldn't bear to think of it dragging on. I think if that happens I'll take an overdose of something.' He saw the expression on my face and came over to hug me. 'Don't be sad. I don't mean to be morbid. I'm just trying to be truthful with you.'

Brian was a vegetarian, and he had cooked us a delicious vegetable lasagne. We began to relax, and by the time we were having dessert – his version of sherry trifle – we were laughing at his stories of the fashion industry. I stayed until almost midnight, and then I reluctantly got up to leave. Brian put his hand on my arm. 'You haven't asked me about what you really came here to discuss,' he said quietly. 'You wanted to talk about John, didn't you?'

I sat down again. 'Yes,' I admitted. 'I'm at my wits' end, Brian. I don't know what to do for the best. There are times now when I actually don't like John any more, but then I see the other side of him and I feel guilty for ever having doubted him.'

Brian was silent for a moment. Then he said: 'I think the problem is that you and David have been thinking that if you could just give him the company, just get him into the Met, just get more bookings or more rehearsal weeks, John would suddenly be happy. But it isn't going to happen. The only thing that would really make him happy would be if someone could absolve him from his own genius.'

Jane invited me over for drinks one afternoon. It was getting dark as I crossed Broadway and made my way past the Ballet Shop and the Empire Hotel. Jane was already sipping a large vodka and tonic. 'Scotch?' she asked.

'Thank you,' I said. 'Just a small one.'

She poured me a triple and sat back in her chair, looking at me shrewdly. 'Having trouble with John?' she asked. I nodded. 'Let me guess,' she went on. 'He doesn't want to skate, doesn't want to tour, doesn't like half the other people in his company . . . Am I right so far?'

'Yes, you are painfully accurate.'

Jane laughed. 'My dear, I've seen it all a million times. You have to learn not to worry about what John wants. He's an artist. He's difficult and self-centred. Sometimes he can be a royal pain in the backside, but he's not actually a lost cause. I'll phone him and see if

I can get anywhere with him. Perhaps I can cheer him up. I can tell him about next year's Met engagement and what he needs to start thinking about.'

Meanwhile, I pursued the possibility of raising donations from some of the established arts benefactors in the USA. I had a long meeting with the noted businessman Asher Adelman, but no immediate offer of help was forthcoming. He did, however, offer to hold a fund-raising party in his apartment later in the year. 'We might be able to raise ten or twelve thousand from that,' he said.

I met with Met board member Frank Taplin, who was chairman of a major industrial concern and hugely wealthy in his own right. He was an old friend of Bill Judd's and I was hopeful that he might be able to bring in some corporate funding. It soon became apparent, however, that Frank's main interest was in being able to play piano during the 1985 Met engagement. 'I could play some jazz and John could skate to it,' he suggested. I didn't encourage the idea, because it was exactly the kind of situation that we had worked so hard to avoid. It seemed that even donations came at a price.

I called David in Vail. 'I'm afraid you'll have to help me,' I said. 'If we divide the list of creditors and take half each, perhaps we can persuade them to work with us so that we don't find the company plunged into bankruptcy.' For the next four days we sat on the telephone, David in Vail and I in New York, and talked to people about paying out our debts. Each of them asked what our income potential was for the coming twelve months, and at what intervals they could expect payments. Everyone made it clear that, if we were able to make a reasonable offer, they were prepared to accept it. The question was, where was the money to come from?

I went to see Catherine Gevers. 'What work do you have for us?' I asked.

'The potential of an arena date in February, at the University of Philadelphia. They would need to use tape and they pay very little, but at least it would be work.'

'That's it? A week in a college campus with canned music? Bill Judd was booking engagements like that when the company was completely unknown.'

'Well,' she said, 'there's the 1985 Met and Kennedy Center bookings.'

I was furious. 'Those dates are our own – again because of Bill Judd's efforts. What I want to know is, what has CAMI done for us?'

She smiled. 'Two hundred and fifty thousand dollars seems quite substantial to me. I think that's quite a contribution to bring to the table.'

'I wish that were true,' I told her, 'that it is a contribution. But, like everything else, it has to be paid back. There is a three-thousand-three-hundred-dollar-a-month interest payment on that loan and the clock is ticking on the principal. If we don't get work soon – *additional* work – then we won't be in a position to repay it.'

At the beginning of the following week, we were in for yet another shock. Going through the paperwork Darryl had left behind, I found a pile of unprocessed cheques in the back of his drawer. They were made out to the IRS, various union funds and the government. It took me an hour to discover that these had been entered into our books but not mailed. Unfortunately, the money to cover them was no longer in the account; we owed far more money than Darryl had indicated. What he *had* paid was thousands of dollars to a 'Mr N. Barnett'. Nate had been on the payroll all along.

Jane was concerned about our predicament and she offered to do what she could to help us. I talked to her about Darryl and she told me I must be very careful if I was to accuse him of theft. He had, theoretically, had control of the budget and it would be difficult to establish that he had acted improperly in hiring Nate. 'But what about the other stuff? The IRS, the unions and the government?'

'You still have to be cautious. Before you can accuse him of what you consider to be misappropriation of funds, you have to be sure you have all your evidence lined up.'

'It makes me so angry when I think that John and David and I weren't drawing salaries at all.'

'I know,' she said. 'I do understand. But perhaps you should have. Who said you couldn't? And besides, there isn't much point in suing someone who has no money.'

The company left for Scandinavia at the beginning of November. I had planned to fly down to see John, but had woken up one morning unable to get out of bed. Every time I moved, a searing pain shot through my body and I had to be taken to hospital in an ambulance.

The doctors could find nothing physically wrong with me, and decided I must be suffering from acute stress. 'It can do funny things to you, almost as though the body is telling you to take it easy for a while.' I was given a dose of Valium and sent home to rest. I called David, only to find he had suffered a severe anxiety attack at almost exactly the same time. He had gone to Vail Infirmary thinking he was having a cardiac arrest. 'What did they tell you?' I asked.

'Told me I was under too much pressure and sent me away with a bottle of Valium tablets.'

I chuckled. 'We're both going to end up as drug addicts!' I said. 'Will you be all right to go to Scandinavia?'

'Wouldn't miss it for the world,' David quipped. 'What could be more restful than a vacation with the John Curry Skating Company?'

John had undergone a period of relative equilibrium, but in the final days before departure he had become recalcitrant and morose. The day before he left, he complained of severe pain in his knee. David called me to ask what we should do about it. 'Obviously he doesn't want to go,' he said. 'But I suppose this could be real.'

'What does Rob think?' I asked.

'He's not sure either, but he does think it might be John's way of getting out of the tour.'

'Then get his bags packed and drive him to Denver this afternoon,' I said. 'He can fly into New York today and I'll make an appointment with the Doctors' Hospital. If they say he can't go, we can collect on the key-man insurance. If he is all right, then I'll meet you all at Kennedy tomorrow with John, and he can go with you.'

John saw his surgeon, who examined his knee thoroughly, and told me it seemed absolutely fine. 'I think it's just a touch of nerves,' he said. 'There's no reason he can't go to Scandinavia.'

John was contrite and I took him out for dinner. 'Talk to me about the state of the company,' he said as we waited to be served. 'How are things?'

This was a difficult moment for me. If I told him the whole truth, I honestly believed he could not possibly deal with it. Too much was riding on our ability to survive the next few weeks, and to have John collapse in the middle of it would spell the end of the company. I told him as much as I felt he could handle. 'Things are tough,' I said. 'We didn't do well in Chicago, but you must know that already.'

He nodded. 'I don't think it was such a failure, considering. I think people liked it, and if we go back again I think we could do much better.' I was delighted to hear him talk this way.

'Exactly,' I said. 'We just have to work very hard to raise some funding, and we need to get work for next year.'

He looked at me. 'How are CAMI doing? Have they got us any dates at all?'

'In a nutshell, no,' I told him.

'Then let's fire them, Elva,' he said. 'Let's get someone who can help us. You and Bill Judd did better than that.'

The next morning I took him out to Kennedy. He was more positive since our discussion, and I realized with a pang of guilt that he needed to talk like this. I thought how much easier it would be if we only had someone who would really help us. Of all the people we had so far involved, only Bill Judd had come through. The rest had talked about professionalism, but fallen short of our expectations. 'You know,' John said as we waited for the Denver plane to arrive, 'if you and David wanted to stop, I would understand. There would be no disgrace in it because we have achieved a great deal.' It was a tempting idea, but we couldn't possibly walk away from the company's debts at this point. We had no choice but to continue.

46

In Copenhagen the promoter, Strom Olsen, welcomed them all and took them on a tour of the city before settling them into a very nice hotel near the World Arena. David and Strom went to the bar for a beer and a sandwich. 'How are the Copenhagen dates selling?' David asked.

Strom shrugged. 'Not so well,' he said. 'Nor the Göteborg Arena either. But the Bergen Opera House is almost sold out.' It seemed that the established cultural audiences accepted the concept of artistic skating much more readily than the usual ice-show audiences.

At five o'clock, John banged on David's door. 'Can I see you for a moment?' he demanded. David, who was trying to rest for a while, put the light on and opened the door. As soon as he saw John's face, he knew something was wrong. 'I've just been across to the arena,' John announced. 'It's bad enough that we have to play an arena when I had been promised that we wouldn't need to do that again. But, accepting that it is an unavoidable imposition, then who on earth decided it was all right to have the rink surrounded by commercial signage?'

David pulled on his jacket. 'It's news to me,' he said. 'We weren't told anything about signs.' He walked over to the arena with John, and went into the auditorium. There were signs all round the edge of the ice. 'I won't skate with those things there,' John said. 'It's against everything we stand for.'

David found Strom and confronted him with John's ultimatum. 'You will have to remove them, or there won't be a show,' he told him.

'Then you will be sued, and I won't pay you anything,' Strom retorted. 'When Victor Hochhauseur booked this date, he said nothing about signage. It wasn't given as a restriction.'

David went to see John. 'John, you have to do this. I know how you feel about it, but if you refuse the tour will be cancelled. We may even be sued.'

John sighed heavily. 'It doesn't look as though I have any choice, does it?' he said quietly. 'Could you please leave now, David? I'm very tired. I want to go to bed.'

In New York I was flat on my back again. This time I had reached down to retrieve a bathtowel and found I was unable to straighten up. Another trip to the hospital had resulted in nothing more than an injection to relieve muscular tension. 'Take a rest,' the doctor said.

David called from Copenhagen and told me about the latest problem. 'I think it will be all right now,' he said. 'But John isn't very happy about it.' The following evening, my phone rang again, and Rob was on the line from Denmark. 'It's John,' he told me. 'He injured himself in the show tonight.' I froze: this was the news I most dreaded to hear.

'What happened?' I asked him.

'It's difficult to say exactly, but I believe he did it deliberately so that he wouldn't have to do this tour. Gayle told me that he was lying down in his dressing room until right before he was to go on. He didn't warm up. He just stood at the edge of the ice and he didn't even stretch. It happened almost immediately he began to skate.'

'Let me speak to John,' I said. 'Is he there?'

John sounded decidedly cheerful. 'I'm injured,' he announced. 'I will have to come back to New York. The others can carry on without me. They'll be fine.'

David was furious. 'Strom is threatening to sue us all,' he said. 'He was so angry tonight he almost put his fist through a wall. The tour can't continue without John. As long as he is absent, they'll cancel. Copenhagen is already off.'

'Get him on a plane first thing tomorrow. Tell Strom not to cancel anything else until we hear what they say at Doctors' Hospital. It may be that he's faking, and if that's the case then I'll send him right back again and the tour can carry on.' Before I hung up I spoke to Rob again.

'I'll look after the company while John is away,' he said, 'but I want you to know that I cannot continue to be around this kind of behaviour. It's too demoralizing for us all. It seems as though John is trying to destroy everything.'

I met John at the airport. He was in a wheelchair and was smiling happily; he didn't seem to be in any pain. We went straight to Doctors' Hospital and John's surgeon examined him carefully. 'A slight sprain,' he said. 'Nothing serious at all. With the proper rest, it will be as good as new in a few days.'

John seemed to be annoyed, and when I said I would make a return reservation to Copenhagen for the weekend he told me he had no intention of going back. 'John,' I said quietly. 'I have rarely felt anger towards you – in fact, I don't think I have *ever* been really cross with you in the time we have worked together – but you're going too far this time. You're jeopardizing all of our livelihoods at the moment, and you're wearing us out. How can you expect the company to respect you when you have just broken one of your most fundamental rules in front of them? Didn't you always tell them that the number-one safety precaution was to warm up thoroughly before a performance? You knew you would be injured if you skated cold like that. Tell me the truth – is it what you hoped for?' He was silent a while. Then he said:

'I don't want to do the Scandinavian tour. I don't want to continue. Please tell me that the company can go on without me.'

'I can't tell you that, John. You haven't reached that point yet. But if you can just keep going for another year or two, then I promise you that you will be able to retire.'

John flew back. There were no further protests from him and he was careful to rest his leg. The Göteborg dates were cancelled and we received no income for the lost performances; consequently the skaters had to be satisfied with rehearsal pay. There was a feeling of resentment, not only towards John but also towards David, and this manifested itself at a company meeting. JoJo was uncharacteristically critical, and because of her wide professional experience her views were accepted readily. For the first time since the formation of the company, David felt he was losing control of the situation.

By the time they arrived in Bergen, John had recovered sufficiently to be able to perform. The dates were all sold out and Strom was able to advance David some cash to take care of the lighting crew, John Paull III and some of the ice costs. Kevin himself waived his fee. 'I don't need it,' he said. 'Use it to cover some of the other stuff. I know how tough it is for you at the moment.'

David called me after the opening night. 'It was magic,' he said. 'Perhaps the best yet. I made a video of the performance – I just had a feeling I should do that.' Rob also called.

'John seems fine now,' he said. 'He skated really well tonight. It's the venue – this is the most magnificent opera house, with glass walls overlooking the mountains. It makes such a difference to the way John feels about performing.'

'What about the company?' I asked.

'There is some resentment over the pay cut,' he said carefully. 'They feel there should be insurance to cover the loss. There's some sense that perhaps things haven't been handled very well.'

'By David?'

'Well – yes, I suppose so.'

'Rob, that's so unfair,' I said. 'He had to cope with John's so-called injury, which turned out to be self-inflicted. But you all know that. Surely they're intelligent enough to know that the insurance company won't pay out under those circumstances?'

'But Strom told JoJo that he had given David ten thousand dollars.'

'He did,' I told him. 'It should have been twenty-five thousand.

It didn't even cover all the basic costs – freight, transportation, hotels, crew, expenses, insurance. Rehearsal pay for the skaters in Copenhagen and Göteborg was an additional expense that wasn't allowed for in that money.' I stopped for a second. 'Surely they don't think David kept any of it for himself? He's put thousands of dollars on to his credit cards on behalf of the company and he doesn't even take any to make the payments on them. He uses his Pro Skate income.'

'I know,' Rob said. 'But I don't think they understand about that.'

While the company was performing in Bergen, Bill Judd suffered a massive heart attack in New York. He was admitted to hospital and was in intensive care for several days. 'He might pull through,' the doctors said, 'but if he does he will have to be very careful. He will be extremely weak.' I went to see him, and the first thing he asked was about the company.

'They're fine,' I lied. 'Bergen was magnificent. A huge success.'

'And John?' he asked anxiously. 'How is he?'

'He's in marvellous shape, Bill. Everything is splendid.'

Tears filled his eyes and began to spill down his cheeks. 'Oh, my dear!' he said, clasping my hand. 'I am so pleased.'

Pro Skate was scheduled for 10 and 11 December, and most of the company were involved. John had prepared some new pieces for himself, plus a lyrical solo for Nathan called 'Sunset', set to music by Grofé. Over the two days of competitions, the company members consistently drew standing ovations from the audience, and the artistic judges singled them out for praise. John himself brought the proceedings to a halt, as the audience cheered, stamped and whistled after his beautiful rendition of Ravel's *La Valse*.

John had been unanimously chosen as the Skater of the Year, and I had asked Dorothy Hamill if she would make the presentation to him right after the Team Championship. She made an eloquent short speech and handed him the crystal obelisk. He kissed her, took the microphone and electrified the audience with an impassioned speech about the state of ice, and what he felt should be done to change things. He spoke touchingly of his concern for his company members, of their dedication and hard work and his pride in their achievements. Then he turned to look at David and me and thanked us for 'never giving up the faith, and for achieving the impossible against all odds'. I felt a cold shiver run down my spine. I knew John was totally sincere, but for some reason the accolade felt like an epitaph.

We had a party afterwards, and John was in a happy, joking mood. Sander Jacobs was there, and before the party was over he had promised John $150,000 to pay for a new rehearsal session and to enable him to choreograph the *Firebird*. 'None of this money must be used for any other purpose than this,' Sander said. 'This is specifically to make the new season possible. It is not to be used to pay any debts.'

At ten-thirty, the door of the restaurant opened and Bill Judd came in. I was horrified: he was supposed to be in hospital still, under strict supervision. He was very shaky, walking with the aid of a stick, and had lost a great deal of weight. His face was chalky white and his voice was as thin as an eggshell, but he smiled at me in delight and hugged me tightly. 'Bill!' I said. 'What are you doing here? You're supposed to be in bed.'

'My dear, I wouldn't have missed the Pro Skate party for the world. Now, how about a glass of champagne?' John sat with him for a while, holding his hands, and told him how much he meant to the company. Then he said: 'Bill, if you will agree to let me take you back to the hospital, then I promise you can come down to Vail and see me in rehearsal in February. Is that a deal?'

A wide smile broke across Bill's face. 'Oh, I shall look forward to that, dear boy. That *will* be a treat.'

'Thank you,' I whispered to John as he steered Bill out to a waiting taxi. 'That was really sweet of you.'

Bob Strauss, an old friend of mine and a theatrical manager, gave me some advice over the matter of booking. 'CAMI are the wrong company for you,' Bob told me. 'You need someone young and aggressive, and I know just who to bring you to.' Right after Pro Skate I went with him to an office at West 57th Street and Broadway. The lift took us to the second floor, and we stepped out into a colourful waiting room, done out in 1950s style. SPOTLITE, the neon sign announced. We were in the offices of Bob Williams, the country's top comedy agent, who managed a wide variety of acts including rock groups and magicians. Suddenly Bob himself emerged and bounded towards us with his large hands held out. He pumped my arms up and down, beaming. He was a tall, handsome man who exuded a magnetic charm and more energy than a power station. 'Hi!' he said. 'I hear we need to find some bookings for an ice show. Come on in and tell me all about it.'

Three hours later, he called one of his agents into the room. 'Chris,' he said. 'We're gonna be taking care of John Curry and his ice company. Set up a full-scale meeting tomorrow morning and let's get someone on to this full time. We need to move!' He walked over and draped both arms around Bob and me. 'I need to do a little homework tonight, but tomorrow afternoon I want to meet Mr Curry. Can you arrange that?'

Spotlite threw themselves into the project wholeheartedly. By the time I brought John to meet Bob, he already had a feeling for what was possible. 'Sit down,' he commanded. 'Now – first I want to tell you that I have done my homework and I am proud to be able to represent your fine company. We are gonna be able to do a whole lot for you. Right now, I can tell you we have canvassed most of the suitable theatrical venues in the country and every one of them is interested.' He stopped for a moment, and eyed John carefully. 'I also want to tell you, sir, that I'm convinced your company could be working year-round.' He let out a hearty laugh and slapped his thigh. 'Just needs booking!'

By the time we left, John was smiling. 'I liked him!' he told me. 'Let's get rid of CAMI immediately.'

'We have to tell Jane first,' I said. 'We need her on our side.'

We took her to dinner in a Chinese restaurant near Lincoln Center, and she listened attentively. 'I think you have no choice at this point,' she said. 'You must keep the company working and, if CAMI aren't doing the job, then better you find someone who will.'

John was due to return to England for Christmas, and the day before he left we had lunch together. Afterwards we walked in the cold winter sunshine and John told me that he was feeling better about himself than he had for a very long time. 'I don't know why,' he said. 'Perhaps it's because I have begun to believe in us all. I don't have that awful feeling of doom hanging over me any longer. Let's all have a lovely Christmas with our families, because we will have to work very hard next year.' In some ways it was the most positive he had ever been, but I couldn't help feeling that it was a temporary remission. Some part of me knew that our problems were far from over.

47

By early January Bob Williams had managed to pencil in almost $2,000,000-worth of guaranteed bookings. I sat down on his sofa heavily. It was hard to take in. 'You're joking?'

He laughed. 'I don't joke about things like this. Your company is a hot item. You should have been working right along.' He looked at me seriously. 'We need to handle this carefully,' he said. 'Once you send CAMI a letter to tell them they're out, the shit is gonna hit the fan good! They ain't gonna like it one bit. So I have a suggestion – why don't we ask them to come up here and meet with me, and see if we can't handle the company on their behalf? It seems to me that they don't have the time to pull it off, but they do have a contract with you. This way, they keep your contract and they can protect their investment. And you get to work! Make sense?'

Three agents and the President of CAMI, Ronald Wilford, came that afternoon. Bob was in an expansive mood, dispensing vintage brandies and funny stories freely. David Foster, Catherine Gevers and Andrew Baker said nothing, but Ronald was quite talkative. Finally, he got up and motioned to the agents to do the same. 'Interesting,' he said. 'We need to go away and think this over. We'll be back to you.' He ignored me, and they all filed out.

As soon as the lift doors closed behind them Bob propelled me back to his office. He let out a shout of laughter. 'Did you see Wilford's face? He wondered what he was doing with a chap who specializes in gagsters! And those agents – no wonder you didn't have any bookings!' He was suddenly serious again. 'They ain't gonna let me handle this for them, I'm afraid. You'll have to fire 'em, because I can't go any further until they're officially notified of your intentions.'

John called me from England. 'Have you fired CAMI yet?' he demanded. 'I want them out.' We arranged for him to return in mid-January, and put the company on notice that rehearsals would begin on the 20th. The break had done everyone good, and spirits seemed much higher. I went to see our lawyer Shelley Cammacker, and asked if he would write the letter to CAMI officially firing them. 'I doubt they will make a fuss,' he told me. 'They can't claim to have done anything for you. If it came down to it, you could get out of the contract on the basis of non-performance.'

David worked with Joe Concilio to sort out the complicated financial situation. He made arrangements with every creditor, including the Chicago Musicians' Union, and offered to make regular payments from performance income. He promised to supply a list of dates and anticipated revenues as soon as it was available. He explained we were in the process of changing booking agent, and this seemed quite acceptable to them all. By the end of the week, all the debts were listed, with indicated repayment schedules.

An appeal for funds went out, but met with lukewarm response: we received a total of $1,000 in donations. Mark Grayson worked hard to put together a printed appeal to foundations and charitable trusts, poring over the names of potential sources and making a shortlist. We had some charming letters from Canadian children who had seen the company in the autumn of 1983 and formed a support group, who told us they had never forgotten the wonderful experience and hoped we would be back soon. But only two people to date had made substantial donations: Vernon Taylor, a philanthropist from Denver, and Kit Wright from Connecticut, who both gave $10,000.

Early February in Vail was cold and snowy, and I felt a sense of gloom over the company again. I sat in rehearsals and watched the embryonic choreography, and thought it very effective even at this early stage. John was in a foul mood, shouting criticism and actually screaming at some of the skaters. He sent Adam and Scott off the ice for yawning, and they came to see me. 'This is not fair!' they said.

'Just swallow it,' I told them. 'If John thinks I'm interfering, it will just make it worse for you.' John left abruptly as soon as the session was over, but I stayed behind to talk to Rob.

'Things are not good,' he told me. 'John seems disturbed. I'm not really sure why.'

I saw John later that evening, and he was in a peculiar mood. I was astonished at the difference in him since December. He was snappy and sarcastic and seemed irritated by my presence for the first time that I could remember. I stayed long enough to eat dinner, but left as soon as I could. Something was terribly wrong, but I had no idea what it was.

Back in New York, I went to see Jane again. She appeared to be solicitous, and offered me a large whisky on the rocks. I sipped it gratefully and poured out my concerns about John. I didn't realize it at the time, but it was a major error of judgement. I thought of her as a friend to all of us, in spite of her occasional tantrums. 'I don't know how much longer we can go on like this,' I told her. 'We're so exhausted. If only we could have a rest.'

April called me that weekend, to tell me that Jane Herman was down in Vail. 'Did you know she was coming?' she asked me. 'I thought it was strange you didn't warn me.'

'No,' I said. 'Where is she staying?'

'With John. And there's something else you should know – Jane called a meeting with the company today and she banned me from the arena until it was over. Don't you think that's odd?' I thought it decidedly odd. For the first time it occurred to me that we could lose the company. I met David in a dingy bar, and told him my fears. He listened silently, and then buried his head in his hands and let out a long groan. 'Oh, my God,' he said. 'So much at stake, so much still to do. How can we fight someone as powerful as Jane?'

'I don't know,' I said. 'I don't think we can, but you mustn't reckon without John. He would never let anyone harm us. We've come through too much together, the three of us.'

Three days later we were sitting in the Pro Skate office going over the list of corporate charitable foundations with Mark and Sara, when the phone rang. 'I have something to tell you,' John said quietly. 'I have been talking things over with Jane Herman, and I have just had a meeting with CAMI. I feel it is best if I get professional management for the company to see if I can make it work. I am very grateful to you and David for what you have done, but I no longer feel able to trust you. I hope you will accept that this is for the best.' I felt as though I had been dropped from a great height. I could hardly breathe.

'Just a moment,' I said. 'I want to take this in the other room. I'll put you on hold.' I couldn't say anything with Mark and Sara staring at me curiously; I needed to be alone. I couldn't remember feeling a worse sense of shock in my life.

'Who is it?' asked David.

'One of the skaters,' I told him, and left. In the back office, I picked up the phone again. 'John?' I felt my voice trembling. 'Please – we need to talk about this. Why didn't you tell me you were coming into New York? I would have met you.'

'Jane picked me up,' he told me. 'And she's waiting now to take me to the airport again. I want to get back to Denver.'

'But I need to see you,' I said. 'We have to talk about this. You can't just throw us out like this, without even a meeting.'

'Yes I can,' he said coldly. 'Jane has made me aware of many things I knew nothing about. Things that were a shock to me. I had no idea my company was in such dire financial circumstances and that the Musicians' Union had blacklisted us. I should have been told these things.'

'Did she tell you we had made arrangements to pay all these people off?' I asked. 'We are not in any danger.'

'I think you don't understand,' he told me. 'I am letting you go. I'm not really interested in your explanations, so don't waste your breath. Maybe with new management we can be successful. If not, then at least I will have tried.' I heard the phone replaced in its cradle and the line went dead.

Somehow I managed to make small talk with Mark and Sara and shortly afterwards they left. David put a hand on my shoulder. 'What the hell was that all about?' he asked. 'All the colour drained out of your face. I thought you were going to pass out.'

'It was John,' I told him. 'He has just called to tell us that we are no longer part of the company. He has fired us.'

David let his breath out sharply and I saw his eyes fill with tears. 'You can't be serious?' he said.

'I'm afraid I am,' I said. 'Jane went down to Vail and told him all the details of our financial obligations without telling him any of the pay-out arrangements we had made. She has suggested to him that he replace us with professionals. He met with CAMI too, and it seems they are back in the picture.'

David looked at me in dismay. 'So that's it? Just like that? It can't be.'

'David, we're going to have to accept it. We both knew that the day might come when John lost faith in us too. Well, that day has now come. There isn't very much we can do about it.'

David looked at me and shook his head. 'Poor John,' he said. 'They'll never be able to make it work. They would never go through what we have. I think he'll go under.'

I walked over to David and put my arms around him. I knew how much he was hurting. The John Curry Skating Company had been part of our lives for so long that it would be an immensely difficult loss for us to accept. We both felt as though part of our beings had drained away, but even more intensely we experienced the fear that parents feel for a child who has moved beyond their circle of protection. There was nothing more we could do to help John.

48

The finality of John's phone call left David and me in a state of shock. Quite apart from the enormous emotional impact of his decision, there were some purely practical consequences which would need to be addressed. We asked Shelley Cammacker for his advice.

'The truth is that John can refuse to work with you, but only on condition he assumes the responsibility of the company. Either he, or someone of his choice, must take over the administration in all its aspects. This will include dealing with the company debts. You need to make a list of all the creditors, including yourselves, and indicate the current status of each. You will then need to resign as directors of the company, because otherwise you will continue to be liable. You should also know that you are entitled to substantial compensation for your contributions to the company and for the manner of your dismissal.'

David and I discussed our situation at great length. We made the decision not to press for any compensation, but simply to ask for our loans to the company to be repaid. We would also ask for assurances that the company would be run by people who cared about it and had its best interests at heart. This was all submitted to John's legal counsel, Patricia Crown, in documented form and in due course she indicated that John was ready to accept the stated conditions. Our tenure was effectively at an end.

One night I received a call from Rob McBrien. He sounded terribly tired. 'This is all so sad,' he said, 'but I did want you to know that I understand how you must both be feeling. This could all have been handled so differently, but you must have known that there was always a possibility John would turn against you.'

'We knew intellectually, of course,' I told him. 'But in our hearts we never believed it could happen.'

Timmy Murphy sent us a letter, stating very simply: 'Dear Elva and David, I love you both. Timmy.' It meant a great deal to us, because he was the only skater who ever expressed any concern. From the rest there was just a curious silence.

We did, however, eventually receive a letter signed by all the skaters in the company. It had obviously been written for them, and it spoke of an appreciation of our central role in developing the ensemble and of their affection for us; it also beseeched us to step aside and allow the company to be 'run by a staff of broad range and experience, each working full-time in their area of expertise'. I felt tears running down my face as I read it. 'They speak to us as though we were extraneous personnel, standing in the way of progress,' I said to David. 'Don't they know we longed for such help? And how can they now afford all this? Where has the money suddenly come from?'

'Go and talk to Bill Judd,' David suggested. 'He might be able to suggest a way of handling all this.' Bill was still frail from his recent illness. He clasped my hands and said:

'My dear, you mustn't allow this to hurt you so. I have worked with artists all my life and sooner or later most have turned on me. One almost has to expect it. You have made the mistake of becoming much too close to John, and living only for the fulfilment of his dreams. Now you need to take time to rediscover yourself and to remember those things you believe in. Most important of all, you must not let bitterness enter your heart – John has hurt himself far more than he has hurt you. Your pain will heal, but John's pain will be with him always.'

Shelley Cammacker informed us that John was still legally under contract to *Symphony on Ice*. When the non-profit entity, the John Curry Skating Company, was formed, his agents had not sought to assign his existing contract. 'What can be done?' I asked.

'Nothing at this end,' Shelley told us. 'But Jack Sakazaki could well hold John in breach of contract.'

'I doubt it,' I said. 'Jack is one of the company's major creditors. It's in his interests to keep John working.'

Rob wrote, appealing to me to find a way to release John from his obligations to Jack. He told me the Met and the Kennedy Center had already cancelled the summer seasons because of the fear of injunctions. 'If this threat remains,' he warned,

> then there is a strong possibility that John will never skate again. I beg you to do this one last thing for John. I know you can. You have done wonderful things for him – emotionally, and materially – and for all these skaters who have worked so long to achieve their places in this company . . . if you allow this to collapse now, you will not only end John's career but also Patricia's, Cathy's, Dita's, Jim's, etc. None of them will have a forum where their skating is accepted, and this high development of the sport will die, perhaps never to be recovered.

David read the letter carefully. 'What makes Rob think you are able to do anything?' he asked. 'We've been stripped of all our influence and bargaining power. I think the only person who could alter this situation is John himself.'

'He'll never do it,' I said. 'He won't apologize to Jack. His advisers must have thought about all this when they recommended he get rid of us. It seems so strange to be ostracized on the one hand, and asked to help on the other.'

By early April David and I were beginning to accept the situation. We still felt as though a vital part of our lives had been ripped away, but we were prepared to sign the final documents effecting the change-over of the company. It was time for us to move on. Patricia Crown, however, had a further shock in store for us. She telephoned Shelley to tell him that John had changed his mind: he had decided to retire from skating altogether and had already returned to England to pursue a career as an actor. He had disbanded the company.

The impact of this latest development was devastating. We were now responsible for all the company debts, and yet we had no access to any of its assets. The copyright in most of the choreography rested with John, and he had withdrawn permission to use it; the ice equipment was in the name of his personal company; and the most important assets of all – John and the skaters – were now totally unavailable to us. We were effectively paralysed.

Shelley warned us that we now had no alternative but to sue John. 'He has been ill-advised,' he told us; 'but you must now cover yourselves. You have been left in an untenable position and there is no attempt whatsoever to relieve any of the pressures on you. I must say, I am at a loss to understand the logic behind this stance.'

Sean McGill was the one person who might be willing to shed some light on the matter. He had been very close to John, and I called him to ask if he could advise me. He was forthright: 'John has retired because he will not contribute to any production which will benefit you, David or Jack Sakazaki. You have apparently asked him for payments he doesn't feel you merit.'

I was stunned. 'But Sean,' I told him, 'David and I have waived our right to compensation. All we have asked is that the loans we made to the company be repaid. David, in particular, advanced tens of thousands of dollars and it isn't reasonable to ask him to sacrifice that. Surely you can understand?'

Sean was silent awhile. Then he said: 'All I know is that John will not be involved if you and David receive anything from the proceeds of performances.' I realized it was useless to pursue the matter.

'Thank you for listening, Sean,' I said, and hung up. I wrote to John in England explaining that, if it would make a difference to his decision, David and I were willing to forfeit any monies due to us personally. I hoped this letter might do some good, but he didn't reply.

Bob Williams put forward an intriguing proposal at the beginning of May. 'I have all these expressions of interest from theatres around the country,' he told me. 'They didn't know who John Curry was, only that we were offering a beautiful classic ice company. Why don't you put together a new company – call it the American Ice Ballet – and create a full-length work, perhaps one of the Tchaikovsky ballets? You could take so much from each performance and apply it to paying off the Curry company creditors. And you could also begin to earn some money for yourselves at the same time!' It sounded like a splendid solution. Mark Grayson helped us to prepare some promotional materials, and within a few days we were receiving some very enthusiastic responses. It appeared that Bob had come up with a solution that could both help us and satisfy the creditors.

Our optimism was crushed again when Bob called to let me know that the word had gone out that the American Ice Ballet was not the John Curry Skating Company. 'This is ludicrous,' Bob fumed. 'She can't do this. How does she expect you to repay your debts if you aren't allowed to work? You can't stop now.'

But we did stop. The fight had gone out of us. It was obvious that David would have to declare bankruptcy; there was no other way for him to extricate himself from the situation, because so many of the JCSC debts bore his name. He was deeply depressed, and expressed real anger for the first time since I'd met him. 'You spend your whole life trying to be a good person,' he said, 'and trying to pay your dues and help where you can. Then something like this happens and everything you've worked for falls apart. Why? What did I ever do to anyone?'

I waited until he was calmer, then I told him: 'We'll get through this, David. You'll go bankrupt, and I will have to give up my apartment. Neither of us has anything left, but the important thing is for us to accept it, because if we become bitter or vindictive we'll never recover. We can only get over it if we let go of it.'

'I know,' David said. 'You're right. But the thing that hurts the most is that no one ever asked to hear our side of the story. We spent so many hours listening to the skaters' problems, and fighting with John on their behalf. Mark Hominuke and JoJo would have been history if we hadn't gone to bat for them. So why won't they speak to us now?' I said nothing. Only time could heal David's pain and frustration. But I did wonder silently what John's advisers had hoped to achieve by their extraordinary course of action. Perhaps they simply hadn't realized the complexity of the endeavours which had brought the John Curry Skating Company into existence. It had survived against all the odds, and if we had followed the accepted rules of good business practice there never would have been an opening night on the stage of the Metropolitan Opera House.

In June we saw advertisements in the *Washington Post* for a summer-season engagement. THE JOHN CURRY SKATERS, they read: *A triumphant return to the Kennedy Center*. They quoted the reviews from the previous year's appearances, and listed all but three of the original ensemble members. Most of the pieces developed over the past two years were also detailed.

Kevin called us: 'They've asked me to go down to make the ice, but I refused. I don't like the way you've been treated.'

'You should go,' I told him. 'I really appreciate your loyalty, but you need the work.'

'Not that badly,' he replied.

The John Curry Skaters were clearly the same entity as the John Curry Skating Company, but they were appearing at the Kennedy Center under the guise of a random group of performers who just happened to have appeared together before. 'What a farce!' Bob Williams said. 'It's so obvious they've done this in order to avoid paying any of the debts.'

Shelley was desperately worried about the new development. 'You must now seek injunctive relief,' he insisted. 'If you don't, you will be liable for prosecution from the creditors. They will quite rightly see this as an attempt to circumvent the obligations you have to them.'

'But it's nothing to do with us!'

'The creditors don't know that, and they may choose to believe you are involved. You have represented to them that John has retired, and that the company has been disbanded. Now it appears that John had not retired at all, and is appearing with the same company these people invested their money in. You dare not let it go unchallenged.'

'We swore we wouldn't sue John under any circumstances,' David said.

'I understand,' Shelley replied. 'But you are now faced with what could be interpreted as a conspiracy to defraud. The assets are being withheld from you because someone – and I doubt it is John himself – has masterminded this way of avoiding any obligation to the former company. It is crystal clear that this current engagement is only possible because of the amount of time and money invested in the original company. It is ludicrous to suggest that this is in any real sense a separate entity. Even the reviews are of last year's perform-ances. You have no choice but to seek an injunction pending suitable arrangements to repay the creditors.'

Any petition for injunctive relief must be accompanied by a hefty bond. (This is because the legal action freezes all activity, denying people the means to earn money. If the injunction is not granted, the petitioner must be able to compensate for lost earnings.) We had no idea where to find such a sum, and held a meeting of the creditors to discuss the situation. Lewis Rappaport was willing to start a fund, and Bob Williams and Sander Jacobs agreed to contribute the balance between them. Bob Harley agreed to do the legal work without payment, and we spent the next three weeks preparing the petition. 'If only it hadn't come to this,' David said miserably. 'We didn't even want to stop them performing. We just wanted them to treat the creditors properly.'

'David, just think about it for a moment. John has a history of refusing to compensate those he grows tired of. He had finished with us, and he wanted us out of his life completely. Ergo, the last thing he would have wanted was for us to benefit from any performances he did. It's not a mystery.'

The arbitrator in Washington heard our petition and refused to grant the injunction. Bob was not surprised: 'We were asking a Washington judge to prevent the Kennedy Center from doing business,' he said. 'It was never on the cards.' The judge's summation included the statement that he made 'no judgement as to the merits of [our] claims'. We were free to pursue them before a civil authority if we chose to do so, but we preferred to let the matter die. The engagement in Washington went forward, and the reviews were ecstatic. However, the two-week season showed a loss of over $400,000.

When he read this in the papers, David howled in frustration. 'Shit!' he yelled. 'They lost as much in two weeks as we lost in two years. And they had the nerve to accuse us of mismanagement!'

'The problem is,' I told him, 'we don't even know who "they" are.'

The Washington episode was the swansong of the John Curry Skating Company. The ensemble never performed as a unit again, even under a phoney name. Nathan Birch, the youngest member of the troupe and John's greatest hope of a successor, has worked valiantly in the interim to form and nurture a company called the Next Ice Age. It is based in Baltimore and, although Nathan does not have the funding to keep the skaters together on a regular, permanent basis, he does manage to arrange performances once or twice a year. The Next Ice Age has 501(c)(3) status, and Nathan has become the first ice choreographer to receive a grant from the USA's National Endowment for the Arts. His work has been lauded by the *Washington Post*, and eventually he will emerge in his own right as a full-time artistic director. Nathan visited John in 1992 and, although John was too ill by that time to be able to take any active part in the Next Ice Age, he did have the satisfaction of knowing that his work continued to flourish.

The skaters scattered to take up other employment, though none of them lost their feeling of attachment to John. Dita and Jim married, and now teach in the southern United States. Cathy went on to obtain a law degree, and practises in Boston. Patricia married Stanley, and took up a new career as an actress. Timmy gave up music and joined Nathan in Baltimore to become the Co-Director of the Next Ice Age. They have also been jointly involved in revamping the *Ice Capades* for Dorothy Hamill, who purchased the show in 1993. Dino was sadly killed in an aeroplane crash in California, and Dorothy remarried, to a sports psychologist, Ken Forster. She is now the proud mother of a little girl. Mark Hominuke moved to upstate New York, where he teaches skating, and Scott Driscoll went on to become the star of the Asian version of *Ice Capades*. David Santee lives and teaches in the Chicago area, and Adam Lieb teaches at a rink in Long Island. Lori Nichol returned to Toronto, where she now teaches, and Jack Courtney continues to live and work in Colorado Springs. Peggy Fleming has two beautiful children and has become a successful entrepreneur in the San Francisco area. Janet Lynn moved with her family to Minneapolis, where her husband works for the FBI. JoJo Starbuck has founded her own production company in New York City, and Charles Barker has earned a solid reputation as a freelance conductor, as well as conducting the Met orchestra in New York. Gayle returned to the theatre, and Kevin operates a highly successful ice-making business.

Bill Judd had a second heart attack and died in early 1987, in Long Island. West Nally went out of business, and Jack Sakazaki continues to promote attractions out of Tokyo. Victor and Lillian Hochhauser are still running a very successful agency out of their Hampstead offices, and Steve Leber continues to promote major arena spectaculars from his offices in East 55th Street. Richard Lenchner works for a leading computer organization, and is married to a dancer from the Twyla Tharp company; they have two young children and live in New York. Bill Weylock runs a marketing research bureau, and Rob McBrien runs a skating school in New York's Sky Rink.

Today, David and I are able to look back on our years with the company without pain. We are proud of the role we played in its remarkable achievements and feel we were privileged to be a part of what we now see as a part of skating history. We never did sue John, and our love and admiration for him is undiminished. The fact that he was lost to us was simply the price we had to pay, and there are no regrets for the years we spent with him and his extraordinary ensemble. For my part, I remember John as I first knew him – the will-o'-the-wisp child-man who created such astonishing beauty on the ice, and was so utterly vulnerable in his own life. He was a rare and sensitive artist; a sweet human being who was driven to the edge of madness by the ghosts of his own past.

Epilogue

It may seem strange to say this now, but I knew in 1984 that I was going to die from AIDS. I had this shockingly powerful revelation, as I was walking along the street in New York. It was so sudden that I believed it utterly. I was passing the Bergdorf Goodman store, and I can still remember catching sight of myself in the window, and thinking how calm I looked. No one could possibly have known that I had just received a death sentence.

49

Perhaps the reason that John accepted the passing of his company with relative equanimity was that in his soul he really did not want to continue. He had taken his gifted troupe from the mountains of Colorado to the wilds of Canada and the heat of the desert. He had presented them in Tokyo, Honolulu and Bergen, in the Royal Albert Hall, the Metropolitan Opera House and the Kennedy Center. He had groomed and polished them, pushed and cajoled them, praised and punished them and turned them into a magnificent and mature ensemble of artists. Now the thing that he wanted most in all the world was for them to carry on without him. He was tired of performing and wanted to be left in peace.

He knew as early as 1985 that there was a distinct possibility he might contract AIDS, since two of his recent lovers – Brian Grant and Sean McGill – were HIV-positive, and a former lover had just died of the disease. He went to visit Brian in New York and told him, 'I am so inspired by the calm way you deal with your illness. If it should happen to me, I hope I can be as brave as you.'

He discussed with his agent, Jean Diamond, the potential of taking up a new career as an actor. Jean had always understood John's unique position in the entertainment world and she recognized his need to move away from skating. His unequalled talent on the ice had become an immense and crippling burden to him and he wanted to become part of an established tradition which did not depend on him for its existence. He was cast in a production of *Privates on Parade* which ran for several weeks at the Roundabout Theater in New York. He received some very favourable reviews and, to his intense pleasure, the critics seemed unaware of his former career as an Olympic champion and the founder of the world's first artistic ice ensemble.

In 1987, he was diagnosed HIV-positive. 'I was terribly ashamed.

I wasn't afraid of dying, but I was terrified that people would find out about it. I felt I had failed everyone. Let them all down. It took me a very long time to get over that concern.' He went home to visit his mother with the intention of telling her about his illness. 'I tried for three days to get the words out, but they wouldn't come. In the end I left again without discussing it with her.'

In 1991, John developed full-blown AIDS, and he went back to England to live with his mother in Binton. 'I had no desire to remain in the USA. I needed to be surrounded by people I loved and I wanted to live peacefully in the country.' The disease changed his life profoundly. 'It may be difficult to understand, but in some ways it was a relief to me. I had been feeling this terrible guilt because I wasn't skating. I had been regarded for so long as the standard-bearer for artistic skating, the crusader, the mentor . . . I never felt I could stop without causing irreparable harm to those skaters who worked in my field. There was no one else, you see. But when I got AIDS, I realized I couldn't live their lives for them. They would either pick up the torch and carry on, or the art form would die out. I had done all I could. I was finally able to let go of it all.'

Those who were close to him marvelled at his calm acceptance of the illness. He seemed to be at peace, spending his days happily cultivating a flower garden behind the house, reading and making needlepoint pictures. He would listen to music on his Walkman, mostly classical but with an occasional David Bowie or Sting tape. 'I always wanted to do an ice ballet set to David Bowie's "Space Oddity". It would have worked so well.' His inner turmoil seemed to have subsided and he went quietly about his daily routine, living each day as it came.

As the months passed, there were periods of severe sickness. He was in hospital only as much as was completely necessary (his worst episode being a bout of toxoplasmosis), and he always returned to Binton as soon as possible. 'Mother is splendid. She promised me that she would look after me at home, even when things got really bad. I don't want to die in a hospital bed. I feel safe in my own room.'

John had several good friends who visited him frequently. These included the musical star Millicent Martin, and Gillian Lynne, the choreographer of *Cats*, at whose wedding John had been best man. His constant companion, however, was the actor Alan Bates. 'Alan gives me a strength and serenity which are very important to me. He is a wonderful mixture of eccentric thespian and worldly-wise intellectual, and he is a warm and compassionate man with a deep sense of family.' During the last months of John's life, Alan took him to Cornwall for a holiday. They travelled down by train, and when they arrived at the hotel, the manager noticed that John was walking with a stick. 'Have you hurt your leg?' he enquired.

'No,' John replied. 'I have AIDS and I need the stick to help me walk. But thank you for asking.'

In February 1994, John watched the Winter Olympics on television. For two weeks he followed the events intently, and when Jayne Torvill and Christopher Dean failed in their bid to recapture the ice-dance title he was critical of the judging. 'It makes no sense at all,' he said. 'Jayne and Chris were clearly the best, but unfortunately the system is wide open to bias and corruption. Skating is a subjective sport and there is no way to challenge an opinion. It took me back to my own Olympic victory. I chose the most virtuoso piece of music I could find – the *pas de deux* from *Don Quixote*. I did an obvious piece of choreography to it and arranged my programme so they could see the degree of difficulty clearly. When it was over, all the judges came to me and said: "Magnificent! It's amazing how much you have improved since last year." The Olympics were over by this time, so I decided to tell them the truth. I said: "This was my least complicated programme for the past four years. It had fewer jumps, fewer spins and less footwork, but I set it up to *look* more difficult." Such is the nature of our amateur institution.'

John gave an interview to a young journalist in early March. 'I can identify with all skaters who have artistic inclination and ambition. The thing that unites us is that we all love the beauty, excitement and joy of skating. Young artists must free their minds and their bodies so they can create work which is unique. They must be true to themselves, and bring to the skating palette their own special colours. That is what will make the art form grow. They must keep pushing the boundaries.'

On 14 April 1994, John spent a peaceful day in his garden. He sat in a chair, breathing the scent of the flowers and feeling a gentle breeze against his face. He went to bed early, tired from all the fresh air. His mother always slept with her door open, in case he called out in the night. At about three a.m. she awoke with a start, sensing that he needed her. 'I don't know what disturbed me on this particular night, because John had made no sound. When I went into his room, he was lying quite still with his eyes open. When he saw me, he smiled. "Hello," he said, and stretched his hand towards me. Before I could grasp it, he had died. He must have been at peace, because he still had the smile on his face.'

Index

Adelman, Asher, 272
Albert Hall *see* Royal Albert Hall
Alexander, Ron, 83–5, 88, 90, 157–8
Allen, April, 259–60, 262
American Federation of Television and Radio Artists (AFTRA), 239–40
Anichini, Rita, 145, 148, 159, 161, 162, 173, 180, 181, 185, 213
Arie Crown Theater, Chicago, 258, 265, 266–8

Baker, Andrew, 282
Ballard, Billy, 138–9
Barker, Charles, 161, 162, 173, 178–9, 181, 184, 200, 201, 202, 203, 204, 223, 229, 230, 232, 233, 236, 239, 252, 293
Barnes, Clive, 234
Barnett, Nate, 219, 229, 269–70, 273
Bates, Alan, 206, 298–9
Bergen Opera House, Norway, 215–16, 275, 278–9
Berghoff, Nancy, 119
Bernstein, Leonard, 166, 235–7
Berry, James, 155, 257, 259
Birch, Nathan, 152–3, 154, 155, 172, 175, 176, 185, 187, 202–3, 234, 256, 265, 279, 293
Birmingham, 3–30, 42
Blaisdell Arena, Hawaii, 155, 189, 190
Bliss, Tony, 193, 228
Bolton, Pete, 200–1
Bonnefous, Jean-Pierre, 88, 126, 193, 232, 248
Bowser, Jim, 119, 128, 133–4, 230, 288, 293
Bridges, Lloyd, 90–1
Brigadoon, 97–8
Bristol Hippodrome, 81, 82–3
British Junior Championships (1967), 33

British Men's Championships (1970), 37
British Men's Championships (1974), 56
Brown, Harry John, 142–4, 161
Brown, Lorna, 120
Butler, John, 82–3
Button, Dick, 48, 99–100, 102, 103, 104

Cammacker, Shelley, 220, 283, 286, 288, 289, 291
Canada, 54, 104–9, 156–7, 162, 163, 168
Carson, Margaret, 165–6, 192–3, 196, 214, 223, 226, 235
Challenge of Champions, 99
Charlton, Warwick, 71
Chicago, 258, 260, 263–4, 265–70
Cohan, Robert, 88
Cohl, Michael, 100–1, 102, 103, 105, 107, 108, 112, 114, 121–2, 125, 127, 131, 138–9, 140, 191
Colorado Springs, 50–2, 55, 56, 58
Columbia Artists Management (CAMI), 116, 213, 254–5, 257–9, 260–1, 269, 273, 275, 280–4, 286
Concilio, Joe, 155, 163, 168, 216, 250, 255, 283
Copenhagen, 275–7
Courtney, Jack, 120, 131–2, 134, 293
Cousins, Robin, 56, 101, 103, 104, 105–6, 108, 146, 148, 150–1, 152, 195
Cranston, Toller, 47, 52–3, 54, 63, 66, 74, 95–6, 104–6, 108, 110–11, 113, 114, 139, 140
Crisp, Clement, 205
Crown, Patricia, 287, 289
Curry, Andrew, 3, 5, 6, 11, 28, 66–7

Curry, John
  on amateur skating 'establishment',
    33, 44, 50, 52, 59–63, 77, 103,
    172, 299
  as competitor, 11, 14, 23, 29, 33–4,
    37, 38, 39, 44–5, 46–8, 52, 56,
    58–60, 61–6, 72–4
  and drugs, 83, 85, 91, 157
  eating disorder, 15–16, 33, 89, 165
  and father's suicide, 27–9, 67, 183,
    211
  sexuality, 67–9, 81, 97, 211–12
  on skating technique, 9–10, 22, 32,
    49–50, 119
  on skating as art form, 7, 11–12, 15,
    24, 30, 33–4, 47, 61, 65, 78–9,
    90
  see also Curry, Joseph
Curry, Joseph, 3–8, 13, 16–20, 21, 23,
    24–9
Curry, Michael, 3, 5, 6
Curry, Rita, 3–9, 11, 12, 13, 15, 17–20,
    21, 22, 23, 24–30, 42, 66–9, 117,
    298, 299–300

d'Alessio, Clem, 170–1
Darrell, Peter, 79–80
Davies, Keith, 109, 112, 113, 119, 127,
    176, 187, 197–9, 207–9, 239,
    257, 259
Davos, Switzerland, 33, 34, 35–6, 37–8
de Mille, Agnes, 97–8
de Velder, Ann, 152
Dean, Christopher, 299
Dean, Laura, 154, 179, 192, 204
Denver, 124–9, 132–4, 199
Diamond, Jean, 205, 297
Diamond, Neil, 172
Dobson, Pat, 129, 225
Dobson Arena, Vail, 129–30, 131, 218,
    262
Dodd, Craig, 205
Dodd, Patricia, 119, 143–4, 172, 175,
    192, 193, 234, 240, 243, 248,
    262, 263, 288, 293
Dodson, Darryl, 218–19, 223–4, 226,
    229, 237, 239, 241, 243, 244–5,
    246–7, 250, 253, 255–6, 258–9,
    260, 263–4, 265, 266, 269–70,
    273
Dotson, Editha ('Dita'), 152, 154, 225,
    230, 231, 240, 267, 288, 293

Doucet, David, 260
Driscoll, J. Scott, 217, 283, 293
Dubai, 149, 162, 165, 207, 208–10
Dunfield, Peter, 39, 41–2
Dylan, Bob, 91

Electric Ice, 148, 150–1, 152–3, 205
Equal Opportunities Commission, 257
Equity, 240
Erhard Seminar Training (EST), 56–8
European Championships,
    Copenhagen, 52
European Championships, Geneva,
    58–61
European Championships, Zagreb, 46

Fassi, Carlo, 49, 51–3, 55, 57–60, 63,
    65, 68, 69, 70, 72–4
Fassi, Christa, 51–3, 55, 63, 65, 73–4
Fauver, Billy, 218, 231, 253
Feld, Eliot, 220, 228–9, 234
Feld, Kenneth, 138
Felt Forum, Madison Square Garden,
    88–9
Fire Island, New York, 93, 98, 109,
    110
First Choice, 132, 138–9
Fleming, Peggy, 51, 76, 102, 106, 108,
    110–11, 113, 114, 293
Fonteyn, Margot, 7
Forster, Ken, 293
Foster, David, 213, 214, 254, 257, 258,
    260–1, 264, 268–9, 282
Foulkes, Cathy, 88, 119, 126, 175, 188,
    194, 209, 232, 234, 243, 249,
    253–4, 288, 293
Fredonia College, New York, 142–4,
    148
Friends of the John Curry Skating
    Company, 195, 235

Garmisch, Germany, 55
Gelb, Peter, 213, 258
Gerschwiler, Arnold, 30–3, 34–8, 43
Gevers, Catherine, 258, 260–1, 272–3,
    282
Gold, Shelley, 214
Goodheart, Skee, 39
Göteborg Arena, 275, 278
Graham, Dr and Mrs, 51
Grant, Brian, 55, 56, 88, 89–90, 161–2,
    270–1, 297